Yearbook of Comparative and General Literature IV

". . . a clearing-house, a rallying point
a source of information and of strength . . "

Yearbook of Comparative and General Literature / *Vol. IV*

NEW YORK

RUSSELL & RUSSELL · INC

1965

THE UNIVERSITY OF NORTH CAROLINA
STUDIES IN COMPARATIVE LITERATURE
FIRST PUBLISHED IN 1955
REISSUED, 1965, BY RUSSELL & RUSSELL, INC.
L.C. CATALOG CARD NO: 53-62589

PRINTED IN THE U. S. A.

YEARBOOK OF COMPARATIVE
AND GENERAL LITERATURE IV

published in collaboration with

The Comparative Literature Committee

of the National Council of Teachers of English

and

The Comparative Literature Section

of the Modern Language Association of America

W. P. Friederich, Editor
University of North Carolina

Horst Frenz, Associate Editor
Indiana University

1955

TABLE OF CONTENTS

Part One

Part Two

148614

Part Three

Part Four

Reviews of Professional Works

. . . and of Recent Translations and Editions

Part Five

Bibliography of Comparative Literature, 1952-1954

PART ONE

COMPARATIVE LITERATURE IN THE SOVIET UNION, TODAY AND YESTERDAY

Gleb Struve
University of California, Berkeley

In approaching comparative literature studies in Soviet Russia it is necessary not to lose sight of one cardinal fact: totalitarian Communism as it is practised today in Russia denies on principle such a thing as independent, objective scholarship (the very word "objective" when used by Communists is derogatory; "bourgeois objectivism" is a term of vituperation). Like literature itself, literary scholarship in the Soviet Union is a handmaiden of the Communist Party. But this complete subordination of it is the end result of a more or less gradual process, and, just as in the history of Soviet literature, it is possible to distinguish three main periods in the history of Soviet literary scholarship: 1) a period of relative freedom, approximately from 1917 through 1929, when it was not necessary for a literary scholar to be a Marxist, when most of the best works in literary history and theory of literature were produced by non-Marxists, the so-called Formalists who found themselves in an open clash with the official Marxist teaching,[1] and when some of the Marxists at least allowed themselves the luxury of more or less independent thinking; 2) the second period, which covered the 'thirties and, on the whole, lasted through the war years (though the war period constituted in itself a sort of interlude of relative freedom) and which was characterized by so-called "Socialist Realism" in literature (this implied a severe clampdown on every species of "Formalism") and by the growing insistence on compliance with the strict Marxist doctrine where literary scholarship was concerned. This, when carried to its logical conclusion, meant complete subordination to the current Party line, as was clearly demonstrated in 3) the third period, which was inaugurated by the famous resolution of the Central Committee of the Communist Party, in August 1946, which emphasized the necessity of rooting out the relics of bourgeois mentality in Soviet literature, and more particularly the spirit of "servility before the capitalist West." The implementation of that resolution in literature, the theatre, and arts in general, as well as in literary scholarship, came to be associated with the name of the late Andrey Zhdanov, and the whole

---

[1] On Russian Formalists and their contribution to literary scholarship, see: Victor Erlich, *Russian Formalism: History-Doctrine*. Slavistic Printings and Reprintings, edited by Cornelis H. van Schooneveld, Leiden University, IV. 's-Gravenhage, 1955. Cf. also Manfred Kridl, "Russian Formalism," *The American Bookman*, 1944, pp. 19-30; V. Žirmunskij, "Formprobleme in der russischen Literaturwissenschaft," *ZSP*, I (1925), pp. 117-152; B. Tomashevski, "La nouvelle école d'histoire littéraire en Russie," *Revue des Etudes Slaves*, VIII (1928), pp. 226-240; N. Gourfinkel, "Les nouvelles méthodes d'histoire littéraire en Russie," *Le Monde Slave*, VII (1929), pp. 234-263; and A. Voznesensky, "Problems of Method in the Study of Literature," *SEER*, VI (June, 1927).

period has been rightly described as the Zhdanov era.[2] Under this Zhdanov dispensation, comparativism became a term of abuse, and those practising it in literary scholarship or literary criticism, became guilty of a mortal sin. To set the scene in greater relief, it is perhaps best to begin with this latest period and then work one's way backwards. This account in reverse order will make it clear that while comparative literature today is practically taboo in the Soviet Union, it was by no means a negligible quantity in the period preceding 1946.

I.

The campaign against "servility before the West," unloosed by Zhdanov, was in full swing when, in the spring of 1947, the well-known Soviet writer Alexander Fadeyev, who after World War II had become general secretary of the Union of Soviet Writers, read a report on "The Tasks of Literary Theory and Criticism"[3] before a meeting of the Board of that Union. It contained, among other things, an attack on Isaac Nusinov, a well-known Communist critic and literary historian, who back in the 1930's had been regarded as one of the pillars of Marxist orthodoxy and one of the principal exponents of Socialist Realism. Nusinov came under fire because of his book entitled *Pushkin and World Literature* (1941). This six-year-old book was in the main a discussion of Pushkin's treatment (in his "Little Tragedies" and some other works) of certain universal literary themes, motifs, and images. Some of the material which went into the making of this book had been published by Nusinov before in a volume which the Social Sciences Section of the Soviet Academy of Sciences brought out to mark the centenary of Pushkin's death.[4] Neither this earlier paper nor the 1941 book aroused any special attention at the time. Nor did they contain anything strikingly new. But now Fadeyev taxed Nusinov with "servility before the West," with minimizing Pushkin's originality, and with regarding Russian realism as a sort of appendix to Western European literature. Fadeyev asserted that Nusinov's main purpose was to demonstrate that "the greatness of Pushkin consists in his being a 'European,' and in his having found his own answers to all the questions posed by Western Europe." Nusinov was said to be preaching the purely abstract "eternal" and "universal" themes.[5] His

---

[2] For a more detailed account of the Zhdanov era, see G. Struve, *Soviet Russian Literature: 1917-1950*, University of Oklahoma Press, 1951, chapter VII.

[3] Fadeyev's report was printed in *Literaturnaya Gazeta* and later reproduced, with some deletions, in the review *Oktyabr'* (1947, No. 7). Another version, with some of the original passages restored, appeared in the symposium entitled *Problems of Socialist Realism* (Leningrad, 1948).

[4] "Pushkin and Images of World Literature," in *IAN OON*, 1937, No. 2-3, pp. 431-502.

[5] Fadeyev might have recalled an earlier book by Nusinov called *Age-Old Images* (Moscow, 1937): it contained a long study of the Promethean myth in literature through the ages, as well as essays on *Don Quixote*, Shakespeare, and Byron. The book was written from the Marixst point of view.

book, said Fadeyev, teemed with names of European writers and poets, "with Nusinov hopping, carefree, from one century into another." Amidst that procession of names there flashed the name of Pushkin, and "now it was he who was carrying on something initiated by a Western European writer, now again it was some Western European author continuing something in the wake of Pushkin." Nusinov's book, asserted Fadeyev, had nothing to do with Marxism. He was not even up to the standards set by the Russian revolutionary democrats.[6] Fadeyev recalled Belinsky's words, "It is high time we stopped admiring things European just because they are not Asiatic," and his contemptuous reference to "coolheaded sceptics, abstract humans, passportless tramps amidst mankind." Such "passportless tramps," said Fadeyev, must be exposed mercilessly.[7] And he went on to suggest that the source of such "conceptions" was to be sought in the teaching of Alexander Veselovsky, whose followers were still active in Soviet academic institutions.[8] The Veselovsky school, according to Fadeyev, was responsible for servility before the West of a certain section of Russian literary scholars, both in the past and in the present. A proof of this could be seen in a booklet entitled *Alexander Veselovsky and Russian Literature* and published by the University of Leningrad as recently as 1946. Its author was Professor V. F. Shishmaryov[9] and it was edited by Professor M. P. Alekseyev, author of a number of studies dealing with Russia's literary relations with the West. Fadeyev accused Shishmaryov of admiring all that was worst in Veselovsky and of being himself awestruck by the long list of names of German scholars among whom Veselovsky was "able to utter *his* word on the subject of 'poetics of the plot'." While admitting that Veselovsky was an important scholar who had accumulated a vast factual knowledge in the field of philology and linguistics, Fadeyev charged him with having broken

---

[6] That is, Belinsky, Chernyshevsky, and Dobrolyubov, the three nineteenth century pioneers of social-utilitarian criticism in Russia.

[7] This expression, alongside that of "rootless cosmopolitans," came to be widely used in the subsequent anti-Westernist campaign.

[8] Alexander Nikolayevich Veselovsky (1838-1906), Professor of General Literature in the University of St. Petersburg, a scholar of exceptional erudition and remarkable productivity, was one of the pioneers of comparative method in the study of literature. His first major work was written in Italian and published in Bologna (*Paradiso degli Alberti*, 1867-69). His Russian work *The Slavic Tales about Solomon and Kitovras and the Western European Legends of Morolf and Merlin* (1872) inaugurated a whole series of comparative studies in folklore and medieval literature. He also wrote fundamental works on Boccaccio and on the Russian poet Zhukovsky in the context of European Romanticism. His "Three Chapters from Historical Poetics" (1895) had a great influence on Russian literary scholars of the present century. He also wrote innumerable shorter studies in Russian, German and Italian.

[9] Vladimir F. Shishmaryov (b. 1874), Professor of Romance Philology in the University of St. Petersburg, and later Leningrad, author of a book on Clément Marot and of numerous studies in French language and literature.

away from the great Russian revolutionary-democratic literary tradition, and of having substituted shallow Western bourgeois positivism for materialism and true historicism.

Fadeyev's attack on Veselovsky, even though the corresponding passage for some reason was deleted from the printed version of his report as it appeared in *Oktyabr'*,[10] gave rise to a systematic campaign against the "survivals of the Veselovsky school," which came to be identified both with servility before the West and with the comparative approach to literature. In its issue for September 1947, *Oktyabr'* published an article by V. Kirpotin, one of the leading Marxist critics, who had been particularly zealous in denouncing various manifestations of servile attitude toward the West. Entitled "About the Attitude of Russian Literature and Literary Criticism toward the Capitalist West," the article began with an attack on Alexey Veselovsky, a lesser and less-known younger brother of the great Alexander and author of a book called *Western Influence in Russian Literature* (5th ed.; Moscow, 1916), which overstressed the theme of influences and therefore lent itself well to criticism. Kirpotin now accused Alexey Veselovsky of considering all that was backward in Russia to be of purely Russian origin, and all that was progressive to be a result of borrowings from the West. He pointed out the one-sidedness of this approach and said that until recently almost nothing had been done to show "the enormous and beneficent influence of Russian literature on the literature of other countries, although no one questions the fact of this influence." Kirpotin then suggested that Alexey Veselovsky's book was a product of his brother's school of would-be historical comparativism, and that it was followed by numerous books and articles by other literary scholars who developed all the weak points of their master. "What an enormous literature was produced to prove that Gogol derived from Hoffmann or from Jules Janin, that Griboedov was born of Molière, that *Boris Godunov* came from Shakespeare, that Dostoevsky emanated from Balzac, Schiller, Dickens and the European detective novel, that Turgenev came out of Molière [*sic!* Mérimée?], *Slovo o polku Igoreve* out of the Turkish folklore, the *byliny* out of Byzantine literature, etc., etc." Kirpotin quoted an article by Professor A. S. Orlov in which the latter had suggested applying the comparative method to Russian medieval literature and following in the footsteps of such nineteenth-century scholars as Buslaev, Veselovsky, and Zhdanov, "with due allowance for a deviation by means of Marxism." This suggestion by the eminent specialist on early Russian literature made Kirpotin exclaim indignantly: "Marxism cannot be applied as 'an allowance for a deviation' to non-Marxist theories and conceptions. Marxism is not just one of the theories placed alongside others; it is a new and higher qualitative achievement of man's theoretical thought . . . "

Three months later the same review published four more articles on the subject of Alexander Veselovsky and his followers. Two of them,

---

[10] This passage was, however, restored when Fadeyev's text was reproduced again in *Problems of Socialist Realism* (Leningrad, 1948).

one by N. Glagolev[11] and the other by I. Dmitrakov and M. Kuznetsov,[12] followed the anti-Veselovsky line of Kirpotin, with Dmitrakov and Kuznetsov singling out as their main target a recent study in comparative folklore by Professor V. Propp, of the University of Leningrad (*The Historical Roots of the Fairy Tale*, Leningrad, 1946). Propp was denounced as a follower of Veselovsky and a disciple of such "bourgeois-idealist" scholars as Frazer, Taylor, Frobenius, and Wundt; he was accused of "bourgeois cosmopolitanism," of shearing Russian folk tales of all their national characteristics, and treating their motifs as borrowings from foreign, Western and Oriental, myths and rituals. In the two other articles an attempt was made to defend Veselovsky. One was by Victor Shklovsky, the one-time boisterous leader of the Russian Formalists,[13] who certainly owed some of their views to Veselovsky. Shklovsky had enough courage to describe Veselovsky as a great scholar and even a genius and to ascribe Fadeyev's strictures to a misunderstanding. Veselovsky, wrote Shklovsky, had tried to substitute historical poetics for German normative aesthetics; "he was a genius . . . whom we cannot by-pass, whose work is indispensable to us." Mentioning that the Formalists had often referred to Veselovsky, Shklovsky added: "but Veselovsky is no more answerable for their theories than Aristotle is for Boileau." The last article was a short but dignified defense of Veselovsky's ideas by Professor Shishmaryov.[14] He admitted that Veselovsky was neither a Marxist nor a consistent materialist. But studying abroad did not imply "servility"—did not Glinka or such great scholars as Sechenov, Mendeleyev, and Butlerov all study abroad? In Russia, Veselovsky, who specialized in general literature, could not learn from anyone. He was influenced by Benfey, but with him the theory of borrowings took on a new form. Shishmaryov then proceeded to justify Veselovsky's idea of "borrowings" and "influences." Strictly speaking, he said, there was no such thing as "migrating" plots, that is, those which become part of a given literature by accident; there were only "assimilated" plots. In every literature there were elements of outside influences and borrowings, but a literature did not thereby lose its national character. The influence of Hoffman on Gogol did not make the latter any less Russian, just as the influence of the Spanish picaresque novel did not turn French novels into Spanish works. Sherwood Anderson was influenced by Chekhov, but he did not become any the less American because of that. It was Pushkin who said that "imitation is not . . . a sign of intellectual poverty," and it was Gorky who said to those who criticized the theory of borrowings that a borrowing can produce a more valuable result. Veselovsky was concerned with establishing why and how foreign themes were assimilated or old

[11] "Concerning A. N. Veselovsky's Conception," *Oktyabr'*, 1947, No. 12, pp. 182-86.
[12] "Alexander Veselovsky and His Followers," *ibid.*, pp. 165-174.
[13] "Alexander Veselovsky, Historian and Theoretician," *ibid.*, pp. 174-182.
[14] "Alexander Veselovsky and His Critics," *ibid.*, pp. 158-164.

themes renovated, that is, with establishing the *qualitative* changes which the process of assimilation produced in the assimilated material. The question of "foreign" and "own" had less interest for him than the question of *how* the foreign had become assimilated and reinterpreted.

This article by Shishmaryov was apparently the last to be published in defense of Veselovsky's comparative method. The very next month *Oktyabr'* came out with a new opus by Kirpotin under an ominously long and ponderous title: "About Servility before the Capitalist West, about Alexander Veselovsky, about His Followers and about Things That Matter Most."[15] It contained an outspoken attack on comparativism and further strictures on Veselovsky and Nusinov. Here are, briefly summarized, the main points of Kirpotin's indictment:

(1) Servility before the West and the ensuing low estimate of the importance of Russian literature are clearly connected with the uncritical attitude towards Veselovsky's heritage. The name of Veselovsky is being used to pass a mimicry of Marxism for the genuine article.

(2) The problem of estimating Veselovsky's heritage is linked up with that of training new contingents of literary scholars and critics in Marxist-Leninist methods. It is a problem of today, not of yesterday.

(3) Shishmaryov's earlier assertion (made in 1938) that the comparative method introduced and perfected by Veselovsky has now become a commonplace, and that we are all either his pupils or his pupils' pupils, fully accounts for the case of Nusinov. Nusinov tackled his subject as a comparativist, as a follower of the obsolete comparative method. That is why he was unable to show the originality and the independence of Pushkin and had to stress his dependence on alien problems and alien attitudes to life. Hence the inescapable deduction that the West did not accept Pushkin simply because he did not offer it anything new. Nusinov's book is an illustration of how *today* Veselovsky's comparativism is camouflaged as Marxism.

(4) There is no need to demonstrate the bankruptcy of comparativism as a method of investigation. It results in an isolation of literary facts, it leads to pure art and formalism, against which Soviet criticism still has to contend.

(5) When Shishmaryov maintains that the influence of Veselovsky can be traced even in those scholars who do not refer to him as their master, or are even unaware of their dependence on him, he must have in mind endless comparativist studies, such as Zhirmunsky's works on Byron and Goethe in Russia, Leonid Grossman's writings, Nusinov's book on Pushkin, etc.

(6) The theory of borrowings, from which comparativism proceeds, is in itself a fallacy. Comparativists detach literary facts from the generating social environment and consider them without regard to the class struggle, the national peculiarities, and the economic bases of international intercourse. Russian comparativists always regarded Russian

---

[15] *Oktyabr'*, 1948, No. 1, pp. 3-27.

literature as the one that borrowed its motifs, plots and forms from outside, from the West or from the East. They argued as to who borrowed what and where, but the very fact of borrowing was never contested.

(7) The idea of "development" as a circle or a series of self-repeating circles has led Veselovsky's followers to the theory of so-called stadialism,[16] according to which literary facts are considered regardless of their genesis, their historical environment, their chronology and their locale, but merely with reference to their "analogousness." Stadialism as applied to literature implies parallel cyclical development without borrowing. By using the abstract concept of stadialism, the comparativists argue outside space and time. Stadialism becomes a mechanical device, allegedly capable of explaining literary facts outside their historical context. The theory of stadial development in comparative literature[17] is fatalistic and pessimistic, it reduces everything to numerous repetitions and fails to account for the real progress of mankind or for national peculiarities.

(8) It is a good thing that Veselovsky's followers have as yet failed to give final shape to the theory they preach, but we must signalize its dangers, all the more so since it is being preached more insistently in academic teaching than in writings. It must also be borne in mind that in its most elaborate and thorough form the theory of stadialism was propounded by Spengler.

Kirpotin concluded his article by pointing out to those who tried to defend Veselovsky that the discussion about the means of doing away with servility before the West was not prompted by any "outside considerations," that it was being carried on in an open forum, and that its literary and political significance were there for everybody to check. In fact, the predominantly political significance of this "open forum" discussion soon became evident. Soviet journalists, critics, and scholars began to vie with each other in denouncing various manifestations of "Veselovskyism," which became synonymous with "bourgeois liberalism," "cosmopolitanism," and above all "comparativism" in literary history and literary criticism. The name of Alexander Veselovsky, hitherto little known outside the circle of specialists in literary history, came to be bandied about in the daily press and in literary periodicals. A month later, the review Novy Mir published an even more violent attack on Veselovsky and his school by the critic Anatoly Tarasenkov.[18] And before another month passed, Kul'tura i Zhizn', the official organ of the Central Committee of the Communist Party, came out with a weighty editorial which amounted to the official excommunication of the Veselovsky school:

---

[16] More will be said below about this theory, advanced among others by Zhirmunsky.

[17] Kirpotin took care to dissociate "stadialism" in the history of literature from the linguistic theories of Marr, which at that time still reigned supreme.

[18] "Cosmopolitans in Literary Scholarship," Novy Mir, 1948, No. 2, pp. 124-137.

even Kirpotin was reprimanded for his moderation and indecision in attacking it.[19]

Some of the individual manifestations of the anti-Veselovsky and anti-comparativist campaign in the Soviet press were absurd and ridiculous beyond belief. Thus, the authors of the first volume of the new *History of French Literature*, undertaken by the Soviet Academy of Sciences in 1946 under the editorship, and with the participation, of several leading Soviet scholars in the field (Mokul'sky, Shishmaryov, and others), were taken to task for their constant references to the influence of French writers (such as Boileau, Molière, La Fontaine, and others) on Russian eighteenth-century literature. A similar accusation was brought up against the editors and authors (again all of them leading specialists in their field, such as Morozov, Alekseyev, Zhirmunsky, Elistratova, and others) of a *History of English Literature* which began to appear in 1943: they were guilty of the crime of mentioning the influence of Swift, Richardson, Fielding, and Sterne on Russian writers of the eighteenth century, an influence that had never before been disputed by Russian scholars. Boris Eichenbaum, author of some of the best studies of Tolstoy, was pilloried for speaking of Tolstoy's debt to Schopenhauer's philosophy. *Literaturnaya Gazeta*, the official mouthpiece of the Union of Soviet Writers, which was particularly zealous in ferreting out the comparativist "heresy," fulminated against those who were responsible for a program of courses for Soviet theatrical institutes, because they had "insulted" the Russian nineteenth-century dramatist Ostrovsky by suggesting that in one of his plays he had used the age-worn device of "recognition," which he was said to have taken over from the Greek comedy via Molière and other European dramatists. Dangerous "comparativist" tendencies were detected in one of the standard histories of the Russian theatre published

---

[19] "Against Bourgeois Liberalism," *Kul'tura i Zhizn'*, No. 7, March 11, 1948. In the new edition of the *Great Soviet Encyclopedia* (1951), in which many articles have been drastically revised and some names have disappeared altogether, there is a short unsigned article on Alexander Veselovsky. He is described as "one of the theoretical precursors of Formalism." His work on Zhukovsky is said to be "an obvious application of his bourgeois comparative method to Russian nineteenth-century literature," and his views in general are characterized as "reactionary cosmopolitan" and as "one of the sources of servility before the West." Few of Veselovsky's own works are mentioned and the references to literature about him are confined to Fadeyev's contribution to *Problems of Socialist Realism* and the 1948 *Kul'tura i Zhizn'* article. In the earlier edition of the same *Encyclopedia* (1928), the article on Veselovsky was written by P. Sakulin. It was at least four times longer and the bibliography of writings about Veselovsky included fifteen titles. Referring to Veselovsky's comparativism, Sakulin wrote: "The comparative historical method which had already been applied by Benfey, Dunlop and Felix Liebrecht, and by Pypin in Russia, found in Veselovsky a brilliant representative. He was not a mere disciple, but one of the founders of this method which he had placed on a firm historical-cultural basis. The causal dependence of literature on social and cultural conditions of the time was always clear to V."

in 1929. Its author, Vsevolodsky-Gerngross, was described as "an idealist and a formalist, an inveterate representative of the 'comparativist' school . . . a fierce and militant champion of foreign, and especially German, influence on the Russian theatre." Specifically, Vsevolodsky-Gerngross' "crime" boiled down to his linking up the origins of the Russian theatre in the seventeenth century to the German troupe of Pastor Gregory—a well-documented fact to be found mentioned in all general textbooks of Russian literature, including those written since the Revolution. Leonid Grossman, best known for his studies of Balzac and Dostoevsky, was belabored by an obscure but zealous critic for suggesting that in Lermontov's poetry there are many Oriental, including Biblical, motifs. Even the authors of the officially approved *History of the U. S. S. R.* by Pankratova and others did not escape censure: they had spoken of the influence of Leibnitz, Helvetius, Rousseau, Mably, and Raynal on Alexander Radishchev, as many of their predecessors had done before them. (To meet such criticisms, the 1951 edition of D. Blagoy's standard University textbook of Russian 18th-century literature was carefully pruned of most of the references to foreign influences on Russian drama, poetry, and satirical journalism, which its earlier edition had contained.) One of the glaring examples of this anti-comparativist witch-hunt was the above-mentioned case of Professor Propp's book on the sources of fairy tales. Published as recently as 1946, it was favorably reviewed by Zhirmunsky and other eminent scholars. When the campaign against Veselovsky began, this book was attacked by Dmitrakov and Kuznetsov (see above, note 12) and denounced as "un-Marxian" and "a survival of Veselovskyism"; the well-known critic Tarasenkov (see above, note 18) said that it looked more like a Berlin or London telephone directory than a University of Leningrad publication, for Propp had the effrontery to quote lavishly from such international authorities on folklore and anthropology as Frazer, Lévy-Bruhl, Boas, Kroeber, Frobenius, and others.

While every suggestion of a Russian author having been influenced by a foreign model was regarded as an insult to the Russian genius and hence a mortal sin, the "comparative" approach in reverse, so to speak, was not only tolerated but even encouraged, and Soviet scholars and critics were urged to study the influence of Russian, and especially Soviet, writers on European and American literature—for instance the influence of Gorky on Jack London, Upton Sinclair, and Theodore Dreiser. Thus Leonid Grossman, cut off from his proper field of studies, was obviously encouraged to publish, in 1948, an insignificant article about the influence of Mayakovsky on Louis Aragon. It was also permitted to discuss the influence of Tolstoy on Romain Rolland. In recent years there have been numerous studies of the influence of Russian writers, past and present, on the literature of the so-called "People's Democracies," that is, Poland, Czechoslovakia, Bulgaria, Hungary, and Rumania. Now and then a healthy note of reaction against the excessive minutiae of uncritical comparativism was sounded in this campaign, but most of it was ludicrous and had nothing to do with true literary scholarship.

Soon Propp was to be the first of a number of leading literary scholars to mount the rostrum in a big auditorium in the University of Leningrad and recant his "comparativist" errors. He was followed by the flower of Soviet literary scholarship, by men like Zhirmunsky, Eichenbaum, Dolinin, Gukovsky, and Alekseyev. Letters of repentance were also sent by Tomashevsky, Azadovsky, Desnitsky, and Shishmaryov, who were unable to attend the meeting. The report of the meeting said that Shishmaryov's letter did not satisfy the gathering, but in any case he went as far as voicing his complete agreement with what *Kul'tura i Zhizn'* had said about "cosmopolitanism," "servility," and the necessity to "combat bourgeois scholarship resolutely." The meeting, which was called in response to the article in *Kul'tura i Zhizn'* (similar meetings were held in other Universities), unanimously passed a resolution proclaiming Veselovsky a typical representative of "bourgeois-liberal academic scholarship" and his method "diametrically opposed to Marxism" and stating that "formalism and bourgeois cosmopolitanism are inseparable from Veselovsky's teaching." It also spoke of Shishmaryov, Zhirmunsky, Alekseyev and Azadovsky as active partisans of Veselovsky, and of Eichenbaum, Tomashevsky, and others as their abettors. The true significance of the charges leveled against all these distinguished scholars, and of the *mea culpas* demanded from the penitents, may be best gathered from the following passage from the statement read at the meeting by Zhirmunsky, one of the principal accused: "I have in mind in the first place liberal-bourgeois cosmopolitanism in scholarship which—at least in the past—appeared to politically nearsighted people to be just an innocent pastime of abstract learning, but which, used demagogically by present-day American imperialists, has revealed itself as a real threat to freedom and national independence of the peoples of the world."[20]

II.

Most of those who, in 1947-48, were accused of preaching the "hostile" and "alien" views of Veselovsky in Soviet Universities had, ten years earlier, taken part in a special volume published by the Social Sciences Section of the Academy of Sciences of the USSR in honor of the centenary of Veselovsky's birth. The volume for the most part consisted of papers read at the meeting of the above-mentioned section on February 27, 1938, and was preceded by a short editorial note which described Veselovsky as

[20] For some further details of this meeting, probably unique in the annals of literary scholarship, see G. Struve, "Witch-Hunt Russian Style: The Soviets Purge Literary Scholarship," *The New Leader*, April 2, 1949. A detailed report of the meeting appeared in *Literaturnaya Gazeta* for November 13, 1948. Little has been heard since of some of these scholars, e.g. Eichenbaum, Dolinin, and Gukovsky. It is significant that numerous flattering references to the last-named, one of the best specialists in eighteenth-century literature in the Soviet Union, have been removed from the already mentioned latest edition of Blagoy's textbook, and his works do not figure in Blagoy's bibliography.

"a remarkable Russian scholar, student of literature and linguist," and which stated that the papers read at the meeting "threw light on the many-sided scholarly works of our famous compatriot."[21] The general tenor of this handsome tribute to Veselovsky as a Russian scholar of international caliber may best be judged by the concluding lines of Professor Alekseyev's paper: "The role of Veselovsky in world scholarship is enormous, even though his influence on Western literary-historical thought and the popularity in the West of his most important works were to some extent limited. Doctor of one of the oldest Italian Universities, the University of Bologna, corresponding member of the Munich and Vienna Academies, Veselovsky enjoyed all-European recognition mostly on account of his earliest works. His later and maturer works, those in which he had outstripped Western European scholars in his universalism and in the breadth and depth of his literary-historical generalizations, were less known in the West. Nevertheless Veselovsky secured international recognition for Russian literary scholarship. There is no doubt that young Soviet literary scholarship which follows a different but a more certain path, having assimilated from Veselovsky's works all that is most valuable in them, will achieve a still wider dissemination among the scholars of the entire world." A little earlier in his paper, quoting Eberhardt Sauer's pessimistic verdict on the achievements of the German *Stoffgeschichte* on the threshold of the present century, Alekseyev expressed the opinion that, had Sauer known the fragments of Veselovsky's *Poetics of Plots*, he would have admitted that "the first truly scientific attempt at a *Stoffgeschichte* had been made by a Russian and that his unfinished work had left far behind all similar attempts by his Western contemporaries." Whatever reservations were made by the authors of this tribute to Veselovsky were all made in the name of Marxism, to which all of them had to pay lip-service—though, as a matter of fact, only one of them, Professor Desnitsky, as far as I know, was a Marxist and a Communist. There was no attempt to discredit Veselovsky's comparativism: in fact, its validity, especially when it came to Veselovsky's folklore studies and his work in medieval literature, was fully recognized.

Two years before, in 1936, an attempt was made by a Soviet scholar to reconcile Veselovsky with Marxism and to lay down the principles of Soviet comparativism. This was done by Victor Zhirmunsky, who later, in 1948, was to be branded as an active follower of Veselovsky. Zhirmunsky had begun his scholarly career before the Revolution with a study of German Romanticism. In the early post-revolutionary years he was prominent as a moderate fellow-traveler of Russian Formalism and author of a number of valuable works dealing with versification and theory of

---

21 *IAN OON*, 1938, No. 4, 138 pp. The volume contains five longish studies: V. F. Shishmaryov, "Alexander Nikolayevich Veselovsky;" V. M. Zhirmunsky, "A. N. Veselovsky's Historical Poetics"; V. A. Desnitsky, "A. N. Veselovsky in Russian Literary Scholarship"; M. K. Azadovsky, "A. N. Veselovsky as a Student of Folklore"; and M. P. Alekseyev, "A. N. Veselovsky and Western Literary Scholarship."

literature (*Introduction to Metrics, Problems of Theory of Literature,*
etc.) In 1924, Zhirmunsky published an excellent study of the reception
of Byron in Russia (*Byron and Pushkin*), following it up with a monumental monograph on Goethe in Russia and several other studies in
comparative literature. His exposé of Marxist comparativism of 1936
was given in the form of a paper entitled "Comparative Literature and
the Problem of Literary Influences" and published in the Bulletin of the
Social Sciences Section of the Academy of Sciences of the U.S.S.R.[22] It
is interesting and important enough to deserve a detailed analysis.

Zhirmunsky began by drawing an analogy with Marr's teaching about
the unity of the glottogonic process which, in accordance with the view
that was compulsory at the time, he described as "one of the most significant achievements of Soviet scientific thought."[23] In literature, too,
said Zhirmunsky, it was necessary to rise above national exclusiveness
and postulate the unity of literary processes. Hence it was possible to
compare analogous literary phenomena arising in the identical stages of
the social-historical process, regardless of whether there was or was
not a direct interaction between those phenomena. This led to the elimi-
nation of the traditional narrow concept of "literary influences," which
contradicted the use of the word "comparative" in other disciplines where
the comparison of analogous phenomena rested on general laws of development ("comparative anatomy," "comparative grammar," "comparative mythology"). Veselovsky had understood the comparative method in
this wider sense. For him the social-historical lawfulness (*zakonomernost'*,
Gesetzmässigkeit) of certain literary facts was demonstrated by their repe-
tition in analogous historical conditions. This idea underlay his ambitious
but unfinished *Historical Poetics*.[24] Veselovsky proceeded from the idea
of the unity and organic regularity of the process of development of world
literature in its social conditioning. This enabled him to compare as
socially equivalent such phenomena belonging to one and the same stage
of development as old Germanic poetry, ancient Greek poetry, and the
poetry of North American Indians, or as the *Iliad* and the *Kalevala*, the
funeral ritual in *Beowulf* and the Abyssinian lament about Balay, etc.
Veselovsky's *Historical Poetics*, according to Zhirmunsky, was the last
attempt made by bourgeois literary scholarship at a large historical synthesis. Its failure was due to his methodological errors, his positivism

---

[22] *IAN OON*, 1936, No. 3, pp. 383-403. It was originally read as a
paper at the inauguration of the Western Section of the Institute of
Literature on December 5, 1935.

[23] After 1950, Zhirmunsky, in line with other Soviet scholars, was to
join in the chorus which denounced Marr and his doctrine.

[24] Veselovsky's studies pertaining to this subject were republished under
this title, as late as 1940, with a long introduction by Zhirmunsky in
which the important place of Veselovsky in European literary scholarship
was duly stressed. In 1941, Professor M. Alekseyev published in the
learned journal of the University of Leningrad (*Uchonye Zapiski*, Philology series, No. 8) some fragments of Veselovsky's *Poetics of the Plots*, with
his comments.

and empiricism, his aversion to all philosophical speculation, to all *a priori* generalizations. After Hegel, there had been a decline of historical thought in the nineteenth century, an inability to produce a general historical synthesis; its place was taken by an endless accumulation of empirical facts. In the second half of the nineteenth century, so-called "general literature" had ceased to exist as a discipline; all that remained was national literatures and the intra-national intercourse among them (the so-called "literary influences"). Later, and especially after World War I, bourgeois literary scholarship, especially in Germany, returned from the philological analysis of empirical data to various types of *geistesgeschichtliche Synthese* (Gundolf, Cysarz). Soviet literary scholarship, on the other hand, developed on the basis of the laws of social development discovered by Marx and Engels. "The Marxist conception of the historical process for the first time enables us [wrote Zhirmunsky] to construe 'world literature' not as a simple sum total of national literatures, consisting . . . of a motley assortment of empirical facts, but as an organic (gesetzmässig) development of social (class) ideology on the basis of social-economic relations. The building up of general literature is the most urgent task confronting Soviet specialists in Western European literatures. The comparative method, understood not as a separate methodology but as a method of research, will occupy a very important place in general literature and in history of art. Comparison should serve as a device for ascertaining the regularity of literary phenomena which correspond to certain stages of social development."

Zhirmunsky then proceeded to illustrate his thought with some examples of "analogies" in literary development. Here are some of them:

(1) The heroic epos: German sagas, Russian *byliny*, Serbian historical songs, Mongol epics, all these betray many similarities. There is no doubt that many coincidences between the Russian *byliny* and the Western European epics on the one hand, and the Oriental (Iranian and Turkish) epic tradition on the other, which used to be attributed to borrowings, must be regarded as such analogies of literary development.

(2) The poetry of the troubadours and minnesingers has been compared with the analogous, and for the most part earlier, developments in Arab literature. Numerous parallels fail to solve the complex problem of direct influences of medieval Arabic poetry upon Provençal poetry. Rather, we are concerned here with a case of analogous development in similar conditions of feudal civilization. In the Christian West, the Provence was undoubtedly the source from which the poetry of chivalry spread. But even here the comparative study of the Provençal, Italian, Spanish, and German material reveals such a far-reaching similarity of poetic ideology and lyrical themes that "the mechanical imitation of imported models appears as an analogy of poetic thought, conditioned by general prerequisites of social development."

(3) The baroque period: Marinism in Italy, Gongorism in Spain,

the Metaphysical School in England, the poetry of the Thirty-Year-War period in Germany—or analogous tendencies in the genesis of the bourgeois drama and the family novel in eighteenth-century England and France—or similarities between the Lake poets and the early German romantics (Novalis, Tieck).

But analogies and influences were closely interlinked. The influences were determined in the first place by irregularities, contradictions, and delays which characterize the development of class society. More backward countries sometimes repeated the phase through which the more advanced countries had already passed. In Europe, from the age of feudal absolutism on, one could trace a certain sequence of literary (and, more generally, ideological) influences, the sources of which are to be sought in turn in the more advanced countries: the fourteenth to sixteenth centuries are the age of Italian Renaissance; the seventeenth century, of French classicism; the eighteenth to nineteenth centuries, of English and French bourgeois realism. Backward countries passed through a period of predominantly imitative literary development (German literature in the seventeenth and early eighteenth century, Russian literature before Pushkin; Germany remained passive until the time of *Werther*, Russia until the second half of the nineteenth century).

In pre-class society, influences played a minor part. In most cases there were coincidences based on analogies of development (here Zhirmunsky once more evoked Veselovsky, his theory of polygenesis of motifs and his distinction between motifs and plots). In medieval literature, influences already played a greater part. France was the main source of such influences in the feudal period. An important part in the transmission of influences was played by translations. Thus, early Russian narrative literature was made up mostly of translations. Migrating plots testified to the absence of a specifically national content in medieval literature. Nor did the individuality of the author play a decisive role. It was only in modern times that both the national peculiarities and the individual initiative became conspicuous factors (Byronism, George-Sandism, the influence of Goethe and Dickens). The concept of influence must be specified and circumscribed, said Zhirmunsky, and he formulated the following three principal reservations:

i. Similarity could be due to identical social-historical conditions. This was particularly true of similarities of a more general order—those of genres, styles, aesthetic principles, ideological trends. Here one had to do with analogies which did not presuppose a direct influence. In any case the existence of analogous trends in national literatures was a *conditio sine qua non* of intra-national literary influences.

ii. Influence was not a fortuitous mechanical push from outside, not an empirical fact of individual biography, not a result of chance familiarity or infatuation with a fashionable literary model or current. All influences were organic and socially conditioned. For an influence to become possible, there had to be a demand for ideological import, a pre-existence of analogous trends. While the literary genre of bourgeois drama or family novel in eighteenth-century France was encouraged by importations from England, a tendency toward its appearance must have pre-existed in French literature.

iii. All literary influence implied a social transformation of the model, that is, its more or less consistent adaptation to local peculiarities of social development and local demands of the class in its social practice. For a literary historian who was studying an individual case of literary influence, the question of the differences in the social background was no less important than that of similarities. (Zhirmunsky illustrated this point from the case of Milton and Klopstock).

The problem of influences, Zhirmunsky continued, was today unpopular both among the Soviet scholars and in the West, with the sole exception of the French comparativists who were diligently accumulating factual data without any general theoretical premises or conclusions. The problem of influences was discredited by the works of the so-called philological school. Modern literary scholarship in Germany (Gundolf and his followers) either ignored literary influences or denied their importance. This was due to the anti-historical trend of that school. Among Soviet literary scholars one could observe a somewhat wary attitude toward literary influences, for they were associated with a formalistic comparison of literary facts regardless of their social significance. Against this approach to the problem of literary influences (as an example Zhirmunsky cited his own work on Byron and Pushkin) it was necessary to point out that any fact of literary influence was an ideological, and hence a socially significant, fact. Thus interpreted, the study of influences would become an integral part of the study of literature as a specific variety of class ideology. Zhirmunsky recalled here the recent fallacy of "Pereverzevism,"[25] which undialectically had opposed ideology to social-economic relations, and he cited as a typical example of this Ulrich Vogt's study "Lermontov's *Demon* as a Style Phenomenon" (1928). Vogt, although perceiving similarities between Lermontov's poem and the works of Byron, *a priori* rejected all possibility of Byron's ideological influence on Lermontov and spoke of their "belonging to the same style, not only literarily but also social-economically."

In Marxist literature, Zhirmunsky went on, the problem of ideological influences was first posed by Plekhanov. Some of Plekhanov's statements, however, had led to serious misunderstandings. Plekhanov maintained that "the influence of the literature of one country on that of another is in direct ratio to the similarity of social relations in the two countries." Consequently, it did not exist when that similarity was nil. As an example,

---

25 On Pereverzev and "Pereverzevism" (which, in 1930, was denounced as "vulgarization of Marxism"), see Edward J. Brown, *The Proletarian Episode in Russian Literature, 1928-1932*, New York, 1953; also *id., The Russian Association of Proletarian Writers (1928-1932)* (Microfilm, Columbia University, 1950).

Plekhanov referred to the African Negroes on whom European literature had not had the slightest influence. Plekhanov further asserted that a literary influence worked one way when one of the two nations, because of its backwardness, could not offer anything to the other from the point of view of either form or content. (Example: French literature of the eighteenth century influenced Russian literature without undergoing the slightest influence from the latter.) Finally, an influence was reciprocal when, as a result of a similarity of social conditions and therefore of cultural development, each of the two nations could borrow something from the other. (Example: French literature, while influencing the English, was in turn influenced by it.)

Disagreeing with Plekhanov, Zhirmunsky asserted that the second, and not the third, case of literary influence was the most common. The intensity of literary influences depended not so much on the similarity of social relations during the identical stage of social development, as on the discrepancies and delays in such development, provided its general direction was similar. The influence of England on backward Germany, or of France on Russia in the eighteenth century, had been much greater than the literary interaction between Germany, France, and England in the post-World War I period, when they had reached the same level of social development. Thus, the influence of European literatures on African Negroes (which Plekhanov had denied on insufficient grounds) and the opposite influence of Negro art (which Plekhanov could not have foreseen) were witnesses to the wide diapason of such influences on different levels of cultural and social development.

Some of Plekhanov's followers had interpreted his thesis in a narrow and one-sided way. Hence the common sociological conclusion about the identity of the social basis and the class genesis of literary works as a necessary condition of literary influences. It would be easy to cite a number of cases when a writer—or at least some aspect of his work— by being reinterpreted had exercised an influence in a socially alien milieu. Chateaubriand's *René*, with its pessimism and anti-social propensities of a disillusioned émigré nobleman, was influenced by Goethe's *Werther*, which was imbued with the progressive, and on the whole optimistic, ideology of a rising class. Another such example was to be seen in the influence of the Greek tragedy (each time reinterpreted, as it were) on the classical French tragedy of Racine, on the philosophical-political French tragedy from Voltaire down to Marie-Joseph Chénier, on Goethe's *Iphigenia*, and on Hofmannsthal-Strauss's *Elektra*, which is so typical for the decadent period. If the influence of a writer had been confined to the literature with which he had a completely identical social basis, it would have been impossible to speak of Shakespeare's life through the ages, of the fate of Goethe's heritage in Russia or of *Cicero im Wandel der Jahrhunderte*. From the standpoint of such ordinary sociologism one would have to question the validity of the heritage of gentry-bourgeois literature in a Socialist society, or the possibility of Shakespeare's influence on Soviet dramaturgy, and so on. The possibilities of creative or theoretical re-interpretation were not endless, but their limits were wide enough. Beyond those limits, there began either indifference or a hostile reaction.

"It must be therefore admitted," Zhirmunsky concluded, "that for literary influences to be possible it is not necessary to have an *identity* of the social-economic basis . . . It would be enough to have a certain *similarity of social conditions*, which would allow this or that aspect of the imported model to be utilized or reinterpreted in the ideological clash of classes." Therefore a proper place was to be given in the Marxist science of literature to a comparative study of literature and of intra-national literary influences, understood not as a special method, but as a set of problems. The study of the literary processes in their national isolation had always led bourgeois scholarship to a narrow provincialism of outlook and to a harmful and fallacious nationalist approach. Marxists had to study separate national literatures within the world literary process as parts of a single process of social-historical development, taking account both of national pecularities and of intra-national interaction. "The history of Russian literature, just as the history of other national literatures, must not be severed from world literature of which it is a part."

This paper by Zhirmunsky is the most thorough and the best reasoned statement known to me of the problem of comparative literature as seen by moderate and independent Soviet scholars. It was made at the time when an openly non-Marxist approach to literature, such as was still possible in the 1920's, was no longer permitted. Much of it is therefore couched in Marxist or semi-Marxist jargon, and the whole smacks of eclecticism. It is an attempt to reconcile Marxism with Veselovskian comparativism, to avoid the pitfall of "vulgar sociologism," and at the same time to ward off in advance a possible accusation of "formalism" (hence a somewhat ambiguous and cautiously worded rejection of one's own "formalistic" work.) Zhirmunsky had always shown a propensity for compromise, for striking a happy medium (such was, for instance, his attitude in the earlier Marxist-Formalist controversy), but his concept of comparative literature was broad enough. Today it would be rejected outright, while Zhirmunsky's attack upon "narrow provincialism of outlook" and upon "harmful nationalist approach," addressed to "bourgeois" scholarship, would sound like bitter irony.

We have already seen that Zhirmunsky was one of the main targets in the post-War anti-Veselovskian campaign. But back in the 'twenties and early 'thirties it was he and his fellow-victims, all those who were to be branded as "comparativists," "rootless cosmopolitans," and even "passportless tramps,"—men like Tomashevsky, Eichenbaum, Grossman, Alekseyev, and others—who were responsible for most of the studies in the field of comparative literature and for keeping an eye on general literature in their University teaching. Most of these studies naturally were concerned with the influence of Western European literature on Russian writers or the reception of European writers in Russia (we saw that Zhirmunsky spoke quite frankly about the "passivity" of Russian literature until the second half of the nineteenth century).[26] Zhirmunsky's own *Byron and Pushkin* (1924) and *Goethe in Russian Literature* (1937) have already been mentioned. He also wrote about Pushkin and Western European literatures. Pushkin's relations with French literature were studied extensively by Tomashevsky and others. Among those who studied Pushkin on the comparative plane were also the veteran pre-revolutionary scholar M. Rozanov (Pushkin and Italian writers), M. Alekseyev ("Pushkin in the West," Pushkin and English literature), the late D. Yakubovich (several studies on Pushkin and Walter Scott), and others. Leonid Grossman specialized in Dostoevsky on the one hand and in Balzac on the other ("Balzac and Dostoevsky," "Dostoevsky and Europe," "Balzac in Russia") ; he also wrote on Tolstoy and Stendhal and on various other contacts between Russia and the West. N. Piksanov, a well-known pre-revolutionary scholar and a specialist on Griboedov, gave a definitive study of Griboedov and Molière (1922). Turgenev's relations with the West were studied by Sakulin, Alekseyev, and others.

In the way of more general works one might include *Russian Romanticism* (1927), edited by A. Beletsky. There were also several studies dealing with the relations between Russian and foreign literatures in the eighteenth century (Pumpyansky on Kantemir and Italian literature, on Tredyakovsky and the German rationalists, etc.) One must also mention such valuable collective undertakings as the three Franco-Russian volumes of *Literaturnoe Nasledstvo* (*Literary Heritage*), published in 1937-39 and containing among other things a wealth of unpublished material concerning Voltaire, Joseph de Maistre, Mme. de Staël, Chateaubriand, Balzac and other French writers. A similar Anglo-Russian series was being prepared for the press during the war, but was never published, no doubt because of the anti-Western and anti-comparativist turn in Communist policy after 1946; it was to contain unpublished letters of Sir Walter

---

[26] The Formalists, especially during their early, "militant," period (in the early 1920's), rejected the traditional approach to the intra-national influences. This may be best seen from the following passage in Tomashevsky's French article (see note 1): "Cette notion de la détermination interne de l'évolution littéraire a particulièrement attiré l'attention des chercheurs sur les causes nationales dans les révolutions littéraires; elle a entraîné quelque négligence des influences étrangères. Les relations internationales sont l'objet d'une étude scrupuleuse, mais en constatant le transfert des idées et des faits littéraires d'un pays à l'autre on se préoccupe surtout d'éclaircir quelles sont les causes nationales qui ont déterminé le recours aux modèles étrangers . . . L'influence de Dostoevskij et de Tolstoj sur le roman français est un problème de l'évolution nationale du roman français, et non point un fait imposé de l'extérieur qui aurait détourné la littérature française de son cours naturel. L'assimilation d'éléments étrangers est essentiellement un acte d'adaptation préalable. La littérature des traductions doit donc être étudiée comme un élément constitutif de la littérature de chaque nation. A côté du Béranger français et du Heine allemand il a existé un Béranger et un Heine russes qui répondaient aux besoins de la littérature russe et qui, sans doute, étaient assez loin de leurs homonymes d'Occident." In the main, this idea was incorporated by Zhirmunsky in his scheme outlined above.

Scott, George Borrow, Dickens, and other English writers. The special Goethe volume of *Literary Heritage,* published for the centenary of Goethe's death, is also of great value and interest. Most of the other pre-War volumes of that publication devoted much space to the theme of Russia's literary relations with the West. The same is true of many works dealing with Russian literature; it was seldom treated in isolation from world literature, foreign influences were unashamedly admitted, and cosmopolitanism in the good sense of that word characterized many of these literary studies. When all the Russian *addenda* to the Baldensperger-Friederich *Bibliography* are completed (the original volume had many gaps and inaccuracies), it may surprise some people to see how much was done in Russia since the Revolution in the field of intra-national literary relations in the widest sense of that term. The titles listed above represent but a small selection.

It should also be mentioned that in the 1920's, when the so-called Formalists played the dominant role in Russian literary scholarship, a great number of works were published dealing with problems of general poetics, in which the comparative approach played an important part: *e.g.,* Zhirmunsky's *Introduction to Metrics* (1925) and *Rhyme: Its History and Theory* (1923), Tomashevsky's *Theory of Literature* (1927), Tynyanov's *The Problem of Verse Language* (1924), Shklovsky's *Sterne's "Tristram Shandy" and the Theory of the Novel* (1921). An international approach was also to be found in such "synthetic" attempts of the late Pavel N. Sakulin as "The Sociological Method in Literature" (1925), "A Synthetic Scheme of History of Literature" (1925) and "Theory of Literary Styles" (1928), as well as in his *Russian Literature and Socialism* (1924). Sakulin was a representative of non-Marxian eclectic sociologism.

The above mentioned example of the Anglo-Russian volume of *Literaturnoe Nasledstvo,* which never saw the light of day, is a good illustration of how literary scholarship in the Soviet Union depends on extra-literary considerations, those of domestic and/or foreign policy. Other examples of this—from the opposite end, as it were—may be seen in the sudden popularity of Western and "comparative" themes during World War II, when the Soviet Union became an ally of Western democracies. In the academic publications of this time such themes were given a place of honor. Here are some titles picked at random from the wartime volumes (1941-44) of the University of Leningrad Publications in Philology: V. M. Zhirmunsky, "Byron and the Modern World;" B. G. Reizov, "Chateaubriand and the Rise of the French Historical Novel (*Les Martyrs*);" E. I. Mikhlin, "Literary Theories of Early French Naturalism;" N. A. Sigal, "Bodenstedt, the Translator of Lermontov;" M. P. Alekseyev, "On the Links Between the Russian and the English Theatre at the End of the Seventeenth and the Beginning of the Eighteenth Century;" S. D. Balukhaty, "A. M. Gorky and English Culture;" G. A. Bialy, "V. G. Korolenko and America;" M. P. Alekseyev, "English Language in Russia and Russian

Language in England;"[27] M. L. Tronskaya, "From the History of Sterne-anism: Theodor von Hippel." Today most of these studies would probably be banned as "servile," "cosmopolitan," and what not. Had not Balukhaty (a noted Gorky and Chekhov scholar) died in 1945, he would undoubtedly have been berated for assembling so carefully all those utterances of Gorky which testified to his respect and admiration for English culture and British tradition. As for Bialy, in his article on Korolenko and America he not only spoke of the positive sides of the American way of life, but described Korolenko as "an enthusiastic admirer of (Victor) Hugo and in many ways a disciple of European Romantics." Today both Gorky and Korolenko are used only as texts for anti-American and anti-European invectives. So far, there seems to be no real change in the intellectual climate, and one can say that comparative literature today simply does not exist in Russia. Even the publication of new material bearing on Russia's literary intercourse with the West has been influenced by the general anti-Western attitude and therefore limited and one-sided. Nor can one say that Kirpotin's suggestion about the necessity of studying the influence of Russian literature on the West has so far borne fruit. Such a "promising" subject as the influence of Chekhov outside Russia has not been tackled by any Soviet scholar, and it is doubtful whether in their present enforced isolation from the West they would be capable of coping with it. Even compared with the 1930's, the knowledge of the West in Russia seems to have declined very noticeably.

----

[27] This study of some 60 pages is much wider than its title would suggest: it deals with the whole subject of Anglo-Russian cultural intercourse from the sixteenth century to our day and contains a wealth of information on translators, intermediaries, channels of reciprocal information, and so on, and is full of stimulating suggestions for further research.

P.S. At the Second Congress of Soviet Writers (the first since 1934), which took place in Moscow in December 1954, Boris Ryurikov, the editor of *Literaturnaya Gazeta*, in his report on "The Main Problems of Soviet Literary Criticism," mentioning the campaign against "pseudo-scholarly, idealistic science" resulting from the fight against anti-comparativism, noted also the excesses of that campaign. "Here too," said Ryurikov, "we could not do without some vulgarization: there were some critics who denounced as treason every single word about the influence of this or that Western writer on a Russian writer, and affixed the label of servility. We reject the attempts of the vulgarizers to fence off the history of Russian literature from that of world literature—such attempts are anti-scholarly and alien to our outlook." Ryurikov said that the real meaning of the anti-cosmopolitan campaign was not so much in pinning down the errors of Veselovsky and his disciples, as in "drawing attention to the *positive* task of laying bare the deep roots which bind literary geniuses to the people which produced them and to the country which nurtured them." This and some similar utterances at the Congress signified a definite change of official tactics. Even more emphatic warnings against neglecting or undermining Western European and American achievements came recently from Soviet scholars in other fields, especially in the sciences. There is no doubt that we have to do here with a new Party line in international relations. How this change of policy will affect actual developments in literary scholarship remains to be seen. The fact remains that the latter is subordinate to the Party line.

THE GROWTH OF COMPARATIVE LITERATURE IN THE NETHERLANDS

A. M. M. P. van Eupen

Institute of Comparative Literature
State University of Utrecht

The following article can give only a very superficial sketch of Comparative Literature in the Netherlands. A complete history does not yet exist, although individual studies have been published on various aspects of our field.[1] Moreover, this article will have to separate the Northern Netherlands from Flemish-speaking Belgium. But in spite of the political separation of North and South in 1830, there exists an ever-growing wish for cooperation between the scholars of the two countries. This wish finds expression in the joint Congresses of Philology (dating from 1897) and in a joint composition of a *Literary History of the Netherlands* under the editorship of Professor F. Baur.[2]

In the second half of the eighteenth century, at a time when the language, the literature, and the manners of the higher classes were completely gallicized, while the bulk of the population basked in the past glory of the Golden Age of Holland, Rijklof Michael van Goens (1748-1810) was the first Dutchman who had the courage to defy public opinion and to attack the principles of French Classicism.[3] He held that it was more important to absorb the spirit of the great classics than the texts alone, and he also advocated the study of modern foreign literatures and in particular the literary-aesthetic ideas of Lessing, Mendelssohn and Riedel. Riedel's *Theorie der schönen Künste und Wissenschaften* was especially influential on Hieronymus van Alphen, the brother-in-law of Van Goens.[4]

The outbreak of the Napoleonic Wars and the occupation of the Netherlands dealt a sharp blow to our self-respect and stimulated the desire for new national activities. In 1797, the first chair of Dutch language and

---

[1] Baur, F. De vergelijkende methode in de literatuurwetenschap. **Album** Vercoullie I, p. 33-45. Brussel 1927.

Baur, F. Literatuur, haar geschiedschrijving en methodes. **Geschiedenis van de Letterkunde der Nederlanden I, Inleiding.** 's Hertogenbosch/Brussel 1939.

Brom, G. Geschiedschrijvers van onze Letterkunde. Amsterdam, z.j.

Gielen, J. Komparatistisch uitzicht in onze Nederlandsche Literatuurgeschiedschrijving. Nieuwe Taalgids XXXI, 1937, p. 1-26.

Vries, D. de. De vergelijkende literatuurstudie. **Neophilologus XX,** 1935.

[2] Geschiedenis van de Letterkunde der Nederlanden I- . . . 's Hertogenbosch/Brussel 1939- . .

[3] Wille, J. De Literator R. M. van Goens en zijn kring I. Zutphen 1937.

Boer, P. J. C. de. Rijklof Michael van Goens (1748-1810) en zijn verhouding tot de literatuur van West-Europa. Diss. Amsterdam 1938.

[4] Koe, A. C. S. de. Van Alphen's literair-aesthetische theorieën. **Diss.** Utrecht 1910.

eloquence was established at Leyden, our oldest university. Matthew Siegenbeek (1774-1854), the first occupant of this chair and a strong admirer especially of Greek literature,[5] may be mentioned for his "Critical Comparison Between Vondel's Lucifer and Milton's Paradise Lost" in which he used Vondel as an illustration for his patriotic belief that the Golden Age of Dutch literature had produced men and works that could well be placed on the same high level as foreign masterpieces.[6] This trend towards a literary rebirth produced also a second comparative essay of significance, "The Epigram," in which its author, Joannes Lublink the Younger (1736-1816), tried to arrive at a sharp definition of a genre by tracing it through several literatures back to the Greeks and analyzing its various aspects.[7] A second treatise by Lublink, "About Criticism," is important not only as a contribution to literary criticism in the Netherlands but also as a discussion of some sound principles of comparatism.[8]

More important than J. P. van Cappelle, who in 1821 wrote a "Treatise Concerning the Influence of Dutch Literature upon High German Literature in the Seventeenth Century,"[9] was William de Clercq (1795-1844), who in 1822 won the first prize in an essay-contest of the Royal Dutch Institute. It dealt with the question of the influence which foreign literatures, especially those of Italy, Spain, France, and Germany, had had upon the language and the literature of Holland from the beginning of the fifteenth to the beginning of the nineteenth centuries. It was our first literary history based upon truly comparative methods.[10]

From this time on, scholars consciously began to continue and to complete the work initiated by William de Clercq. In 1823, there was established, in Amsterdam, an English Literary Society for the purpose of advancing the knowledge of English literature in Holland, and among its first results was an essay by N. G. van Kampen (1776-1839) on "The Influence of English Literature on Dutch Literature."[11] Other disciples of William de Clercq turned to the study of medieval Dutch literature—a trend entirely natural in view of the very great predilection for the Middle Ages felt by most European romanticists. The *Horae Belgicae* of

---

[5] Over de handhaving van den echt Nederlandschen geest, in de beoefening der fraaije letteren en kunsten. Museum IV, Haarlem 1817.

[6] Beoordeelende vergelijking van den Lucifer van Vondel en het Verloren Paradijs van Milton. Museum IV, Haarlem 1817.

[7] Verhandeling over het Puntdicht. Nieuw Algemeen Magazijn van Wetenschap, Konst en Smaak III, stuk I, p. 125-162.

[8] Verhandeling over de Kritiek. Nieuw Algemeen Magazijn van Wetenschap, Konst en Smaak III, stuk I, p. 455-484.

[9] Cappelle, J. P. van. Bydragen tot de geschiedenis der wetenschappen en letteren in Nederland, p. 169-272. Amsterdam 1821.

[10] Verhandeling van den Heer Willem de Clercq ter beantwoording der vraag: welken invloed heeft vreemde letterkunde, inzonderheid de Italiaansche, Spaansche, Fransche en Duitsche, gehad op de Nederlandsche taal- en letterkunde, sinst het begin der vyftiende eeuw tot op onze dagen? Amsterdam 1824, 1826[2].

[11] Kampen, N. G. van. De invloed van de Engelsche letterkunde op de Nederlandsche. Amsterdam 1836.

1830 by the German Hoffmann von Fallersleben contained many medieval
Dutch songs which had been collected with the help of scholars like W.
Bilderdijk, N. G. van Kampen, M. Siegenbeek and others. This encouraged further indigenous activities of which the center was W. J.
A. Jonckbloet (1817-85), who, in 1842, established the Society for the
Advancement of Ancient Dutch Literature. This society prepared the
first exact editions of the most important medieval Dutch literary texts
and provided them with scholarly comparisons with the corresponding
texts of their sources (mainly French). Through his enthusiastic work
on medieval Dutch and French literature, Jonckbloet also prepared the
ground for the later professorships of modern languages in Groningen.
Jonckbloet should also be noted for his *History of Medieval Dutch Poetry*
of 1851, which was modelled on the work of Gervinus[12] and for his scholarly *History of Dutch Literature*.[13]

During the period from 1830 till 1880, literary criticism pioneered
further corrections of taste and indicated the path which authors and
literary historians were to follow later. Potgieter (1808-75), one of the
champions of "surrounding Holland with Europe," in 1837 established the
important periodical "De Gids" which is still in existence today and which
during its first fifty years served as the great center of literary life in
the Netherlands. It fought against slavish imitation, not only of the
French, but also of the historical novels of Sir Walter Scott—for historical
novels, like every other work of art, should always be true and national.[14]
"De Gids" promoted the idea of attempting historical theories of various
genres and, in so doing, it demonstrated the strong influence of history
on the various forms of art.[15] It also advocated thematology and de-
fended its importance.[16]

All these endeavors led to the important Movement of the Eighties,
when all the ideas promulgated before reached their finest fruition. By
1880, the study of the Dutch language and literature had proved its
right to exist; in fact, owing to the efforts of Jonckbloet, it was possible
to take a degree in this subject from 1876 on. In Leyden, Jonckbloet was
appointed to become professor of Dutch literature, its history and its
aesthetic criticism. Groningen established lectures on French, English
and German, and in his opening lecture in 1878, B. Symons delivered a
remarkable plea on behalf of Comparative Literature, interpreting the
field as a study both of the common cultural heritage of nations and of
mutual literary influences.[17] Symons, who had completed his scholarly

---

[12] Jonckbloet, W. J. A. Geschiedenis der Middennederlandsche Dichtkunst. Amsterdam 1851.
[13] Jonckbloet, W. J. A. Geschiedenis der Nederlandsche letterkunde.
Groningen 1868-1872.
[14] De Gids 1837, I B, p. 331-345.
[15] De Gids 1838, I B, p. 461-473; 521-535.
[16] De Gids 1839, M, p. 152-168; 202-215.
[17] Over de wetenschappelijke beoefening der moderne talen. Rede
Groningen 1878.

training at Leipzig, and his colleague A. G. van Hamel, who had studied in Paris and Bonn and who, in 1884, became professor of French at Groningen, both fought to obtain a solid academic status for the study of Dutch and foreign literatures. Jonckbloet's successor at Leyden, Jan ten Brink, should be noted for his *Literary History of the Netherlands in the Nineteenth Century, Biographies and Bibliography, 1830-80*, which in its Introduction contained a survey of Romanticism in the Netherlands and of the foreign influences at work.[18] One year later, in 1889, there also appeared from his hand *The Epistolary Novel, 1740-1840, Specimen of Comparative Literary History*, a rather feeble attempt to study the essence and the history of a genre.[19]

A more significant continuator of Jonckbloet's endeavors than ten Brink was G. Kalff, whose dissertation, in 1883, dealt with the Dutch and German "Lied" during the Middle Ages[20] and who, when appointed to a professorship at Utrecht in 1896, inaugurated his lectures by a vigorous defence of thematology.[21] Kalff hailed thematological theses by his students as significant contributions to comparative literary history,[22] and in an article of 1916, "General and Comparative Literature; a Lack in Our University Education" he visualized a natural development from national literary history to the literary history of foreign countries, to a general history of literatures, and finally to a last stage, to Comparative Literature.[23] His important, though unfinished, *Literary History of Western Europe, Fifteenth and Sixteenth Centuries*, was edited by his son after his death in 1923.[24] Outstanding among Kalff's contemporaries to complement his work was Professor J. Prinsen, a specialist for the eighteenth century, whose comparative methods applied not only to Dutch literature[25] but also to general European literature. His studies on the novel and the drama of the eighteenth century are as yet unsurpassed.[26] Besides this, Prinsen has been the stimulating force for several comparative dissertations concerning foreign influences.

Success was achieved when Groningen was the first to establish a Germanic-Romanic Institute in 1915 and when, six years later, new aca-

---

[18] Geschiedenis der Noord-Nederlandsche Letteren in de XIXe eeuw. In Biographieën en Bibliographieën, 1830-1880. Amsterdam 1888.
[19] De Roman in brieven 1740-1840. Een proeve van vergelijkende letterkundige geschiedenis. Amsterdam 1889.
[20] Het Lied in de Middeleeuwen. Diss. Leiden 1883.
[21] Taalstudie en Literatuurstudie. Rede Utrecht 1896.
[22] Haslinghuis, E. J. De Duivel in het Drama der Middeleeuwen. Diss. Leiden 1912.
[23] Algemeene en vergelijkende Literatuurgeschiedenis. Een leemte in ons Hooger onderwijs. Vragen des Tijds 1916, p. 451-476.
[24] Westeuropeesche Letterkunde I, 15de-16de eeuw. Groningen/Den Haag 1923.
[25] Prinsen, J. Handboek tot de Nederlandsche letterkundige geschiedenis. 's Gravenhage 1916.
[26] De Roman in de 18e eeuw in West-Europa. Groningen-Den Haag 1925. Het Drama in de 18e eeuw in West-Europa. Zutphen 1931.

demic statutes brought university examinations and degrees in modern philology within reach of all. Chairs for modern languages and literatures are either being created or consolidated at all Dutch universities up to this very day. With the comparative idea generally accepted by them, it became necessary to establish a methodology. This was largely done by a Belgian scholar, Professor F. Baur, a continuator of the work of G. Kalff, who published his "Comparative Method in the Science of Literature" in 1927. In his Introduction to the first volume of his ample *History of the Literature of the Northern and the Southern Netherlands*, Professor Baur likewise supplied a complete method of literary historiography.[27]

Once the study of modern languages and literatures was organized by the founding of chairs and institutes, and a method of investigation was being worked out, the further study of Comparative Literature called for a permanent center which would provide the indispensable materials from all over the world and which would also further the contact with other nations. Hence, in 1948, the founding of an Institute for Comparative Literature at the State University of Utrecht (Instituut voor Vergelijkend Literatuuronderzoek aan de Rijksuniversiteit te Utrecht) under the directorship of H. Sparnaay, Professor of German Language and Literature, a medievalist and Arthurian scholar, and of W. A. P. Smit, Professor of Dutch Literature and a specialist in the sixteenth and seventeenth centuries. The rich output of comparative investigations since World War II bodes well for the continuing growth of Comparative Literature in the Netherlands.[28]

---

[27] See notes 1 and 2.

[28] Some publications which appeared after the second world-war:

Gerhardt, M. I. Essai d'analyse littéraire de la Pastorale dans les littératures italienne, espagnole et française. Diss. Leiden 1950.

Greevenbroek, J. Th. R. van E. J. Potgieter. L'homme et l'œuvre dans leurs rapports avec la littérature française. Diss. Amsterdam 1951.

Gunkel, R. Büchner und der Dandysmus. Diss. Utrecht 1953.

Heybroek, J. F. De fabel. Ontwikkeling van een literatuursoort in Nederland en in Vlaanderen. Amsterdam 1951.

Hoogewerff, G. J. Nederlandsche dichters in Italië in de zeventiende eeuw. 's Gravenhage 1950.

Huisman, J. A. Neue Wege zur dichterischen und musikalischen Technik Walthers von der Vogelweide. Mit einem Exkurs über die symmetrische Zahlenkomposition im Mittelalter. Diss. Utrecht 1950.

Jans, R. Tolstoj in Nederland. Diss. Nijmegen 1952.

Kat, J. F. M. De Verloren Zoon als letterkundig motief. Diss. Nijmegen 1952.

Premsela, M. J. Anatole France en Hollande. La Haye 1947.

Siemers, Th. B. B. Seneca's Hercules furens en Euripides' Heracles. Diss. Utrecht 1951.

Zaalberg, C. A. Das Buch Extasis van Jan van der Noot. Diss. Utrecht 1954.

Zandvoort, R. W. Shakespeare in de twintigste eeuw. Groningen/Djakarta 1952.

PORTUGAL'S LITERARY RELATIONS WITH THE OUTSIDE WORLD*

Francis M. Rogers
Harvard University

The section on Portuguese contributions in the Baldensperger-Friederich *Bibliography of Comparative Literature (BFCL)* may, on first consultation, appear all too brief. It must be used, however, in conjunction with the many other items concerning Portugal (themes, genres, Antiquity, Orient, Italy, etc.) archived in appropriate places throughout the bibliography and its four supplements.[1]

The Portuguese bibliography provided in the present *Yearbook* of necessity has many shortcomings. Its bias in favor of the Portuguese discoveries and overseas expansion in the fifteenth and sixteenth centuries, to the partial neglect of other periods, testifies to the particular interest of the compiler. Regardless of the bibliography's inadequacies, it is clear that literary studies involving Portugal on an international basis are in their infancy. Portugal is amply and ably represented in international geographical circles. Although knowledge of her history is not as widespread as desirable, basic work has been done, and bibliographies and directories of archives are available (D.V.1.). Portugal forms part of the international world of linguistic science, and Portuguese linguistics is regularly included in the standard bibliographies (D.V.6.). With the possible exceptions of the medieval *cancioneiro* poetry, the Inês de Castro theme, and *Os Lusíadas*, Portuguese literature has not entered the international scene. The great Eça de Queiroz can hardly be said to enjoy an international reputation, and the extremely poor translation of his *Primo Bazilio* recently presented to the English-reading world will hardly aid his cause.[2]

---

* The Editors are deeply grateful for the hundreds of new bibliographical items on Portugal collected by Dean Rogers which make it possible to provide this *Yearbook* with a first supplementary chapter on Portugal. Other Portuguese items supplied by Mr. Rogers in this year's Bibliography can be found under the heading of Orient, Spain, France, and England—while again others will be included in later issues. References like D.V.2 mean Book Four (The Modern World), Part Five (Portuguese Contributions), Chapter Two (Camoens).

[1] The following pages in the *BFCL* and supplements contain items on Brazil, by Brazilians, or published in Brazil. They are in addition to Book Four, Fifth Part, Portuguese Contributions (pp. 473-475). *BFCL*, pp. 48, 112, 197, 315, 331, 349, 354, 361, 421, 449, 483, 484, 499, 509, 520, 521, 545, 599, 603, 622, 668, 669, and 675; supplement I, pp. 98, 99, 129, 142, and 143; supplement II, pp. 104, 119, 122, 123, 124, 135, 142, 155; supplement III, pp. 111, 123, 130, 144, 158, and 170.

[2] Eça de Queiroz, *Cousin Bazilio, translated by Roy Campbell with an introduction by Federico de Onís*, New York: The Noonday Press, 1953. This translation was also issued by Max Reinhard in London; for an unfavorable review, see *Atlante*, II (1954).

It is possibly unjust to assert that Portuguese literature is not a part of the world's literary heritage. It would be more accurate to state that scholarship has not yet revealed to what extent Portuguese literature has, in fact, had international ramifications. Hence the great need for many and detailed studies.

For one accustomed to thinking of Portugal's foreign relations exclusively in terms of England, the Portuguese bibliography, perhaps fortuitously, will contain surprises. It reveals the closeness of relations down the centuries between Portugal and Italy on the one hand and Portugal and Flanders on the other. In spite of the studies already published, there is evidence of need for considerably more research concerning Portuguse influences on Italian books. Portuguese deeds of the fifteenth century were the object of all Europe's admiration. Portuguese exploits in North Africa left their echo in an Italian play, *La forsennata principessa*, in which the Prince of Morocco elopes with the Princess of Portugal,[3] and also in a tale in Masuccio's *Novellino* about Alfonso V's generosity in releasing a captive Arab during his Moroccan campaign. Moreover, the travels of the "figliuolo del re di Portogallo" have done the rounds in story form in Italy. A *novella* in Sabadino degli Arienti's *Porretane* tells of them, as does another story taken down from oral tradition toward the end of the nineteenth century.[4]

In recent years the pivotal role of Isabel of Portugal, Philippe le Bon's duchess for thirty-seven years, has attracted the attention of scholars (D.V.2.). This interest will assuredly lead to extended knowledge of the pan-European cultural influence of the court of Burgundy.

The Portuguese additions to the *BFCL* are intended as guides for the direction of future research rather than as a detailed inventory of investigations already completed. Many of the works listed as concerning inter-national relations, although they hardly belong in a strictly literary bibliography, may perhaps prove of worth to the literary historian. Occasionally suggestions are included which may lead to a broadening of our understanding of Portugal's literary contributions. An example is the identification of certain themes as Portuguese, shipwreck and the legend of the seven cities, for instance (A.VI.10.). To allege an influence of Camões on Somerset Maugham may be stretching the evidence (D.V.4.4.). Not so with Kermit Roosevelt, however, and decidedly not so with Melville, who makes direct reference to the giant Adamastor, "Camoëns' Spirit of the Cape, an eclipsing menace mysterious and prodigious," in *Billy Budd, Foretopman,* and describes the *Lusíadas* as the "man-of-war epic of the World" in *White Jacket.* He has also left two poems entitled "Camoëns."

---

[3] Enzo Petraccone, *La commedia dell'arte* (Naples, 1927), pp. 341-349.
[4] Vittorio Imbriani, *La novellaja fiorentina,* 2nd ed., Leghorn, 1877. Gherardo Nerucci, *Sessanta novelle popolari montalesi (circondario di Pistoia),* 2nd ed., Florence, 1891.

Melville owned a copy of Camões' lyrics in the Strangford translation.[5]
The late Professor F. O. Matthiessen possessed this copy and was kind
enough to lend it to me. On p. 40, opposite the line which reads, "And
sweetest eyes that e'er were seen!", was the notation, "Cf. Mrs. Browning's verses on this." Elizabeth Barrett did indeed know Camões (D.V.2.),
as did Wordsworth, and Stendhal, and Chateaubriand. One is tempted to
conclude that the romantic biography of Camões rather than the *Lusíadas*
has fascinated these writers. This biography has become a literary work
in itself, and even New England's Harriet Low (A.IV.3.) succumbed to
its charm while residing in Macau:

> Tuesday [October 13, 1829] we were invited to Mrs. Fearon's to
> take tea and walk in the garden. It is the most romantic place,
> is very extensive, and abounds in serpentine walks. There is a
> beautiful view of the sea, and immense rocks and trees, and several
> temples in the garden. In another part there is a cave in the rocks
> where the celebrated Camoëns wrote his "Lusiad." A bust of him
> stands in the cave. It is a wild and delightful spot.

A perusal of the whole of the *BFCL* in search of Portuguese items has
revealed many *lacunae* in scholarship involving Portugal. Thus, under
B.I.9., what of the *Arabian Nights* in Portugal? As for the Turks (B.I.7.),
Professor Bataillon has pointed out, in his review[6] of Rouillard's study on
the Turk in French history, thought, and literature, that it is time for
methodical studies on the Turk in German, Spanish, and Italian history
and literature. He might have included Portugal, for the "pequena casa
lusitana" was quite as aware of Turks as of Moors. The Infante Dom
Pedro fought both, in person (C.III.10.).

Portugal's great contribution to the scientific and cultural history
of mankind was her transmission of knowledge of the Orient, and of part
of America, to Western Europe, and her transmission of Western values
in the opposite direction. Her glory was the age of discovery and exploration. St. Exupéry, describing in the *Lettre à un ôtage* the tragic
days of 1940 as he observed their impact on Lisbon, indicates the extent
to which she is still affected by her past achievements. This subject,
unlike the less interesting problem of Amadís de Gaula, has been far from
exhausted by scholars. There are no Portuguese entries under D.VII.16.
(Montaigne) and none under D.VII.17. (Rabelais), yet Nicolas de Grouchy
(D.V.7.), who translated Fernão Lopes de Castanheda's *História* into
French, was Montaigne's teacher at the Collège de Guyenne, and the first
phase of the "navigations de Pantagruel" manifests Rabelais' knowledge
of the Portuguese sea road to the Indies. Moreover, when one enumerates
the great collectors Ramusio, Hakluyt, and Purchas, one habitually omits
the first great collector of travel narratives, Valentim Fernandes "the

---

[5] *Poems, from the Portuguese of Luis de Camoens. With remarks on
His Life and Writings. Notes, etc. etc. By Lord Viscount Strangford.
. . . A New Edition*, London, 1824. See Merton M. Sealts, Jr., "Melville's
Reading: A Check-List of Books Owned and Borrowed" (*Harvard Library
Bulletin*, II-IV, 1948-50), III, 119, and IV, 108.
[6] *Revue de Littérature Comparée*, XXI (1947), 623.

German," of Moravia, intermediary par excellence who published Marco Polo, Nicolò de' Conti, and Girolamo da Santo Stephano in Portuguese in 1502 (A.IV.8.).[7]

A genealogy of the editions, and editions of translations, of the Portuguese books on the East, by Francisco Álvares, Dom João de Castro, Garcia da Orta ("Harto, the historian of Goa," in *Moby Dick*), António Galvão, Luis de Camões, Fernão Mendes Pinto, Jacinto Freire de Andrade, Jerónimo Lobo, and many others, would be a most helpful tool. An index merely of the Portuguese narratives in Ramusio, Hakluyt, and Purchas would be a welcome addition to one's reprint file.

I have attempted a genealogy of the sort I have in mind with the *Roteiro de Goa a Suez* of Dom João de Castro. The Cotton MS. of this description of the Red Sea was translated into Latin and published by Matthaeus in 1699, and reprinted in 1738. The Latin was again published by Nunes de Carvalho in 1833 along with the original Portuguese text of the MS., now in the British Museum. Kammerer put Nunes de Carvalho's Portuguese text into French in 1936 and his Latin text into French the following year. Finally, in 1940 Fontoura da Costa published a new edition of the Portuguese text printed by Nunes de Carvalho, but compared this time, so he states, with another MS. in the possession of the Duke of Palmela in Lisbon. To go back to the Cotton MS., it was also done into English and appeared in Purchas (1625) and then in Astley (1745), and then in Kerr (1812), who used both Purchas and Astley. Purchas went into Dutch in 1706 in two editions, folio and octavo, published by Pieter Vander Aa. Astley went into the Abbé Prévost's French (1746), in a quarto edition. Hondt reprinted, and corrected, this French in 1747, and the same year issued a new Dutch translation. In 1749 an edition of Prévost's French appeared in-16, and in 1763 Terracina's Spanish translation of Prévost was issued. Returning to 1747, in that year Astley went into German, by Schwabe, and the following year the German was done into Danish. An illustration of the need for this kind of listing is provided by the fact that no Portuguese scholar, to my knowledge, has been aware of the Danish translation of Castro's rutter.[8]

---

[7] The Lisbon, 1502, edition of the *Livro de Marco Paulo* was reproduced in a facsimile edition, Lisbon, 1922.

[8] *Almindelig Historie over Reiser til Lands og Vands; eller Samling af alle reisebeskrivelser, som hidindtil ere udgivne i adskillige Sprog af alle Folk. Sammendragen ved et Selskab laerde Maend i det Engelske, og nu oversat paa Dansk,* 17 vols., Copenhagen, 1748-62. The Castro text is in vol. I, pp. 196-227, i.e., Book I, chap. xviii; its title is "Don Stephano de Gamas Reise fra Goa til Suez, i det Oiemerke, at forbraende de torkiske Skibe i denne Havn, beskreven ved Don Juan de Kastro, paa den Tid vaerende Skibshovedsmand paa Floden og derefter Statholder og Vicekonge i Indien; oversat og sammendragen af det Portugisiske."

I am indebted to Mr. Palle Birkelund, librarian of the Koneglige Bibliotek in Copenhagen, who, at the request of Professor Jakob Nielsen, my colleague on the Administrative Board of the International Association of Universities, furnished me with the above information. I have been un-

Such is the dissemination received by one Portuguese text on the achievements in the East. These deeds were made known not only by the Lusitanians, but by other great intermediaries, notably the Italian Ludovico de Varthema, the Dutch Jan Huygen van Linschoten, and the French François Pyrard de Laval,[9] the genealogy of whose editions and translations is also complicated, yet necessary for the historian of ideas.

AMERICAN DOCTORAL STUDIES IN GERMANIC CULTURES*
A Study in German-American Relations, 1873-1949

By Ralph P. Rosenberg
Yeshiva University

There is an impressive number of European bibliographies of doctoral dissertations, some of them of long standing, which list, respectively, the theses of all the universities of Canada,[1] Denmark,[2] England,[3] France,[4] Germany,[5] Holland (and Belgium),[6] Russia,[7], Scandinavia,[8] South

---

able to find the *Almindelig Historie over Reiser* in the United States, and it is not in the Biblioteca Nacional, Lisbon. I was led to the Danish by a chance remark of Cox, *Reference Guide to the Literature of Travel*, I, p. 33. This led me to Chr. V. Bruun, *Bibliotheca Danica* (4 vols.; Copenhagen, 1877-1902), II (1886), cols. 399-400, where I found the complete title of the collection. I then asked Professor Nielsen to see if Book I, chap. xviii, was Castro's Red Sea rutter; it was.

[9] See D.V.2. FRANCE. (Cunha Rivara), HOLLAND. (Agostinho, J.), and ITALY. (Spinelli) respectively. There is no complete translation of Linschoten's narrative into Portuguese.

* This article is an enlargement of a paper presented before the Germanic Section at the annual meeting of the Modern Language Association of America in New York City on December 28, 1950. Grateful acknowledgment of indebtedness is due the American Council of Learned Societies, Professor John G. Kunstmann, and the officials and staff of the Columbia University Libraries for innumerable courtesies.

[1] *Canadian Graduate Theses in the Humanities and Social Sciences, 1921-46.* Ottawa, 1951, 194pp.

[2] [S. Dahl]: *Danish Theses for the Doctorate and Commemorative Publications of the University of Copenhagen, 1836-1926.* Copenhagen, 1929, 395pp.

[3] *The Yearbook of the Universities of the Empire* [includes theses for the years 1927, 1928, and 1929 only]; *Index to Theses Accepted for Higher Degrees in the Universities of Great Britain and Ireland.* Vol. I (1950-51), London, 1953, 157pp.

[4] *Catalogue des thèses et écrits académiques,* 1884 ff.; *Catalogue des dissertations et écrits académiques provenant des échanges avec les universités étrangères et reçus par la Bibliothèque Nationale,* 1884-1924; A. Mourier and F. Deltour: *Notice sur le doctorat ès lettres, suivie du catalogue et de l'analyse des thèses françaises et latines, 1810-1900.* Paris, 1880, 442pp.; A. Maire: *Répertoire alphabétique des thèses de doctorat ès lettres des universités françaises, 1810-1900.* Paris, 1903, 226pp.

Africa,[9] and Switzerland.[10] American universities and individual bibliographers, having become aware of the rich source material available for consultation in dissertations, have published not only limited lists of theses for individual American universities and for specific disciplines, such as had been done successfully in Europe, but have compiled, besides, two composite lists embracing the dissertations of a large number of institutions.[11]

[5] *Bibliographischer Monatsbericht über neu erschienene Schul—, Universitäts— und Hochschulschriften.* (Dissertationen . . .), Leipzig, 1889 ff.; *Jahresverzeichnis der an den deutschen Universitäten erschienenen Schriften* [title varies], Vol. I [1885] Berlin, 1887; H. Mundt: *Bio-Bibliographisches Verzeichnis von Universitäts— und Hochschuldrucken (Dissertationen) vom Ausgang des XVI. bis Ende des XIX. Jahrhunderts* [unfinished], Lfg. 1-13, Leipzig, 1936-42.

[6] Dodt (Johannes Jacobus): *Repertorium dissertationum belgicarum . . . 1815-30*, 1835, 146pp. [contains dissertations for both Belgium and Holland. A short supplement by Namur (Jean Pie) was added in 1848]; J. W. Wijndelts: *Catalogus van academische proefschriften verdedigd aan de Nederlandsche Unversiteiten gedurende de jaren 1815-1900.* Vol. I [1815-1900], Groningen, 1901, 52pp.; Vol. V [1815-1900], Groningen, 1903, 70pp.; M. A. Dée: *Academische proefschriften verdedigd te Leiden, Utrecht, Groningen en Amsterdam in de jaren 1877-1899.* Leiden, 1900, 167pp.; *Catalogus van academische Geschriften in Nederland en Nederlandsch Indië verschenen*, 1924ff.

[7] *Ežegodnik dissertacij.* 1936-37. God izd.1-2. Moskva, 1938-40; *Bibliografija dissertacij. Doktorskie dissertacii* 1941-44, 1945ff. Moskva, 1946ff.

[8] Gabriel Marklin: *Catalogus disputationum in academiis Scandinaviae et Finlandiae* [1778-1819], Upsaliae, 1820; Gabriel Marklin: *Catalogus . . .* [1820-55]; Aksel Gustav S. Josephson: *Avhandlingar ock program, uitg. vid svenska ock finska akademier ock skolor*, 1855-90, Uppsala, [1891-97]; Axel H. Nelson: *Akademiska afhandlingar vid Sveriges Universitet och Högskolor läsären*, 1890-91—1909-10, 1911, Uppsala, [1911-12], 149pp.; John Tuneld: *Akademiska afhanglingar . . .* 1910-11—1939-40, 1945, 336pp.

[9] A. M. Lewin Robinson: *Catalogue of Theses and Dissertations Accepted for Degrees by the South African Universities, 1918-41.* Cape Town, 1943, 155pp.

[10] *Jahresverzeichnis der schweizerischen Universitätsschriften* [title varies] 1897ff., Basel, 1898.

[11] Critical material on dissertation literature is relatively limited, *e.g.* Schlichter, J. J.: "A Decade of Classical Dissertations [1900-10]," *Classical Journal*, VII (1911-12), 80-83; Gerig, John L.: "Doctoral Dissertations in the Romance Languages at Columbia University. A Survey and Bibliography," *Romanic Review*, XII (1921), 73-79; Gerig, John L.: "Doctoral Dissertations in Romance Languages at Harvard University. A Survey and Bibliography," *Romanic Review*, X (1919), 67-78; Gerig, John L.: "Advanced Degrees and Doctoral Dissertations in the Romance Languages at the Johns Hopkins University. A Survey and Bibliography," *Romanic Review*, VIII (1917), 328-40; Gerig, John L.: "Doctoral Dissertations in the Romance Languages at Yale University. A Survey and Bibliography," *Romanic Review*, XI (1920), 70-75; Hohlfeld, A. R.: "The Wisconsin Project on Anglo-German Literary Relations" (pp. 3-32) in *German Literature in British Magazines, 1750-1860.* Edited by B. Q. Morgan and A. R. Hohlfeld. Madison, Wisconsin, 1949, 364pp.; Leavitt,

The first of the composite bibliographies in America was published by the Library of Congress for the year 1912 "to fill the need long felt for a publication corresponding in a general way to the works of a similar scope published abroad (p. 7)." It was more than ten years ago while engaged in some bibliographic reconnaissance that I had occasion to scout the excellent lists of American doctoral dissertations compiled by the Library of Congress in all the disciplines for the years 1912 through 1938. This valuable series has, however, some obvious lacunae. It includes only *printed* dissertations, or excerpts thereof, which had appeared either as separate publications or as articles in scholarly journals and acquired and catalogued by the Library of Congress; the majority of American universities have no requirement for the publication of dissertations. Many of those that have had it, are now omitting it entirely, or easing it. Also, the lists go no further back than 1912; the first three American doctorates, not of the honorary type, were granted in 1861 by Yale University, one in Classical Languages and Literatures, one in Philosophy and Psychology, and one in Physics. And, I repeat, the series ceased publication in 1938.

The second major contribution to bibliography of thesis literature in America we owe to the vision and fortitude of the late Donald B. Gilchrist, the initiator and editor of the first six annual volumes of *Doctoral Dissertations Accepted by American Universities*. While this important bibliography contains all accepted dissertations instead of just the printed ones, it does not include any material before 1933-34.[12] Let me make a brief comparison between the Library of Congress lists and the Gilchrist one for the single year of 1938. The former gives the titles of 1013 *printed* dissertations; the latter lists 2768 titles of *accepted* dissertations—almost three times as many. The Library of Congress list for 1938 has included 47

Sturgis E.: "Clearinghouse for Theses," *Hispania*, XVIII (1935), 456-57; Newcombe, Luxmore: "The Accessibility of British University Thesis Literature," Paper read in 1939 before Aslib, subsequently published, unavailable; Record, P. D.: *A Survey of* [the accessibility of] *Thesis Literature in British Libraries*. London, England, 1950, 21pp.; Rosenberg, Ralph P.: "Bibliographies of Theses in America," *Bulletin of Bibliography*, XVIII (1945), 181-82, XVIII (1946), 201-03; Rosenberg, Ralph P.: "American [Doctoral] Studies in Franco-German Literary Relations," *Comparative Literature News-Letter*, IV (December, 1945), 18-22; Rosenberg, Ralph P.: "Doctoral Research in Franco-German Literary Relations at American Universities," Address MLA, 1944; Rosenberg, Ralph P.: "Young Germany in the Light of American [Doctoral] Research," Address MLA, 1948; "American Doctoral Studies in Germanic Cultures, 1873-1950," Address MLA, 1950; Silver, Henry M.: "Publishing of Doctoral Dissertations in the Humanities and Social Sciences," *ACLS News Letter*, II (November, 1951), 7-20; Bliss, Eleanor A.: "Bryn Mawr Studies its Ph. D's," *Journal of the Association of University Women*, XLVIII (1954), 14-16.

[12] It would be unkind not to mention the valuable *Microfilm Abstracts*. A Collection of Abstracts of Doctoral Dissertations Which Are Available in Complete Form in Microfilm. Ann Arbor, Mich., Vol. I ff., No. I, 1938 ff.

universities; the *Doctoral Dissertations* . . . was based on reports from 87 institutions.

The inadequacy of both reference works was the incentive for my undertaking *An Analytic Bibliography of Doctoral Dissertations in or Relating to Germanic Cultures Accepted by [76] American and [6] Canadian Colleges and Universities, 1873-1949. A Study in German-American Cultural Relations.* It was clear that the investigation, were it to have the necessary degree of inclusiveness and completeness, would have to begin with original source material, in this case the individual university archives. The very helpful *Guide to Bibliographies of Theses: United States and Canada*[13] by Thomas R. Palfrey and Henry E. Coleman put me on the right track at once. When, then, the American Council of Learned Societies voted me grants-in-aid-of-research in 1943, 1944, and 1945, I was privileged to begin what turned out to be a forty-thousand mile "See American Universities First" journey over the United States. I visited some eighty institutions of higher learning, checked my preliminary lists against those found in the university catalogs and files, and examined all the theses.

I have found notable discrepancies among library facilities. In one of our famous American libraries I had the services of a messenger who for ten full days patiently lugged heavy-laden carts of dissertations to me. On the other hand, in another institution I had to go through subterranean corridors, stand before an enormous vault far below the roaring city and patiently wait while an eerie air-fan was put into action to prevent my suffocation. At last the special combination was dialed and the huge door swung open with creaks and groans, revealing the university archives—the whole scene in the best tradition of blood-curdling mystery fiction.

Although the greater majority of dissertations are for the degree of Doctor of Philosophy, there is no differentiation made in my bibliography between this degree and the Doctor of Theology or Doctor of Education, for example. This is the general practice in other bibliographies dealing with similar subject matter. Among the special features of my bibliography, which is now complete in manuscript and hopefully awaiting a publication subvention, are the following. It extends from 1873 to 1949[14] inclusive and contains some 2500 items from 76 American and 6 Canadian institutions granting the doctorate. The term "Germanic" is used in its philological sense and includes Austrian, Danish, Dutch, Finnish, Flemish, German, Icelandic, Norwegian, Swedish and Swiss. English, notwithstanding its preeminence, has, for obvious reasons, not been included. For each dissertation listed, with the exception of those in the 1945ff supplement, there are given the complete table of contents and pagination; for each printed dissertation, the place, date and pagination are supplied;

---

[13] Second edition, Chicago, Ill., 1940, 54pp.
[14] The material is being kept up to date and now includes dissertations through 1953. It contains over 2700 items. The end date 1949 has been used in this article because all computations had been made up to this year for my reading paper before the MLA in 1950.

also whether it has been published in full, in part, or abstracted in a university publication. Included, too, are further publications by the candidate in the broad field of his thesis. The bibliography, arranged alphabetically by author and numbered consecutively, encompasses all the humanities in Germanics and contains both a chronological list of dissertations by universities and one by subjects, arranged chronologically, according to the following eight large categories: Comparative Literature, Education, Fine Arts, Literature, Philology, Philosophy and Religion, Psychology, and the Social Sciences. To facilitate its use, there is appended a comprehensive author and subject index with specific dissertation and chapter references, some ten thousand in all. I have attempted, also, to print the bibliography with a minimum of punctuation. Most punctuation has been replaced by planned spacing as is seen in the following entries of my sample page.

Ambrose   Brother [E F Dwyer]   The Influence of H Ibsen on G B Shaw
Fordham 1930   [38]

Introduction   1 Ibsen founder of the new school of drama   2 The development of Ibsen   3 A study of the development of Shaw through Ibsen   4 Shaw's interpretation of Ibsen   5 Shaw's opposition to popular romantic conceptions   6 His views on marriage   7 His departure from his former philosophy   8 Different angles of the approach to life of the two dramatists   9 Comparison of their world theories 10 Both playwrights influenced technically by character and aims   Conclusion   Bibliography   78pp

Bluhm   Heinz S   The Reception of Goethe's *Faust* in England after the Middle of the XIX Century   Wisconsin 1932   [185]

[1] Some aspects of English thought in the 19th century   [2] General consideration on *Faust* in England   [3] Gradual penetration of the idea of Goethe's *Faust* 1850-80   [4] Goethe's *Faust*   A divider of spirits 1880-1900   Appendix   Translations of Part II in the 19th century Bibliography   172pp

[P1] "The Reception of Goethe's *Faust* in England after the Middle of the XIX Century"   *JEGP*   vol 34   1935   pp201-12   [P2] "Recent American Research on Luther's German Bible"   *GR* vol 18   1943 pp161-71 [P3] "The 'Douche' Sources of Coverdale's Translation of the Twenty-Third Psalm"   *JEGP*   vol 46   1947   pp53-62

Cole   Robert T   Responsible Bureaucracy   A Study of the Swiss Civil Service   Part II   Harvard 1936   [Part I by C J Friedrich]
                                                                            [363]
Introduction   1 The systematic concept of bureaucracy   2 The functions of the Swiss civil service   3 The Swiss hierarchy   4 The personnel of the Swiss civil service   5 Impacts upon the hierarchy in Switzerland   The trend toward functional autonomy   Conclusion   Bibliography   Index of authors
Summaries . . . *Harvard* 1936 pp228-30   *Responsible Bureaucracy* A Study of the Swiss Civil Service   Cambridge Mass   1932   94pp

Hazelton   Roger   The Relation between Value and Existence in the Philosophies of N Hartmann and A N Whitehead   Yale   1937 [816]
Introduction   Part I Axiological   1 The problems of value   2 The objectivity of value   3 The apprehension of value   4 The realization of

value   Part II Ontological   5 Some metaphysical foundations of value
6 Value metaphorically defined   7 Goodness and God   Conclusion
Bibliography   320pp
"Discussion on Hartmann's Doctrine of Values as Essences"   *Philosophical Review*   vol 48   1939   pp621-32
Leon   Theodore H   The Mexican Novels of C Sealsfield   A Study of
their Origin, Sources and Historic Truth   Washington (StL)   1936
                                                                  [1139]
Introduction   1 Origin of the Mexican novels   2 Sources of the Mexi-
can novels   3 Historic truth of the Mexican novels   Bibliography
191pp
Final Examination . . . Washington (St. Louis) 1 p   [P1] *The Mexican
Novels of C Sealsfield*   A Study of their Origin, Sources and Historical
Truth   St Louis Mo 1938   24 pp   [P2] *C Sealsfield*   Bibliography
of his Writings together with a Classified and Annotated Catalogue of
Literature Relating to his Works and his Life [with O Heller]   St Louis
Mo   1939   88 pp   [P3] *The Language of C Sealsfield*   A Study of
Atypal Usage [with O Heller]   St Louis Mo 1941   **154pp**

Regarding the earliest American dissertations in Germanic cultures,
the distinction of having granted the first two earned Ph.D.'s in the humanities goes to Yale University, where in 1873 Jules Luquiens, later
Street Professor of Romance Languages at Yale, wrote a thesis on "The
Ablaut in the Indo-European Conjugational System" (dissertation unavailable), and William R. Harper, later the first President of the University of Chicago, in 1875 received the doctorate with a thesis on "Some
Problems Connected with Comparative Indo-European Philology" (the
title has also been quoted as "A Comparative Study of the Prepositions in
Latin, Greek, Sanskrit and Gothic," dissertation unavailable). Both these
doctorates were completed in the department of Classical Languages and
Literatures.   To be remembered is the fact that Classical Philology, both
in Europe and America, was the fountain-head for all subsequent lan-
guage philologies.   The year 1896 is the date of the first dissertation accepted for the doctorate at Yale in Germanic Languages and Literatures.
In 1879 there were two more doctorates granted, one at the University of
Michigan, the "mother of state universities," to William T. Jackson on
"Seneca and Kant" (Dayton, Ohio, 1881, 109pp.), and the other at Cornell
University to Waterman T. Hewett, subsequently Professor of German
there, on "The Frisian Language and Literature" (Ithaca, N. Y., 1879,
60pp.).   In 1880 Harvard bestowed the doctorate on Samuel E. Turner
(d. 1896) for a study on "The Influence of France on English and German
Politics during the Age of Louis XIV" (40pp. holograph).   In 1884 John
Dewey, the American philosopher, completed his Ph.D. at Johns Hopkins
on "The Psychology of Kant" (dissertation unavailable, cf. Milton H.
Thomas: *A Bibliography of John Dewey, 1882-1939*, New York, N. Y., 1939,
246pp.).   The first American doctorate in German literature proper was
awarded to Hugo J. Walther by Columbia University (then Columbia College) in 1886.   The title was "Syntax of Cases in Walther von der Vogelweide."   It is still in manuscript and unpublished.[15]   These theses indi-

---

[15] Rosenberg, Ralph P.: "Hugo Julius Walther," *Germanic Review,*

cate that the inception of interest in Germanic culture from a scientific point of view is contemporaneous with the founding of the American Graduate School: Johns Hopkins in 1876; Columbia in 1880; Clark and Catholic Universities in 1889; Chicago and Harvard Universities in 1890; and Yale and Wisconsin Universities in 1892.[16]

A frequent question asked me is, "Which American universities have had the largest number of theses in Germanic cultures, that is, in all the disciplines?" That distinction is equally divided between the Universities of Chicago and Columbia.[17] Each one has granted some 230 doctorates or somewhat less than ten per cent of the total number of 2500. Following closely is Harvard with 205 theses, next Wisconsin with 160. The overall picture varies somewhat when we consider the number of dissertations from the point of view of the eight large subject categories. For example, in the field of Comparative Literature, Wisconsin, which ranked fourth in the largest number of dissertations granted in all the disciplines, comes to the fore with 36. It is followed by Columbia with 32, and Pennsylvania with 29. In the field of Education, Columbia and New York University are far in the lead with a tie, each with 23. Then comes Ohio State with 6, Washington (Seattle) and Wisconsin with 5 each, and Harvard, Iowa, and Yale with 4 each. In the Fine Arts the results are almost negligible; there have been only 44 in all. Eight of these were written at Columbia and 6 at Harvard. In Literature, Chicago comes first with 75 theses, Wisconsin second with 60, and Columbia next with 56. In Philology, Chicago is again first with 31 theses, Johns Hopkins next with 21, and Yale is third with 17. In Philosophy and Religion, Yale heads the field

---

XXIX (1954),224-29; Rosenberg, Ralph P.: "The First American Doctorate in German Literature," *American-German Review*, XXI (Feb.-March 1955), 34.

[16] Horton, Byrne J.: *The Graduate School.* Its Origin and Administrative Development. New York, N. Y., 1940, 182pp. On p.77 Horton gives the year in which the Graduate School was organized in 28 universities. If the following books are any indication of an important trend, there is a definite revival of interest in the history of American graduate schools. Atkinson, Carroll: *Pro and Con of the Ph.D.* Boston, Mass., 1945, 172pp. [Especially ch. I, pp.11-20]; Bowman, Isaiah: *The Graduate School in American Democracy.* Washington, D. C., 1939, 70pp.; Carson, Ryan W.: *Studies in Early Graduate Education*: The Johns Hopkins, Clark University, The University of Chicago. New York, N. Y., 1939, 167pp.; Hofstadter, Richard and Hardy, C. de Witt: *The Development and Scope of Higher Education in the United States.* New York, N. Y., 1952, 254pp.; Hollis, Ernest V.: *Toward Improving Ph.D. Programs.* Washington, D.C., 1945, 204pp. [Especially ch. I, pp.1-37 and ch. II, pp.38-67]; John, Walton C.: *Graduate Study in Universities and Colleges in the United States.* Washington, D. C., 1934, 234pp.; Pierson, Mary B.: *Graduate Work in the South.* Chapel Hill, N. C., 1947, 265pp. [Especially ch. II, pp.11-31 and ch. III, pp.32-66]; Storr, Richard J.: *The Beginnings of Graduate Education in America.* Chicago, Ill., 1953, 195pp.; Valentine, P. F. (ed.): *The American College.* New York, N. Y., 1949, 575pp. [Especially ch. I, by Valentine, pp.7-29 and the chapter by John T. Wahlquist, pp.516-69].

[17] Cf. footnote 14.

with 45 theses; Harvard is a near second with 37. Columbia is first both in Psychology (8) and the Social Sciences (69). Harvard, Chicago, and California (Berkeley) come second in Psychology with 4 each. Harvard and Chicago have 68 and 67 theses respectively in the Social Sciences. It is impossible to estimate what percentage of these theses have appeared in print because the regulations for the printing of dissertations, in part or complete, vary, not only over the years, but from time to time within the individual institution. The introduction of microfilming of complete dissertations has complicated the problem even more.

The material just discussed gives the following picture when analyzed chronologically. Some four per cent of the total 2500 dissertations were written before 1900. As would be expected, the largest number was written at Yale (23), followed by Cornell (17), by Johns Hopkins (15), and by Harvard (12). Eleven per cent were written between 1900-1913; 20 per cent between 1914-1930; 35 per cent from 1931-1939; and 30 per cent between 1940-1949. A chronological analysis within the eight large subject categories shows that in Comparative Literature 8 dissertations were written before 1900; 59 between 1900-1913; 75 between 1914-1930; 85 between 1931-1940; and 59 from 1941-1949. In Education 3 dissertations were written before 1900; 12 between 1900-1913; 30 between 1914-1930; 38 between 1931-1940; and 26 between 1941-1949. In the Fine Arts 1 dissertation was written before 1900; 2 between 1900-1913; 5 between 1914-1930; 11 between 1931-1940; and 25 between 1941-1949. In Literature 26 dissertations were written before 1900; 99 between 1900-1913; 137 between 1914-1930; 276 between 1931-1940; and 203 between 1941-1949. In Philology 25 dissertations were written before 1900; 23 between 1900-1913; 33 between 1914-1930; 55 between 1931-1940; and 35 between 1941-1949. At a time when the ideal of philology dominated both the European and American academic world, Philology started out before 1900 almost neck and neck with Literature. It has since receded far into the background. In Philosophy and Religion there were 41 dissertations before 1900; 52 between 1900-1913; 64 between 1914-1930; 117 between 1931-1940; and 107 between 1941-1949. From these statistics we observe that the largest number of dissertations in any discipline before 1900 was submitted in the division of Philosophy and Religion. This former position of prominence has not been maintained in the last half century. In Psychology 2 dissertations were written before 1900; 1 between 1900-1913; 6 between 1914-1930; 25 between 1931-1940; and 65 between 1941-1949. In the Social Sciences there were 18 dissertations before 1900; 58 between 1900-1913; 136 between 1914-1930; 227 between 1931-1940; and 231 between 1941-1949. Only dissertations in the Fine Arts, Psychology, and Social Sciences show a steady increase over the years. The other subject categories strongly reflect the vicissitudes of the day.

Of the 2500 dissertations surveyed somewhat less than 20 per cent were written by women,—roughly 1 per cent before 1900, 2 per cent between 1900-1913, 4 per cent between 1914-1930, 8 per cent between 1931-1940, and 5 per cent between 1941-1949. The greater majority, some 40 per cent,

was written in Literature; twenty per cent in the Social Sciences; almost
as many in Comparative Literature, 15 per cent. The remainder was almost equally divided among Philosophy and Religion, Psychology, Philology,
Education, and Fine Arts in descending order. The University of Wisconsin bestowed the doctorate on about 15 per cent of these *doctorandae.*
Columbia followed with almost as many; then came Chicago with 10 per
cent, and Radcliffe and Cornell with 6 per cent each. With the exception
of Radcliffe, a woman's college, I have no satisfactory explanation for the
leading role played by these institutions in higher education for women.
This should be a worthwhile study for an educationalist or sociologist.

The first American doctorates in Germanic cultures granted to women
were awarded at the University of Michigan in 1892 to Caroline Miles
("Kant's Kingdom of Ends," dissertation unavailable) and Eliza R. Sun-
derland ("A Comparison of Kant's and Hegel's Conception of the Relation
of God and Man," dissertation unavailable). One year later Kate A.
Everest ("German Immigration into Wisconsin," dissertation unavailable)
received the degree at Wisconsin as did Marguerite Sweet at Bryn Mawr
("The Third Class of Week Verbs in Primitive Teutonic, With Special
Reference to its Development in Anglo-Saxon," Baltimore, Md., 1893, 49pp.).
To Minnie Highet, who received her Ph.D. at Cornell in 1895 ("Influences
of English Literature Over the Writers of Germany During the Eighteenth
Century," dissertation unavailable), goes the honor of being the first
American woman to obtain the doctorate in German literature. Mention
should also be made of Anna Bowen ("The Sources and Text of R. Wagner's Opera, *Die Meistersinger von Nürnberg,*" Munich, Germany, 1897,
96pp.) and Martha Tarbell ("The German Ballad: History, Four Great
Writers, Characteristics," unpublished, 170pp.). Miss Bowen took her
degree in 1897 at Cornell, as did Miss Tarbel at Brown in the same year.
I have been unable to find the date of the first Ph.D. awarded to an American woman, so that a comparison at this point is impossible. I can say,
however, that these first doctorates awarded to American women in Germanics represent the culmination of the idea current in America during
the last four decades of the nineteenth century of equal opportunities for
women as for men. Signs of this movement are seen in the founding of
women's colleges, the woman suffrage movement, and the growth of
American graduate schools, both in the older universities and in the newly
founded ones, which gradually permitted women to infiltrate higher education.[18]   A unique fact which merits further investigation is that, of
these 14 early doctorates before 1900, Cornell University bestowed almost

---

[18] Woody, Thomas: *A History of Women's Education in the United
States.* New York, N. Y., 1929, 2 vols. [Especially vol. II, pp.333-40]
Vassar was founded in 1861, Smith in 1871, Wellesley in 1875, and Bryn
Mawr in 1880. The dates 1869 and 1890 are significant in the history of
Woman Suffrage. The former was the founding date of the National
Woman Suffrage Association and the American Woman Suffrage Associa-
tion. The two societies were unified in 1890 as the National American
Woman Suffrage Association.

one half,—one in literature, 1 in philology, 2 in philosophy and religion, and 2 in psychology.

About 10 per cent of all the dissertations in Germanic cultures were written in a foreign language, primarily German. Six were written in French and 1 in Italian. The largest number of dissertations in German was completed at the University of Wisconsin (35), primarily in literature and some in philology. Second in this respect was Chicago with 19, followed by New York with 18, Johns Hopkins with 17 and Pennsylvania with 16. It is striking that the five states in which these universities are located are American focal points in German immigration. A survey of the dissertations written in a foreign language for all universities in my bibliography shows that 20 per cent were written from the beginnings to World War I; about the same per cent and number from 1914-1930; about 40 per cent, or equal to the two preceding periods of time, from 1931-1940 (probably due to the large number of refugees who had come to America to complete their graduate training which had been interrupted by Hitler's march on Europe); and a return to the norm of approximately 45 dissertations from 1941-1949. There were 7 dissertations written in German before 1900. All of them were in the field of philology, as was the first by Starr W. Cutting ("Der Conjunktiv bei Hartmann von Aue," Chicago, Ill., 1894, 53pp.) who received his doctorate at Johns Hopkins in 1892 and was for many years Professor of German at the University of Chicago.

The breakdown of the 2500 items into the eight large subject categories gives us the following overview in round numbers. Literature, with some 750 items,[19] touches on the Old High German period, laying somewhat more emphasis on Middle High German literature, with the *Nibelungenlied* (2, 2), Hartmann von Aue (3, 3), Wolfram von Eschenbach (8, 4) and Gottfried von Strassburg (7, 2) occurring most frequently. For German literature between 1300-1600 we find the following names: Brant (5, 2), Erasmus (8, 4), Fischart (3, 2), Melanchton (2, 2), Murner (1, 2), and Sachs (10, 11). American research on the Baroque and Neo-Classicism is negligible,—Gottsched (2, 8), Gryphius (1, 3), Opitz (1, 5), and Weise (0, 4). The main interest is shown in literature of the eighteenth century. Klopstock (4, 8) is touched on, Wieland (11, 23) is emphasized more, but the main authors, as would be expected, are Goethe, Schiller, Herder and Lessing.

There were 82 dissertations on Goethe plus 100 further references to him. The first dissertation was written in 1891 at New York University by William J. Eckoff ("Educational Views of Goethe," unpublished, 53pp.), The University of Wisconsin, under Professor Hohlfeld, produced the largest number of dissertations on Goethe. There were twenty-two.

---

[19] To complete the picture I shall give in parentheses both the number of theses written as well as chapter references and published items found in other theses. All this information is culled from the detailed author and subject index. *E.g.* "Wolfram von Eschenbach (8, 4)" means that there are 8 complete dissertations on Wolfram von Eschenbach; also, there are 4 other [usually chapter] references to him in other dissertations.

Yale University, where Professor Schreiber has been for many years Curator of the Speck Collection of Goetheana, follows with fourteen.

There were 25 dissertations on Schiller plus 50 other references to him. The University of Michigan and Wisconsin share equal honors, for at each of these institutions there were 5 dissertations accepted on Schiller. The University of Chicago follows with three. The first dissertation on Schiller was written by Otto E. Lessing, at one time at the University of Illinois, who in 1901 received the Ph.D. at the University of Michigan with a thesis, "Schillers Einfluss auf Grillparzer. Eine litterarhistorische Studie" (*Bulletin of the University of Wisconsin*, No. 50, Philology and Literature Series, II (1902), pp. 77-204).

There are 16 dissertations on Herder and almost twice that number (30) of references to him. The University of Chicago comes first with three dissertations on Herder, followed by Illinois, Columbia, Stanford, and Wisconsin, at each of which two dissertations on Herder had been written. The first doctorate on Herder was granted to Irvin C. Hatch at Stanford University in 1900 for "Der Einfluss Shaftesburys auf Herder" (*Studien zur vergleichenden Litteraturgeschichte*, I (1901), pp. 68-119).

Fifteen dissertations were written on Lessing. Other references to him total thirty-nine. At Chicago there were 4 dissertations on Lessing, followed by Columbia and California (Berkeley), where two theses were written. The first American doctoral thesis on Lessing was written in 1904 at Yale by Edward Thorstenberg on "Lessing's Appreciation of Color as an Element of Effect in Poetry: A Contribution to the Study of *Laokoon*" (unpublished, ca. 95pp.).

The romantic movement focuses on Tieck (12, 14), as do the 30's and 40's on Heine (16, 18). There is more research in the drama of the nineteenth century than in prose fiction for the same period. It is vigorous in Kleist (12, 12), Grillparzer (15, 14), Hebbel (22, 13), and Wagner (10, 16), and consistent for Keller (12, 8), Fontane (8, 6) and Storm (6, 7). In contemporary literature the name of Hauptmann outstrips all other names. There were 22 dissertations and 16 references to him. The largest number, six, was completed at the University of Pennsylvania where also the first Hauptmann dissertation was written by Martin Schütze, the well-known Chicago Professor of German, who in 1899 submitted a thesis on "Gerhard Hauptmann's Plays and their Literary Relations" (dissertation unavailable). Three Hauptmann dissertations were written at Columbia, Northwestern, and Wisconsin. Other modern authors are Hofmannsthal (4, 7), Schnitzler (5, 6), George (2, 10) and Rilke (4, 6). Even though Thomas Mann (6, 5) is the darling of the American intellectual, and Americans by and large accept him as the lodestar of German culture, he does not enjoy anywhere near the interest of the doctoral candidate as does Hauptmann. Hermann Hesse (1, 4) and Kafka (0, 1) are neglected figures also, even though the latter has been enjoying a popular American vogue at present. To fill in the picture we might add that Thematology has the leading part in this literary procession. There are 98 dissertations and 20 references to motifs. The subjects vary from "actor" to "William Tell." Folklore (9, 5) plays a comparatively unimportant role in our academic parade of literary authors, scholars, and subjects.

The growth of the graduate school in America was accompanied by two parallel and germane movements. One was the attainment of professional status for the language teacher. The other was the opening up of printing sources so that scholarly productivity would not be bottled up in manuscript. Both were united when in 1883 the Modern Language Association of America was founded and when one year later the *Publications of the Modern Language Association of America* were begun.[20] Other periodicals devoted to the publication of scholarly articles and reviews soon appeared. However, they were university publications. For example, *American Journal of Philology* (vol. I, 1880) and *Modern Language Notes* (vol. I, 1886) at Johns Hopkins University; *Monatshefte für deutschen Unterricht* (title varies, vol. I, 1889) at the University of Wisconsin; *Journal of [English and] Germanic Philology* (title varies, vol. I, 1897) at the University of Illinois; *Modern Philology* (vol. I, 1903) at the University of Chicago; *Studies in Philology* (vol. I, 1906) at the University of North Carolina. All of these periodicals are thriving even today. We should not forget to mention the valiant attempt by Columbia University professors to publish in 1903 the first, though short-lived, American *Journal of Comparative Literature*.

Comparative Literature reflects the spirit of "one worldness," which is the key-note of our age. There are a surprisingly large number of studies, approximately 300, in this branch of literature which shows Germany in literary relations with countries in a world-wide periphery of time and space: America, England, France, Greece (2, 0), Italy (2, 0), Scandinavia (1, 0) and Spain (5, 0). As expected, the greatest emphasis is on Anglo-German literary relations. There were 81 dissertations and 32 other references. The University of Wisconsin takes the lead with 14 dissertations followed by Columbia with 10 and Harvard with eight. It was at the last-named institution that Curtis H. Page wrote the first doctorate in 1894 on "Carlyle: his Relation to the German Thinkers, Especially Fichte" (unpublished, ca. 450pp.). German-American literary relations comes next with 48 dissertations and 13 other references. The University of Pennsylvania granted more degrees in this branch of comparative literature than did any other university. There were 13 dissertations at Pennsylvania, followed by Wisconsin with 6 and Harvard with four. The first dissertation in this field was written at Johns Hopkins University in 1892 by Albert B. Faust on "C. Sealsfield (C. Postl) Materials for a Biography. A Study of his Style, his Influence upon American Literature" (Baltimore, Md., 1892, 53pp.). Professor Faust was active at the University of Cornell for many years. Next comes Franco-German Literary relations with 37 dissertations and 19 other references. Wisconsin again takes the lead here with 7 disserta-

---

[20] Parker, William R.: "The MLA, 1883-1953," *PMLA*, LXVIII (1953), Number 4, Part 2, 3-39.

tions, followed by Pittsburgh, Illinois, Columbia, and California (Berkeley) with 4 each. The first dissertation was written in 1897 at Johns Hopkins by Charles F. Woods (d. 1912) on "The Relations of Wolfram von Eschenbach's *Willehalm* to its Old French Source, *Aliscans*" (dissertation unavailable). A striking statistical fact is the large number of dissertations written in comparative literature by women. We must recall that less than 20 per cent of the dissertations in all subject categories were written by women. In comparative literature there were 39 out of the total 166 aforementioned dissertations in Anglo-German, German-American, and Franco-German relations written by women, or almost 25 per cent.

Important are the Wisconsin project in Anglo-German relations (Hohlfeld), with the tangential ones at Stanford (Morgan), California (Price), Northwestern (Jantz), as well as the ones in German-American literary relations at Pennsylvania (Learned), Cornell (Faust), and Harvard (Francke). The culmination of all these movements in comparative literature is seen in the recent founding of three American periodicals in the field: *Comparative Literature News-Letter* (vol. I, 1942, ceased publication in 1946), *Comparative Literature* (vol. I, 1949ff.), and the *Yearbook of Comparative and General Literature* (vol. I, 1952ff.).

Some 200 dissertations in Philology investigate linguistic questions on dialects, grammar and etymology, with an emphasis on Pennsylvania Dutch, which is in harmony with contemporary trends in backgrounds in American cultural heritage.

The Social Sciences:—history, sociology, economics, and politics— are unusually well represented with slightly less than 700 dissertations. Whereas the 700 dissertations on literature give a fairly standard perspective, though somewhat at variance with contemporary trends, the theses in the social sciences reflect more accurately the social and economic interests of the times,—for example, labor problems, cartels, tariff policies, colonialism and imperialism, nationalism and internationalism, and even such controversial topics as Nazism and The Third Reich (17, 23) and Marxism (29, 9). In passing, I cannot help but wonder whether this eager interest in and firmer knowledge of German social conditions by the American graduate student in any small way contributed to the saner attitude in America towards Germany in the Second World War in contrast to the hysteria shown in the First one.

The more than 350 dissertations in Philosophy and Religion run the gamut of names and subjects. Kant (66, 57) and Luther (37, 16) have attained most prominence in this group. Kant, the subject of one of the earliest American doctorates in German cultures, is also the most frequently discussed German philosopher during the subsequent seventy-five years of graduate research. His preoccupation with moral and ethical problems, Hegel's (40, 29) synthesis of ideological conflicts, Nietzsche's (15, 18) revaluation of values, and Luther's virile religious precepts, ideas which form the warp and woof of American philosophic thought, have caused this quartet of German intellectuals to take strong hold in America.

Education, with slightly over 100 dissertations, and Psychology, with exactly 100, like the Social Sciences previously discussed, reflect modern currents of ideas. In Education the emphasis is on contemporary German experimentalists and their influence on American educational philosophers such as John Dewey. For Psychology I need only mention the names of Freud (11, 5) and Rorschach (55, 0), the latter the subject of innumerable dissertations, to make clear their significance for American thought.

The Fine Arts, with only 44 dissertations in the long history of American doctoral research in Germanic cultures, comes at the very end as far as number is concerned. This small figure is not surprising considering the few institutions offering higher degrees in this discipline, and very often those that do, accept original compositions in lieu of a scholarly investigation. Statistically, almost all the dissertations are in music, with art and painting next, followed by a few in architecture. There are dissertations on Bach, Handel, contemporary German musicians and church music; also German architecture, Flemish painting, and aesthetics.

It should be evident from this introductory analysis that the impact of Germanic cultures on the American Weltanschauung is an important one. Since there exist no parallel bibliographic studies in other foreign literatures, we can have no basis for comparison to determine the exact relationship of these influences. However, it is encouraging to note that the interest in dissertation material in languages and literatures, both in Canada and in America, is definitely on the increase, and that the gateway to larger, all-embracing studies has already been opened.[21]

At this point I should like to call attention to another aspect of thesis bibliography for which we have many institutional lists, but for which we have as yet no cumulative bibliography going back to the beginnings,—A Bibliography of American Master's Theses. I have been collecting one for many years on the German Language and Literature, and I have found a great need for such bibliographies in all languages and literatures. The natural scientists have already pointed the way and have also taken the lead. They have just published the first annual list of Master's theses in the natural sciences.[22] Language and Literature groups could well follow suit. In addition, they should publish cumulative lists. Now that Americans are becoming increasingly conscious of their cultural heritage, the two aforementioned bibliographic projects would not only be valid in themselves, but also as a contribution to American relationships with other literatures. One aspect of this program could

---

[21] My article in manuscript on "American Theses Lists in Languages and Literatures" substantiates this statement.

[22] Blesdoe, Barton: *Master's Theses in Science, 1952.* Washington, D. C., 1954, 252pp.

well be a large collection of Master's theses written on the history of the language and literature departments of our colleges and universities. With the exception of sporadic and brief reports, this aspect of research has been neglected. I know of no finer introduction to methodology in research than that of digging in college and university archives, searching for the origins and development of our traditions.[23]

As for my Bibliography, I hope that beyond its strictly functional value it will open up a hitherto closed, vast treasure house of important scholarly source material which, when evaluated, should be a fundamental contribution to the History of Germanic Scholarship in America—a fascinating study which I hope to be able to complete some day.

THE FEASIBILITY OF TRANSLATION

Paul E. Hadley
University of Southern California

Since translated works are the basis of study in both the world literature course and in the broader curriculum of research in comparative literature, it seems appropriate to devote some attention to the question of translation. We tend, however, to proceed upon the naïve assumption that, generally speaking, any literary work may be translated from one language to another, or specifically, that the English language as a vessel can receive whatever the translator may pour into it from other languages, ancient or contemporary, and from the several *genres*, i.e., from the formal essay to the emotional lyric. That this assumption is faulty is discovered as soon as one begins to consult critical opinion.

"Never translate! Translation is the death of understanding."[1] Thus, Sir T. Herbert Warren cites an extreme point of view on the feasibility of translation. A more carefully reasoned, but still negative approach recognizes the difficulty of reading a great work of literature even in the original where no linguistic barrier to understanding exists but that of uneven comprehension. If, says Hiram Roy Wilson, this original comprehension is difficult, then an effort to re-word or to paraphrase the thought in the same language would be less successful, and, finally, the transference of that thought to the framework of another language would

---

[23] As a model piece of research of this type, I should like to call attention to the MSE thesis by Bergenthal, Hugo: "The History of the German Language and Literature in the Curriculum of the College of the City of New York," C. C. N. Y., 1936, 195pp., unpublished.

[1] Sir T. Herbert Warren, "The Art of Translation," *Quarterly Review*, CLXXXII (1895), 364. *Cf.* J. P. Postgate, *Translation and Translations* (London: G. Bell and Sons, 1922), 1.

be nearly impossible.[2]   One is reminded of Plato's magnet symbol which, by showing the decreasing power of inspiration and lessening accuracy of observation, illustrates well the unreliability of poetic and dramatic rendition.

Translating both Content and Form

The task of the translator is thus doubly complicated, as he tries to express not only his author's meaning but also to provide some resemblance to his form and style.[3]   And Tolman cites the German von Humboldt in a similar expression:

> 'All translation,' writes Wilhelm von Humboldt to Wilhelm von Schlegel, the German translator of Shakespeare, 'seems to me but an attempt to accomplish what is impossible.   Every translator must run shipwreck on one of two rocks: either at the cost of the style and idiom of his own nation, he will hold too closely to the original, or at the cost of the original, he will hold too closely to the peculiarity of his nation.   The middle ground between these is not only hard, but absolutely impossible.[4]

And von Humboldt was not addressing himself to the transference of meaning but only of form.   The question of the practicality of a formal, literal translation is a classic argument.   There are, on the one hand, apologists who contend, as did Edward FitzGerald in his Preface to *Agamemnon*, that

> . . . a literal translation of this play, if possible, would scarcely be intelligible.   Even were the dialogue always clear, the lyric Choruses . . . are so dark and abrupt in themselves, and therefore so much the more mangled and tormented by copyist and commentator, that the most conscientious translator must not only jump at a meaning, but must bridge over a chasm, especially if he determine to complete the antiphony of Strophe and Antistrophe in English verse.[5]

This is, of course, the easy way out—to assume that a search for verbal and other formal identities is pedantic.   The translator may content himself with the pretended success of having captured the conception of the original and having transferred that conception by means of adequate

---

[2] Hiram Roy Wilson, "Translations in Relation to the Originals," *The Classical Journal*, XVIII (February, 1923), 265-66.

[3] Flora Ross Amos, *Early Theories of Translation*, Columbia University Studies in English and Comparative Literature (New York: Columbia U. P., 1920), p. 106.   Miss Amos cites North's translation of Jacques Amyot's principle: " . . . the office of a fit translator consisteth not only in the faithful expressing of his author's meaning, but also in a certain resembling and shadowing out of the form of his style and manner of his speaking, . . . "

[4] Herbert C. Tolman, *The Art of Translating*, with special reference to Cauer's *Die Kunst des Uebersetzens* (Boston: Benjamin H. Sanborn and Co., 1901), 24.

[5] Edward FitzGerald, *Letters and Literary Remains* (London: Macmillan and Co., 1903), VI, 267-68.   For a contrary point of view in regard to the same Greek tragedy in English, cf. Robert Browning, *The Agamemnon of Aeschylus* (New York: Thomas Y. Crowell and Co., 1898), 1-2.

equivalences.[6] Indeed, there are undoubtedly writers whose original language is merely a garment, clothing their ideas for the sake of convention, a garment easily replaced by the contemporary dress of any translator in any country. A. V. Dicey suggests Thucydides to have been the kind of writer whose thoughts and mode of thinking were all-important.[7] The present writer is not sure that he would dispense so easily with the form of the *History*, but is ready to concede that there are authors whose thoughts might well be expressed in another form. One would feel quite confident, for instance, that the ideas of Émile Zola could be expressed effectively without the baroque quality of his style. On the other hand, no one would venture to dissociate the orderly thinking of Flaubert or of Gide from the economy of their prose. Dicey claims this same consideration for the Roman historian and essayist Tacitus, in whose works he says " . . . manner plays quite as great a part as . . . substance."[8] Particularly in the case of the poets, it seems dubious that both form and meaning can often be successfully transferred. Certainly there is little reason to disagree with Dryden's judgment of Virgil, who

> . . . being so very sparing of his words, and leaving so much to be imagined by his reader, can never be translated as he ought, in any modern tongue. To make him copious is to alter his character; and to translate him line for line, is impossible; because the Latin is naturally a more succinct language than either the Italian, Spanish, French, or even than the English, which, by reason of its monosyllables, is far the most compendious of them. Virgil is much the closest of any Roman poet, and the Latin hexameter has more feet than the English heroic.
>
> Besides all this, an author has the choice of his own thoughts and words, which a translator has not; he is confined by the sense of the inventor to those expressions which are the nearest to it; so that Virgil, studying brevity, and having the command of his own language, could bring those words into more narrow compass, which a translator cannot render without circumlocutions.[9]

And so one's opinion shifts from the individualism of a dilettante like FitzGerald to the more disciplined approach of a Dryden, and even to the attitude of professorial scholars like Dorothea Clinton Woodworth, who "maintain before students and philistine colleagues alike that there is no such thing as an adequate translation."[10]

Dryden, however, did not fear the rendering of all authors as he did Virgil. He felt himself fully capable of translating Lucretius,[11] and at

---

[6] William Norman Guthrie, "Translation: A Method for the Vital Study of Literature," *Sewanee Review*, XVII (July, 1909), 315.

[7] (A. V. Dicey), "Jowett's Thucydides—I," *The Nation*, XXXIV (Jan. 5, 1882), 15.

[8] *Ibid.*

[9] John Dryden, "Preface to Silvae: Or, the Second Part of Poetical Miscellanies," 1685, *Essays of John Dryden*, Selected and Edited by W. P. Ker (Oxford: Clarendon Press, 1926), I, 257.

[10] Dorothea Clinton Woodworth, "Meaning and Verse Translation," *Classical Journal*, XXXIII (Jan., 1938), 193.

[11] John Dryden, "Preface to Silvae," 258-59.

times he veered close to the romantic concept of translating the sense before concerning himself with the form. For example, he quotes a Renaissance writer, Sir John Denham, with evident approval:

'That servile path thou nobly dost decline
Of tracing word by word, and line by line:
A new and nobler way thou dost pursue
To make translations and translators too:
They but preserve the ashes, thou the flame
True to his sense, but truer to his fame.'[12]

Dryden goes on to say that it is almost impossible to translate literally and well at the same time, for to attempt to copy both the form and the thought of the original involves the translator in a dilemma from which he can hardly hope to escape with credit either to himself or to his source:

'Tis much like dancing on ropes with fettered legs: a man may shun a fall by using caution; but the gracefulness of motion is not to be expected: and when we have said the best of it, 'tis but a foolish task; for *no* sober man would put himself into a danger for the applause of escaping without breaking his neck.[13]

Perhaps this argument over the feasibility of translating effectively both the form and the content of a work of literary art is but an academic quarrel. As Vladimir Weidlé observes, one hears constantly how futile all translation is, but there is no cessation of the practice. Indeed, there is both truth and wit in the remark of Anatole France to his English translator, Lewis May, who had complained of the impossibility of his task:

Vous avez parfaitement raison, mon ami, et remarquez que la connaissance de cette vérité est la première condition de la réussite dans l'art du traducteur.[14]

With full recognition, then, of the impossibility and the inevitability of literary translation of both form and content, let us consider next the difficulties inherent in the transference of the spirit or tone of an original work.

It has been stated that the optimum translation would "arouse in the English reader or hearer the identical emotions and sentiments that were aroused in him who read or heard the sentence as his native tongue."[15] Our discussion of the difficulty of translating both form and content will have prepared the reader to be skeptical of the successful communication of the spirit of an original work. For, as F. W. Newman, goaded by the criticism of Matthew Arnold, came to admit, " . . . how *can* an Englishman read any Greek composition and be affected by it as Greeks were?"[16] There is in a great work of art, as the anonymous author of the article on translation in the *Enciclopedia Universal Ilustrada* says,

---

[12] "John Dryden," Preface to the Translation of Ovid's Epistles," Edition Ker, 238.
[13] *Ibid.*
[14] Vladimir Weidlé, "L'Art de traduire," *Nouvelles Littéraires*, (May 20, 1939) 1 and 6.
[15] Tolman, *op. cit.*, 22.
[16] Matthew Arnold, *Essays* (London: Humphrey Milford, Oxford U. P., 1935), "F. W. Newman's Reply," p. 349.

. . . algo casi inaccesible y sin embargo esencial, ese soplo con
que el espíritu del autor penetra la obra entera, que le da vida,
movimiento, individualidad, y que puede ser comparado justamente
a lo que se llama principio vital en los cuerpos orgánicos.[17]

Certainly it is this "vital principle," this indefinable spirit in the
expression of a writer or even of a nation that often escapes the translator. He can, of course, approximate it through careful word selection
based upon deep and broad research, but one is inclined not to join with
Phillimore in his belief that it can surely be achieved by years of reading
in the original language.[18]

Perhaps the chief barrier to success in translating the spirit of an
original work of genius lies in the infrequent incidence of companionate
genius in the translator. If we must concur with Croce that there is an
"eternal rebirth or re-evocation that poetry undergoes" and that "such
re-evocation cannot become actual otherwise than as the retracing of the
creative process of that expression,"[19] then we must agree that, in the case
of poetry at least, even the reading of a book involves the interpenetration
of minds, the re-creation of the original experience. How much more then
can we demand of the translator who must not only re-create but re-express
that experience using the medium of another language! The task of
the translator is in one sense even more subtle than that of the musician
who, by means of a mechanical instrument, objectifies his understanding
of what the composer has written.[20] It has indeed been suggested that
only a poet can translate a poet, i.e. that there must be creative genius
in the translator of an order not too much lower than that of his author.
It is necessary, however, to indicate the rarity of that phenomenon. Saint-
Evremond especially postulates a lack of confidence in one's own genius
as a prerequisite for becoming a translator!

C'est ce qui arrive à la plupart de nos traducteurs; de quoi ils
me paraissent convaincus, pour sentir les premiers leur stérilité.
Et en effet, celui qui met son mérite à faire valoir les pensées des
autres n'a pas grande confiance de pouvoir se rendre recommand-
able par les siennes; mais le public lui est infiniment obligé du
travail qu'il se donne pour apporter des richesses étrangères où
les naturelles ne suffisent pas.[21]

And those who doubt the feasibility of translation will find support in the
apparently impossible requirement imposed by Frac et Valère: "La

---

[17] *Enciclopedia Universal Ilustrada Europeo-Americana* (Madrid: Es-
pasa-Calpe S. A., 1905-33), "Traducción," LXIII, 508d.

[18] J. S. Phillimore, *Some Remarks on Translation and Translators*,
English Association, Pamphlet No. 42 (Oxford U. P., January, 1919), 12.

[19] Gay Wilson Allen and Harry Hayden Clark, *Literary Criticism, Pope
to Croce* (New York: American Book Company, 1941), 624. The citation
is from *La Poesia* (Bari: 1937), 65.

[20] Lewis Galantière, "On Translators and Translating," *The American
Scholar*, XX (Autumn, 1951), 442.

[21] [Charles de] Saint-Evremond, "Sur nos Traducteurs," in his *Oeuvres*,
Mises en ordre par René de Planhol (Paris: À la Cité des Livres, 1927),
I, 263.

difficulté de traduire est en effet d'apparaître soi, tout en ne cessant pas d'être un autre."[22]   It has been a fortunate and infrequent event when a creative genius like Dante Gabriel Rossetti has been content to devote his own spirit to the revelation of another's.

If the task of translating the spirit or tone of a work seems overwhelming, perhaps it may be expected that the process of finding word equivalents will appear more feasible.

Word Equivalents

". . . nihil esse difficilius quam ex bene Graecis bene Latina reddere."[23] Thus, Erasmus summed up his problems of translation.   He had been trying, he says, to stay as close to the original meaning as possible, but he found no task more difficult than locating proper equivalent meanings. Subsequent translators have sympathized with the sufferings of the *nouus interpres* and have come to the conclusion that absolute fidelity to the meaning of the original can be achieved only by the sacrifice of form. Thus, in the case of scientific and technical treatises, perhaps satisfactory transference may take place.   Even in such material, however, there is a necessity for the translator to choose among synonyms for the expression of relations and qualifications.   Hilaire Belloc considers it naïve to think that this can be accomplished.   He says that there are no such things as exact equivalents between terms in different languages: first, because each word, no matter how simply it is used, is employed with a multiplicity of meaning; secondly, its history, connotation in verse or prose, sound-value, cultural association, "in general all the atmosphere of its being, make it one thing in one language from what it is in another even where the use being made of it is similar."[24]   Schopenhauer expresses himself on the subject more profoundly and scientifically, stating:

> Nicht für jedes Wort einer Sprache findet sich in jeder andern das genaue Aequivalent.   Also sind nicht sämmtliche Begriffe, welche durch die Worte der einen Sprache bezeichnet werden genau dieselben, welche die der andern ausdrücken; wenn gleich dieses meistens, bisweilen sogar auffallend genau . . . der Fall ist; sondern oft sind es blosz ähnliche und verwandte, jedoch durch irgend eine Modifikation verschiedene Begriffe.[25]

He goes on to objectify his position through the use of diagrams.   He employs concentric circles to illustrate those words which find exact equivalents, intersecting circles with different centers to illustrate varying degrees of equivalence, and totally separate circles to show the disparity between words like the Latin *luridus* and the English *lurid* which have

---

[22] Frac et Valère, "Comment traduire les Bucoliques," *Revue Bleue,* LXXI (May 20, 1933), 301d.

[23] Desiderius Erasmus, *Opvs Epistolarvm Des.   Erasmi Roterodami,* Denvo Recognitvm et Avctvm per P. S. Allen (Oxford: Clarendon Press, 1906), I, 393.   Letter 177 to Nicholas Ruistre, Louvain, Nov. 17, 1503.

[24] Hilaire Belloc, "On Translation," in *Selected Essays,* comp. John Edward Dineen (Philadelphia: J. B. Lippincott Co., 1936), 293.

[25] Arthur Schopenhauer, "Ueber Sprache und Worte," *Parerga und Paralipomena* (Berlin: A. W. Hayn, 1851), II, 460.

acquired totally different significations. He also points out the existence
of words like *naïf* in French and *gentleman* in English which evoke concepts having no exact parallel in any other language.
He says:

> Hierauf beruht das nothwendig Mangelhafte aller Uebersetzungen.
> Fast nie kann man irgend eine charakterische, prägnante, bedeut-
> same Periode aus einer Sprache in die andere so übertragen, dasz
> sie genau und vollkommen dieselbe Wirkung thäte. Daher bleibt
> jede Uebersetzung todt und ihr Stil gezwungen, steif, unnatürlich;
> oder aber sie wird frei, d. h. begnügt sich mit einem *à peu près*,
> ist also falsch. Eine Bibliothek von Uebersetzungen gleicht einer
> Gemäldegallerie von Kopien.[26]

Thus, those who doubt the feasibility of translation find evidence on what
might be considered the easiest step of the process. Few writers have put
it so colorfully as the Renaissance Englishman, George Chapman, who,
beset with the problems of rendering Homer, declared that translators
into English

                    . . . may as well
          Make fish with fowl, camels with whales engender,
          Or their tongues' speech in other mouths compell.[27]

Of course, it may be said that only the mediocre translator will com-
plain as to the adequacy of his own language, that if he knew it well
enough or applied himself with sufficient energy to his task, he might find
exact equivalents. Tytler seems to have held this view when he prepared
his famous *Essay on the Principles of Translation* in 1791. He thought
that a translator might through diligent study learn to perceive "those
very delicate shades of distinction in the signification of words,"[28] both in
the original language and in his own. This was particularly necessary,
he said, in translating the works of the ancients. Robert Bridges, however, insists that equivalent terms simply do not exist for the translation
of, say, the metaphysical ideas of the Hebrews or the Greeks into English.
It is not only that the terms are not found, but, he affirms, "our English
words are labels for other ideas, and cannot be readjusted and assorted to
match with ideas that are outside our mental horizon."[29] It is not a
question of energy or of application, he would say. It simply does not
lie "within the compass of human skill."

Constance West points out a slightly different aspect of this barrier
when she observes that words with apparently the same dictionary meaning
have different associative meanings within their several national cultures,

---

[26] *Ibid.*, p. 462.
[27] George Chapman, trans., *The Iliad of Homer* (London: J. M. Dent,
1901, reproduced from the Edition of 1616), I, p. xvi.
[28] Alexander Fraser Tytler, Lord Woodhouslee, *Essay on the Principles
of Translation* (London: J. M. Dent, n.d., reprint of Revised Edition, 1813),
14.
[29] Robert Bridges, "The Bible," in his *Collected Essays, Papers, Etc.*
(London: Oxford U. P., 1934), Essay No. 16, p. 110.

meanings which make them utterly unusable in another tongue.[30] The translator must indeed give attention to the complex problem of the use of synonyms. There is, for instance, the difficulty of finding the exact terms to express minute distinctions in the original, nice discriminations which the translator may have difficulty even in perceiving without profound study. On the one hand there is the natural tendency to use the same equivalent each time a given term occurs in the original.[31] Some languages have to rely upon variations in word order or even upon accent and tone patterns to denote shades of meaning. These differentiations the translator must show through the careful use of synonyms. On the other hand, there is the extreme reluctance in English (and in other modern languages as well) to repeat a word within the same section of a discourse. Postgate calls it an "almost morbid repugnance . . ., due in part no doubt to certain deficiencies, as for example in pronouns, but chiefly to a sensuous dislike of recurrences of the same word or rather of the same sounds."[32] Since older or more primitive languages may have lacked the capacity to achieve this variation, it behooves the faithful translator to repeat his most exact English equivalent. If he fails to do so, he betrays his obligation to render his original.

In this brief discussion we have pointed out that the translation of both form and content is an extremely difficult process and that the preservation of the spirit or tone of an original work imposes a still heavier responsibility upon the translator. In further illustration of the difficulties of translation we have indicated some of the problems of finding proper word equivalents. We might well continue, calling attention to the technical, stylistic, and linguistic barriers which limit the feasibility of translation. In spite of these and other barriers, translation will always be carried on, simply because it is the nature of man as a cultural being to do so. It is fortunate that this is true, since translation is fundamental to the diffusion of literature itself. For the study of comparative literature, translation is an essential point of departure, as it is only when masterpieces are apprehended through the vehicle of the student's own tongue that he has a common denominator for intelligent comparison.

---

[30] Constance B. West, "La théorie de la traduction au xviiie siècle par rapport surtout aux traductions françaises d'ouvrages anglais," RLC, XII (April, 1932), 340.

[31] Isaac Broydé, The Jewish Encyclopedia (New York: Funk and Wagnalls Co., 1909). "Translations," XII, 220c.

[32] Postgate, op. cit., p. 40.

COMPARATIVE LITERATURE FOR UNDERGRADUATES?

Horst Frenz
Indiana University

More than once we have expressed our belief that the *Yearbook of Comparative and General Literature* fulfills an important function as a clearing house for information on comparative literary studies and their place and importance in American education. How much an annual publication of this kind is needed becomes evident from a recent article entitled "Comparative Literature" and published in the January 1953 issue of the *Modern Language Journal.* In this article, Garnet Rees of the University College of Swansea (Great Britain), while recognizing the importance of graduate studies in comparative literature and admitting the validity of research in this field, expresses serious doubt as to the value of comparative literature as an undergraduate discipline and warns against such studies.

To his charge that there are dangers "in the indiscriminate use of comparative literature—the careless thinking, prejudice and *parti-pris*, rash generalization and sanction of a harmful critical method," one must answer that the indiscriminate use of any discipline is dangerous, and that careless thinking and rash generalization are equally objectionable in comparative as well as in other literature courses. Why should courses that cut across the literatures of several countries be more superficial than courses that cover the literature of a century or even a portion of a century in one country? Why should a course in a single major figure be more desirable than a course which combines the works of two or more major writers from different countries? Why should it be more acceptable to compare Shakespeare and Jonson than Shakespeare and Racine?

Professor Rees illustrates his objections to comparative literature courses by discussing the desirability of separate studies in Shakespeare and Racine. Nobody will deny the importance of such courses on individual writers in a student's curriculum; however, Mr. Rees' statement that "if Shakespeare and Racine can be considered in these degenerate days to be representatives of their respective geniuses, it is better for us to accept them as such, with all their violent divergences, rather than to link them together with fragile threads of purely fortuitous comparison" and that "the knowledge and acceptance of national differences are surely as much an aid to international understanding as the discovery of artificial and illusory bonds" reveals a decided misconception of the nature of comparative literature courses. Obviously, Mr. Rees has the strange notion that the study of comparative literature is concerned only with similarities. We maintain that the separate study of the two authors could well be supplemented with a most valuable comparative course discussing writings of both Shakespeare and Racine. Here are two writers working in the same medium both at peak periods in their respective national literatures: a comparative study would point out their achievements, their similarities and, equally important, their differences, and finally their contributions to the total development of the drama and theatre of the western world.

Mr. Rees believes that only persons with "erudition, the experience of mind and method, the absence of *parti-pris* . . ., the subtlety of approach" should undertake the study of comparative literature. Again it is obvious that all of us vitally concerned with the study of the humanities should like to attract mature and superior students. Although such students may be rare, we should, however, not allow this factor to discourage undergraduate programs in any area of the humanities. As a matter of fact, what Professor Rees does throughout his paper is to point out the difficulties inherent in defining, criticizing and teaching literature and then applies them exclusively to comparative literature. If he were to carry his arguments to their logical conclusions he would eliminate the teaching of all literatures—national, international or anything else—and throw out all approaches—historical, textual, aesthetic, etc.—because of the many difficulties and because of the lack of clear definitions. There are students that will profit from the study of one national literature; there are others who will benefit from a broad, that is, comparative, approach to literature, a program which emphasizes the study of several literatures concomitantly.

Mr. Rees makes a great deal of the alleged confusion arising from the various meanings of the term "comparative literature." It is quite true that the study of comparative literature has undergone an evolution and that it does not mean today what it meant a few decades ago. It is equally correct that not all scholars in comparative literature agree on a single definition of the term. However, the same charge may be made against other disciplines in the liberal arts college. The study of English, for example, has undergone considerable changes and the term may, in some cases, refer to English literature alone, and in others, include American literature, and even creative writing, linguistics, or folklore as well.

It has already been said that comparative literature implies the study of several literatures concomitantly which, it might be added, will show the flux of ideas, literary movements, themes, etc. across national and linguistic barriers. The study of influences is really secondary except in interlocking influences of a general character, e.g. those of the romantic movement as a whole in England, France, Germany, Italy, etc. The writers in this movement show common attitudes and approaches to life (which, to the same extent, the 18th century did not have)—it is a total movement. Clearly, it should be studied as such or one can have no deep or broad understanding of it. Familiarity with Goethe adds to the understanding of Shelley or Byron, not because of specific influences, but because Goethe highlights certain ideas common to the whole group and enables one to understand the whole group better. Again it should be emphasized that such a course on romanticism need not replace, but rather supplement courses in certain aspects of romanticism or in certain romantic writers. The actual study of influences may well be reserved to graduate study, not because it is comparative literature, but because it requires specialized techniques of investigation (whether approached comparatively or for one literature only). As a matter of fact, many respectable scholars in comparative literature no longer consider the tracing of influences their main areas of investigation.

Interestingly enough, Professor Rees admits that courses in romanticism, classicism, and "the study of the great literary movements and beliefs" should have a place in the undergraduate curriculum, and thus approves substantially of the kind of program we have set up for undergraduate students in my own institution. Such period courses as the renaissance, enlightenment, romanticism and realism may well form the core of a comparative literature program and may be supplemented with advanced work in at least one foreign language and literature, some familiarity with the classical literatures, and the study of major English and American figures.

That the study of a foreign language, literature, or culture adds to the students' understanding of a foreign civilization and of international problems is generally accepted. Therefore, it is difficult to see why a comparative literature program that deals with the literatures and thought of other nations and emphasizes the importance of foreign languages should not achieve the same results and claim to be "an instrument of international understanding." Such a claim is not, as Mr. Rees seems to feel, just another of many attempts by the advocates of comparative literature to justify the existence of this approach. There is hardly a better way of bringing about international understanding than, for instance, by relating one's own literature and culture to the literatures and cultures of other nations.

And finally a word should be said about the importance of the study of languages in the comparative literature program. Professor Rees ignores the fact that a program which deserves that name necessarily encourages foreign language study. If he were to look at the situation at Indiana University, he would discover that, outside of the foreign language departments, our program is the only one which requires, on the undergraduate level, advanced work in at least one foreign literature offered by the language departments and which encourages the study of a second or a third language. On the graduate level, our program in comparative literature insists on the knowledge and use of foreign languages and is the only department which requires a thesis and two foreign languages for the M.A. degree.

I am convinced that there is a place for undergraduate—as well as graduate—studies in comparative literature in our colleges and that such programs fill an important function in a student's liberal education. I even submit that faculties can profit from a program which, in order to be successful, must call upon the services and resources of persons in various departments. Our program, for example, planned and administered by an interdepartmental committee and supported by the department of English, the foreign language departments, and the department of philosophy, has accounted for an unusually fruitful exchange of ideas for the benefit of faculty and students alike. It is this kind of a program that will prevent isolation within the various fields in the liberal arts and contribute substantially to the strengthening of the humanities.

OUR COMMON PURPOSE

W. P. Friederich
University of North Carolina

Recent discussions on the essence of Comparative Literature in this *Yearbook* have done much to clarify many moot points and, if read in conjunction with European viewpoints expressed in recent issues of the *Revue de Littérature Comparée* and the *Germanisch-Romanische Monatsschrift*, they indicate the road we have travelled since the days of Posnett's first (and now quite untenable) definition of the term Comparative Literature. On the other hand, however, these discussions have also pointed to serious cleavages among us which should not be permitted to develop too far, for the literary—and, I might add, the political—ideals which hold our heterogeneous group together are far stronger and more lasting than occasional divergencies concerning the goals and the methods of Comparative Literature.

Our teaching and, in part, our research in Comparative Literature vary widely, for they are largely circumscribed by the institutions in which we are located and by the type of students available on every campus. The courses given by us range from the lowliest sophomore class about the epic elements in the *Iliad* to the highest seminar for doctoral candidates about the aesthetic of European Symbolism. In our spare time, in our research, in papers read before our colleagues, in articles and books published for a wider audience, we reflect our own tastes, predilections and potentialities: some of us turn to thematology, others to an international study of genres; some prefer the investigation of influences, others turn to the importance of intermediaries; some try to link up their knowledge of two or three literatures with history or religion, others with the fine arts or with art criticism: some conceive of the task before them as a useful excursion into the sociology of literature, while others are capable of permeating their work with the finest aesthetic considerations. It stands to reason that these differences of viewpoints produce works of different degrees of quality and importance, for here again the articles and books may range from treatments of trifling problems to vast and comprehensive studies of great international movements; indeed, they may range from the pedantic to the obtuse. But each work represents what its author can do best, the kind of problem which he wants to pick in this fascinating and new and inviting field which is Comparative Literature. Already Muralt stated that "une des beautés de l'univers c'est la diversité"

—and we can do no less than wish more power to each one of our colleagues, though his predilection may not exactly be our predilection.

For, it bears repeating, that which holds us together is far stronger
than what separates us. We are all resolved to break away from narrow
departmentalization, that bane of colleges and universities, that breeder
of national conceit and ignorance, and we are all united in recognizing
our fellow men across national borders, in acknowledging the very real
significance of their culture and literature, and in studying the impact
they had on us and we had on them. We are all men and women dedicated
to the task of working for a greater understanding among nations and of
emphasizing the common cultural heritage, indeed the common humanity,
in which we all share. I am sure that all of you recall, as I do, classes
in Chaucer which consisted of picking out Kentish or Northumbrian dia-
lectal forms in the text and in which words like Ovid, Italy, France or the
Renaissance were never even mentioned—or classes on New England
Transcendentalism which were given in a complete vacuum, with no
reference to German Idealism or European Romanticism. Today an increasing number among us is determined to put an end to such blindness,
to place a national movement into its larger international context, to
shake off the self-complacency and ignorance foisted upon us by depart-
mental barriers and, by Jove, to learn a handful of foreign languages,
and learn them well, if thereby we obtain the tools of enlarging our
knowledge of literature and of enriching our own life as well as the lives
of our students. If, in possession of his newly acquired faculties, a comparatist wants to rush into the field of thematology, we might agree with others
who hold that the study of the different treatments of the same theme is
not really Comparative Literature at its best—though we cannot help
observing, too, that, for instance, the presentation of the ever advancing
evolution of the concept of the rights and the dignity of womanhood in
the treatments of Jephtha's daughter or of Griseldis is most rewarding,
and that any student of Buchanan or of Dekker could profit by studying
some later versions. Or if another comparatist chooses to derive rather
sweeping generalizations about national tastes and literary predilections
from the investigation of the success or the failure of a great dramatist
like Racine or Shakespeare, or of a literary movement like Classicism or
Romanticism in various nations, we should consider also this to be entirely
legitimate and desirable. Equally acceptable are occasional political interpretations of the popularity or the unpopularity of a certain nation in the
literatures of its neighbors. Such efforts to connect literature with the
multiple political or social activity of the world around us would certainly
obviate the reproach, frequently heard, that the Humanities in general and
Literature in particular have ceased to attract the youth of today because
they operate in a vacuum, an ivory tower removed from all reality—and
the comparatist, who is doubly well qualified to approach these problems
on a broad international front, can be expected to produce more fascinating
and more accurate results than most of his colleagues.

Of course, it is agreed that the proper study of literature is literature, and that the investigation of the traffic of ideas and forms across national boundaries will never absolve the comparatist from the necessity of study-ing the texts themselves, of fathoming the genius and the intellectual and aesthetic greatness that is behind every great work of art. My own and rather strong convictions in this matter are that we should always go back *ad fontes* and that we should never neglect the aesthetic evaluation of a poet—but that we should not overdo it, either. The study of Comparative Literature, of the manifold cosmopolitan interrelationships of literary trends, is enough of a task for any one man; to go beyond that is certainly the exception, not the rule. In our age of specialization, we comparatists have a definite task assigned to us which we should fill to the best of our abilities; in the vast majority of all cases, we cannot and dare not encroach upon other territories. In the importance of our field, we are on equal footing with our colleagues in the Italian, German or French departments; we should help each other, complement each other, but, if possible, not poach in each other's territory. Our colleagues in Italian, German or French supply us with all the biographical information, the textual criti-cism, and the poetic evaluation of a Dante, Goethe, or Hugo, while we supply the international background of the Renaissance or of Romanticism, the crisscross of currents between Italy, Germany and France that helped to make Dante, Goethe and Hugo what they are. I believe that most of us are satisfied with that kind of task; in most cases we would be glad if the individual literature departments acknowledged the dire need for such complementary work and if a few comparatists were associated with the Humanities Division of every university, to take care of that particular mode of investigation for which our training has prepared us. To go beyond this limited assignment and to say that the term "Professor of Comparative Literature" (apart from the old objections to the term "comparative") is really a misnomer and that "Professor of Literature" would far more accurately define our task is something with which, I imagine, only few people would agree. Most of us are not big enough to assume this super-role of evaluating literature in its well nigh boundless totality—and even if we were, we might suddenly find out that it would not be good diplomacy to wish to assume it. We should be content if the individual universities acknowledge us as being on equal footing with the professors of Greek, Italian or American literature—but we most certainly do not wish to supersede them, to appropriate their jobs in addition to ours, and to push them out of their vested interests. That would be suicide, for it would utterly destroy the good will and the friendly col-laboration so many of us have been trying to build up during the past decades—and before we knew it, we might be back where we started from a generation ago: in the wilderness. The Schlegels with their all-encompassing universality would have qualified as "Professors of Litera-ture," and in our times that title might occasionally best be bestowed upon certain practitioners of the art, like Archibald MacLeish or T. S. Eliot—but when it comes to scholars, we would better keep to our special training and assignment.

A few examples will show how the professor of national literature and the comparatist can complement each other, each one practising his own special skill while at the same time learning and borrowing from the other: Mr. Chamard's excellent life of du Bellay and Mr. Vianey's study on Italian Petrarchism in France; Mr. Kittredge's or Mr. Craig's work on the basic greatness of Shakespeare and Mr. Par's studies on Shakespeare in Spain; Mr. Strich's analysis of German Classicism and Romanticism and Mr. Baldensperger's investigation of the movement of ideas during the French Revolution. It does not matter who came first among the two types of scholars, the "nationalist" or the "internationalist," for such beneficial influences occur in either direction. This is the type of coexistence we should strive to achieve; these are the fields in which we can be peers among peers.

There is another reason why we should be satisfied with our task and not impinge—to choose an example at random—upon the New Critics in their cult of evaluating the imagism of Ezra Pound's poems or the symbolism of Kafka's novels: our own age, with the old tragedies and the new hopes of its post-war adjustments, is in dire need of constant reassurance of the political and cultural unity of our Western World. It would seem that today we can afford less than ever to indulge in many fads of subjective aestheticism, for what the younger generation needs is a constant awareness of the cultural unity of all Western civilization and of the constant and fructifying give-and-take that occurs between the great literatures of our world. We may no longer be as boldly optimistic as Wendell Willkie was with his "One World!" concept, but at least we are firmly determined to consolidate the spiritual unity in our half of the world—and in that task Comparative Literature can be of immense importance. Indeed, it may be assumed that many of us have deserted the study and the teaching of individual national literatures not only because we found the narrowness of cultural and academic departmentalization often frustrating, but also because we have espoused a political ideal and because, within the limits of our profession, we want to do our share in the realization of the cherished goal of Western unity. This may be a slightly utilitarian perversion of our primary task, of which, however, we need not be ashamed. In justifying this semi-political aspect of our chosen calling, we realize that it would again be unnecessarily dogmatic—and not in keeping with the tolerant latitude which we are willing to accord to all of our colleagues—if we frowned upon those comparatists who prefer other emphases to the West European-American problem which is dearest to most of us; for those who work in Oriental-Western or indeed in Slavic-Western relations form an equally important element in our present task of breaking down barriers and of building bridges.

The horizons are thus wide enough to enclose within the scope of our field a multitude of scholars with similar cosmopolitan ideals, but with a wide variety of plans and methods to translate these ideals into tangible reality. If the comparatist has any "enemies" whom he should combat with all his might, it is not the hapless colleague who loves thematology, or delves into comparative national psychologies, or traces fussy little influences through fussy little intermediaries. Far more dangerous to our cause is the professor of Spanish who teaches his literature as though nothing important had ever happened north of the Pyrenees, or the professor of English who, partly because of his own linguistic inabilities, does not deign to look at what had been thought and written across the English channel. If we can win over these men to a belated awareness of our common cultural heritage, we might be able to reform also the few "enemies" within our ranks who are not a credit to our earnest purpose. Foremost among those I would mention, on the undergraduate level, the teachers of survey courses who, instead of concentrating seriously on a few Great Books, pretend to give a grandiose World Literature course taught by means of anthologies, with scanty sprinklings of infinitesimal fragments ranging from the *Gilgamesh* epic to just one chapter of *War and Peace* or one act of *The Doll's House*. And on the graduate level our main concern should be with professors who, when given a chance to do comparative work, do so in order to satisfy some dormant jingoism and to carry into literature old political hatreds and prejudices—something which we should consider with profound distaste as the very negation of our finest purpose.

But such matters can be settled by earnest discussions on individual campuses or at national meetings. They need not for one moment disrupt that which should be most important to all of us: the basic unity of all comparatists, of all believers in the international approach to literature.

PART TWO

BENEDETTO CROCE di Aldo Vallone

L'attenzione che Croce ha prestato alle letterature straniere è stata lunga e costante; anzi possiamo dire che essa non è stata mai disgiunta dallo studio e dalla intelligenza dei fatti storici e delle vicende letterarie della nostra storia. Interpretazioni e ricerche, anche quelle più dotte ed erudite, si integrano poi strettamente tra loro in modo da presentare un unitario aspetto, una salda prospettiva: quella della umana civiltà degli uomini. In possesso di un fermo e valido metodo di indagine critica, il Croce ha precisato fonti e origini letterarie, momenti e figure storiche, aspetti e testi fraintesi o dimenticati, famosi o ignoti. Questa opera è durata per oltre sessant'anni, dalle prime monografie storiche ed erudite agli ultimi saggi, sempre in una prosa fine, organica e impregnata di arguzia e umore. Quello che giova rilevare è che il Croce, nel mentre è stato paziente ricercatore di dati minuti e particolari, nello stesso tempo non ha perduto la visione generale e superiore dei fatti. Ogni indagine, ogni elemento di indagine, per quanto a prima vista potesse sembrare marginale, finiva poi col condurre al concreto di un rilievo storico-letterario e filologico. Si ha così l'impressione che tutta l'opera del Croce sia una costruzione compatta e vigorosa, in cui ogni cosa ha una sua ragione e un suo scopo. Ricercando con amore di figlio devoto la storia della sua Napoli non poteva fare a meno di interessarsi della storia e della cultura spagnole, che in un dato momento si intrecciarono con quelle napoletane: ecco perciò nascere, fin dal 1885, un' opera biografico-critica su Lucrezia d'Alagno, amata da Alfonso d'Aragona; e d'allora in poi traduzioni, saggi e memorie accademiche sempre in larga misura.

Gioverà, in queste brevi note[1], citare almeno qualcuna di queste opere (tutte pubblicate via via con rara nobiltà d'arte dall'editore Laterza di Bari). Fondamentale, per la letteratura inglese, rimane il saggio, avviatore di altre fruttuose indagini, su Shakespeare nel volume *Ariosto, Shakespeare e Corneille*, e minori saggi, altrove, su W. Scott, G. M. Hopkins ed altri. Per la letteratura francese sono da ricordare i saggi su Corneille, nel volume citato, su Ronsard, Racine, Molière, Beaumarchais, Chénier, Hugo, Baudelaire ecc. in *Poesia antica e moderna* e su altri autori in altre opere. Notevolissimi poi i saggi su scrittori tedeschi (a parte i filosofi) e spagnoli: tra i primi, Goethe, ampiamente studiato e tradotto in due volumi e che tanto fervore di critica ha incontrato da Santayana al Bahr, e poi Heine, Schiller, Kleist, Chamisso ecc. in *Poesia e non poesia*; tra gli scrittori spagnoli (fondamentale e nuovo per prospettive e rilievi è

---

[1] V. in particolare: C. Antoni—R. Mattioli *Cinquant'anni di vita intellettuale italiana, 1896-1946*, Napoli, 1950, voll. 2; F. Flora *Benedetto Croce* (a cura di), Milano, 1953.

il volume *La Spagna nella vita italiana durante la Rinascenza* e parallela-
mente a questo volume gli altri sul *Seicento*) i saggi su *Lazarillo de
Tormes, Don Quijote, Romanze spagnole*, Lope de Vega, Góngora, ecc. in
Poesia antica e moderna e altrove. L'ampiezza di tali interessi era tale
che il critico con suprema padronanza poteva spaziare dalle letterature
antiche e medievali alle moderne e contemporanee: da Omero, poniamo,
ad Ibsen. Va notato anche che le indagini del Croce si staccano completa-
mente da quelle condotte da molti altri studiosi di letterature comparate, che,
tra la fine dell'ottocento e i primi vent' anni del novecento, occupavano cat-
tedre universitarie, riviste ed istituti di cultura: perchè, mentre al Croce
queste indagini servivano a rinsaldare la sua propria convinzione che ogni
opera è frutto di una individuale visione del mondo e della vita e che perciò
essa va goduta nella sua particolare atmosfera, agli altri studiosi invece le
opere di uno stesso autore o di diversi autori si illuminavano solo se
rapportate tra loro nei motivi di ispirazione, nelle ragioni di canto e nelle
forme espressive.
Roma, Istituto Scientifico di Stato "A. Righi"

NICOLAE IORGA   by Claudiu Isopescu

In the history of humanity Nicolae Iorga (1871-1940) stands out because
of his immense cultural achievements and the unsurpassed number of his
publications: 1,200 books and 23,000 articles and reviews[1]. Among his
numerous and powerful historical writings are the four volumes of an
Essai de synthèse de l'histoire de l'humanité which were singled out for
special praise when he received his *doctor honoris causa* at the Sorbonne.
No less important is his poetic and dramatic work and his literary criticism, which, although he made significant contributions as a scholar and
as one of the few great founders of Comparative Literature, has never been
underscored sufficiently. Since his was not only a work of erudition but
also of art, it is well to bear in mind the many literary and linguistic talents
which he inherited especially from the maternal side of his family; his
early exposure to French language and literature (George Sand, Hugo,
Pichot, Florian); his rapidly increasing proficiency in German, Italian,
English, Spanish, Latin and Greek; and his growing passion for reading
the best foreign classics in the original language. His earliest published
poems revealed the influences of Eminescu as well as of his readings in
foreign literatures, and among his significant translations of this period

---

[1] See J. C. Campbell: "Nicholas Iorga," *SEER*, 1947, 44-59. When
he gave his lecture on "French and Other Literatures in South-Eastern
Europe" at Columbia University in 1930, Iorga was introduced by Mr. John
L. Gerig as "the outstanding personality of the modern world." See N.
Iorga: *My American Lectures*, collected and arranged by Norman L.
Forter. Bucharest, 1932, p. 5.

should be mentioned that of Longfellow's *Evangeline*. This exceptional young man, this "prodigy of memory, knowledge and power of thought" who was to become and remain the spiritual leader of his people for over forty years, naturally finished his university studies in a minimum of time, and an essay on Virgil won for him a scholarship to Italy in 1890. While in Italy, he visited especially Venice and Naples and became engrossed in the works of Verga. A second scholarship enabled him to go to France and enrich further his increasingly encyclopedic knowledge of literature. After his doctorate (1893) he turned to the study of other languages and literatures and in 1895 received his professorship at the University of Bucharest, which he kept until his assassination.

His indefatigable travels and lectures took him to almost all the countries of the Western World. Beginning in 1895, he produced quite an ample library about these travels, telling not only of the foreign countries, landscapes and peoples, but including also critical essays about, or translations from, Carducci, Camoens, Cervantes, Ibsen, Emily Dickinson, Longfellow, Whitman, Sandburg, Tegnér, Wergeland, and others: from the capitals of the North (1904), across Bulgaria to Constantinople (1907), to Germany, Belgium, England (1913), Venice (1914), France (1921), Poland (1924), Yugoslavia (1927), Spain (1927), Portugal (1928), America (1930), and Greece (1931). Even more important than the various books which achieved a similar purpose for the provinces, the landscape, the people and the spiritual values of his own native Rumania (1904-10) was his *Istoria Românilor prin Călători* (1920-22) in which he gave us a new and very interesting historical account of the Rumanians from the fourteenth century to 1860, as seen by foreign travellers and visitors. This very important work is more than a cultural history of Rumania; it also displayed Iorga's vast knowledge of foreign cultures and stressed the significant interrelationship between Rumania and the literatures of the West and of the East.

Though opposed to servile imitation, he was greatly interested in the problem of translations, both as a scholar and as a poet in his own right. Besides his beautiful renderings into Rumanian of some 300 foreign poems, Iorga excelled also as a translator of prose (e.g. Goldoni's *La Locandiera*). In his efforts to make Rumanian literature known abroad, he should be noted, too, for his retelling, in French, of the *Contes roumains* and for his rendition of Eminescu's masterpiece, *Luceafarul*, into French and Italian.

It would be difficult to find another interpreter for his people equally able to present in so personal a way, and often with contributions of his own, the works not only of the major foreign literatures, but even of the minor, such as Byzantine, Neo-Greek, Portuguese, Swedish, Hungarian, Bulgarian or Turkish. Among his critical studies dealing with thematological problems, mention might be made of *La nature roumaine dans la poésie des Roumains*, *L'élément occidental dans le conte danubien et balcanique*, *National Unity in Rumanian Literature*, and *Rome in Rumanian Literature*. Another important group of investigations deals with the

success, in Rumania, of foreign writers like Shakespeare, Molière, Rousseau, Mme de Staël, Alfieri, and many others. Other major works of this great and untiring comparatist include a *History of Romance Literature* in three volumes, which was published by the Rumanian Academy in 1919 and which traced not only the development of these literatures, but also their constant interrelationship and mutual influences (including also the influences of outsiders like Shakespeare) ; everywhere Iorga endeavored to stress the new values of thought, feeling, and art contributed by each Romance literature to the spiritual progress of mankind. A similar purpose can be detected in his five volumes entitled *Books Important in the Life of Mankind*, containing thoughtful analyses that extend from St. Augustine to our own time. In 1911, as part of the celebration of the fiftieth anniversary of Italian unity, Iorga had written, in Italian, a *Short History of the Rumanians*, which dwelled particularly on the cultural and literary relations between Italy and Rumania—and this type of study was later supplemented by his *History of the Relations between France and the Rumanians* (1917), *A History of the Relations between Russians and Rumanians* (1917), *Rumanians and Greeks through the Centuries* (1921), *Poles and Rumanians* (1921) and *A History of Anglo-Rumanian Relations* (1931).[2] Branching out into new fields of investigation, Iorga then published a book on *Art and Literature of the Rumanians; Parallel Summaries*, and also a suggestive chapter in the volume *America și Românii din America* (1930), which deals with the parallelisms between American literature and art. Both these works were meant as forerunners of a gigantic *General History of Universal Literature and Art Shown in Parallel Summaries*, in which the methods of historiology were meant to demonstrate the absolute unity of human life. Of major importance are also his eight volumes of a painstakingly complete and accurate *History of Rumanian Literature* (1901-34), in which he dwelled particularly on the lively literary intercourse of the Rumanians with the rest of Europe; though he was among the first to point to these connections, his findings were later amply corroborated by the more recent studies of Drouhet, Ortiz, Grimm or Cartojan. And finally he wrote two volumes on *Foreign Influences upon the Rumanian Nation* (1923) and *French Ideas and Literary Forms in the Southeast of Europe* (1924), which discuss the impact of Western Europe upon the literatures of Southeastern Europe.

As a member of Parliament, Iorga proposed the foundation of the Ecole roumaine en France, of which he became the director; he was also

---

[2] In his incomplete article "La Littérature comparée chez les Roumains" in *Yearbook* II, 1953, 19-27, Mr. Munteano ignores all this work of Iorga's on comparative literature and merely writes about him that he "multipliait en peu partout . . . les détails et les suggestions." It is also to be regretted that he calls Drouhet's *Le Roumain dans la littérature française* a mere article, for it is a powerful work, rich in information and completely based upon new research.

the editor of the *Mélanges de l'Ecole roumaine*, a series of 22 volumes. He likewise proposed the foundation of the Accademia di Romania in Roma, and later, when he was President of the Board of Education, he proposed that there should be a chair of Rumanian language and literature at the University of Rome. The establishment of this resulted, despite regrettable interruptions since 1946, in 74 essentially comparative theses. In Rumania he was also the founder and the director of the Institute for the Study of Southeastern Europe and of the Institute of Universal History, and he was the editor of the *Revista Istorica*, the *Revue historique du Sud-Est européen*, and the *Bulletin de la section historique de l'Académie roumaine*. Amid this rich and admirable activity, he inevitably became ever more deeply involved in comparative studies.

Iorga's was a truly international mind that believed mankind's real progress could be achieved only through constant cultural interpenetration and mutual understanding among the national and ethnical branches of humanity. His cruel assassination on November 27, 1940, deprived both his country and the rest of the free world of a very great man.
Università di Roma

ALFONSO REYES   por Raimundo Lida

Desde uno y otro extremo de la América hispana, el mexicano Alfonso Reyes y el argentino Jorge Luis Borges han razonado —y con las mejores razones, incluídas las del corazón— su cosmopolitismo literario. ¿Cuál es nuestra tradición?, se pregunta Borges; y se contesta: Toda la cultura de occidente. Reyes ha hecho de parecida pregunta uno de los núcleos más fértiles de su meditación sobre Hispanoamérica. Y su propia obra de escritor es ejemplo de cómo un espíritu hondamente mexicano se desarrolla y enriquece acogiendo en sí los más variados estímulos de la literatura universal.

Él mismo ha evocado (*Pasado inmediato*, México, 1941) sus años de iniciación en la que fué primero "Sociedad de Conferencias" y después "Ateneo de México." Quehacer urgente, la revisión de la literatura nacional, y a él se consagra Alfonso Reyes con su conferencia sobre el poeta Manuel José Othón y, poco después, con un trabajo más amplio y sereno: *El paisaje en la poesía mexicana del siglo XIX* (México, 1911). Lo mexicano siempre y, a su alrededor, ondas más y más vastas de lecturas y reflexiones. Así se nos aparecerá Reyes en sus tempranas *Cuestiones estéticas* (Paris, 1911). Y cuando sus deberes de diplomático lo lleven a Francia, España, Brasil y Argentina, don Alfonso será el gran Embajador de lo mexicano más incitante y duradero. Al cabo de los años habrá logrado presentar así, en imponente galería, los mejores poetas y prosistas de su tierra, y habrá desplegado en cuadros de conjunto los concretos problemas del hacer literario en México. En obras como *L'évolution du Mexique* (Paris, 1923), *Simples remarques sur le Mexique* (Paris, 1926), *Tránsito de Amado Nervo* (Santiago de Chile, 1937), *Letras de la Nueva España* (México, 1948), *La X en la frente* (México, 1952) y el ya citado

Pasado inmediato, quedan fijados algunos de esos brillantes panoramas.

Si su México está cordialmente unido a la América hispana, esa América lo está al mundo entero. La obra de Reyes nos exhorta a "abrir los vasos comunicantes" (*Tentativas y orientaciones*, México, 1944) en procura del más amplio y bienhechor contacto humano. El autor de *The Position of America* (New York, 1950) conoce como pocos el alma de nuestros pueblos —claro que no olvida al Brasil—, y figuras como las de Alberdi y Montalvo, Silva y Darío, Isaacs y Graça Aranha, Rodó y Güiraldes, los Henríquez Ureña y los García Calderón, Gabriela Mistral y Juana de Ibarbourou, Supervielle y Borges, Brull y Florit, aparecen continuamente en su obra. Pero le fascina además el espectáculo del Nuevo Mundo reflejado en Montaigne y Rousseau, en Goethe y Paul Valéry, en Valle-Inclán, Valery Larbaud y Waldo Frank. Ni pierde ocasión de referirse también con agradecida alabanza al Waldo Frank de *Virgin Spain*, y a Havelock Ellis y Jean Cassou, y a Prescott y Washington Irving: grande y noble familia de hispanófilos. Años decisivos para Reyes son, en fin, los que él mismo ha vivido en suelo español, enlazado a aquel glorioso Centro de Estudios Históricos que en Madrid dirigía don Ramón Menéndez Pidal, y a su *Revista de Filología Española*. Allí prepara los textos, prólogos y notas de sus ediciones de clásicos. Allí colabora con Foulché-Delbosc en esas *Obras poéticas* de Góngora (3 vols., New York, 1921) en cuyo prefacio el maestro francés habla del joven mexicano como del "primer gongorista de las nuevas generaciones." De aquellos años de investigación fervorosa y placentera nacerán, no sólo multitud de artículos, sino sus sabias *Cuestiones gongorinas* (Madrid, 1927), sus *Capítulos de literatura española* (México, 1939 y 1945) y otros libros en que la antigua materia se reordena con miras a un público más amplio (*Cuatro ingenios*, México-Buenos Aires, 1950; *Trazos de historia literaria*, de igual fecha y lugar).

La literatura francesa era alimento habitual de aquella juvenil "Sociedad de Conferencias" y aquel "Ateneo de México." De entonces a hoy, nadie más fiel que Alfonso Reyes a esa devoción. En sus *Cuestiones estéticas* ya se nos aparecía reveladoramente atraído por Mallarmé. Nunca abandonará su culto, y a él dedicará uno de sus libros de más bella y suelta erudición: *Mallarmé entre nosotros* (Buenos Aires, 1938). De año en año lo veremos moverse con creciente agilidad por la literatura y el pensamiento francés de todos los tiempos. Relee, pluma en mano, sus clásicos y sus modernos; salta de los unos a los otros; nos muestra de pronto, con una sonrisa, que tal o cual moderno —Henri Massis— no ha entendido cabalmente a tal o cual clásico —Pascal—: red en que se entrecruzan y combinan mil observaciones sobre poetas, moralistas, políticos, eruditos (la novela no deja huella muy profunda en estos comentarios).

Por su primer libro desfilaban también Wilde, Pater y Shaw. Con los años, Alfonso Reyes traducirá a Sterne, a Stevenson y, con especial consagración, a Chesterton. A todos ellos se refiere en sus continuas e inquietas glosas, así como a Thomas Browne, Swift y Samuel Johnson, a Jane Austen y Meredith, a Browning y William Morris, a Oliver Wendell Holmes y a

los dos James de Nueva Inglaterra, a Belloc, a Joyce, a los Huxley. En
tan variado mapa, inclúyase todavía el Portugal de Eça de Queiroz, y la
Italia de D'Annunzio y de Croce, y la Alemania de Nietzsche y de Goethe,
ese Goethe cuya biografía espiritual acaba de dibujar Alfonso Reyes con
rara perfección (*Trayectoria de Goethe*, México, 1954). Aún habría que
añadir otras tierras más exóticas. No vamos a detenernos en ellas. Todas
apuntan, en la obra de Reyes, hacia el aquí y el ahora del escritor, en vivo
diálogo con el lector. ¡Y qué decir de las literaturas antiguas! Virgilio
incita a Alfonso Reyes a contemplar la conquista de México a la luz de los
triunfos de Eneas. Grecia imprime en su obra, desde el comienzo, rastros
variados y frecuentísimos. Con los años, la meditación de los temas helé-
nicos se hará aún más asidua, y lo animará a nuevas empresas. Así habrá
de nacer *La crítica en la edad ateniense* (México, 1941) y, llevado el impulso
de exploración hacia las doctrinas literarias de Roma, *La antigua retórica*
(México, 1942). Y la vena del helenista y la del poeta confluirán finalmente
en un proyecto decisivo: la traducción de la *Ilíada* en muy modernos
alejandrinos aconsonantados. El primer volumen, espléndido, ha aparecido
ya (México, 1951) y don Alfonso avanza a buen paso por el segundo.

Rótulos como "internacionalismo" o "cosmopolitismo" expresarían torpe-
mente, por sí solos, la rara movilidad de espíritu de Alfonso Reyes. Los
diversos planos de su obra ilustran, cada uno a su manera, la rapidez de
síntesis en que se ejercita continuamente este apasionado hombre de
letras. A ejemplos tomados de todas las literaturas y de todas las épocas
acude en ese grupo de trabajos teóricos en que el escritor se concentra
—como volviendo la mirada hacia el íntimo foco de su propia actividad—
en el examen del fenómeno literario mismo: *La experiencia literaria*
(Buenos Aires, 1942), *El deslinde* (México, 1944), *Tres puntos de exe-
gética literaria* (México, 1945). Los elementos a primera vista más dis-
pares, lo superficial y lo profundo, lo presente y lo remoto, tanto en la
geografía como en la historia, se asocian en originales acordes a lo largo
de sus reflexiones sobre formas concretas de cultura. Nada más lícito,
para Alfonso Reyes, que esos acercamientos: "Comparar no es un error.
Sólo confundir es un dislate" (*En torno al estudio de la religión griega*,
México, 1951). En fin, parecidos enlaces relampaguean aquí y allí en
sus poéticos ensayos, en sus narraciones y, claro está, en sus versos. In-
fatigable y ahincado "comparatismo" de un espíritu en permanente ebu-
llición creadora. Y es asombrosa la variedad de los materiales que se
funden en su crisol y reciben la estampa de esta inteligencia vibrátil.
Inteligencia personalísima, y a la vez muy mexicana, hispana y universal,
que "prend son bien où elle le trouve" y que fatalmente lo transforma y
asimila. La sustanciosa medula de cuantos libros —innumerables— llegan
al laboratorio secreto de Alfonso Reyes, está destinada a florecer en
páginas de prosa y verso igualmente inconfundibles, igualmente mexicanas,
hispánicas y universales.

Harvard University

GILBERT CHINARD   by Chandler B. Beall

Gilbert Chinard, throughout a long academic career in America, has not only been a tireless researcher in the field of comparative literature and cultural history, but has also functioned all these years as a magnificent intermediary between the cultures of his native France and the United States. He is remembered at Brown, California, Johns Hopkins, and Princeton as an enthusiastic and inspiring interpreter of French literature to Americans, and as a vigorous and many-sided scholar. He has constantly endeavored, with intelligence, charm, and effective action, to strengthen the ties between his native country and that which is his by adoption. And above all he has made himself the outstanding historian of these ties.

Almost single-handed, Chinard has carved out and pioneered the field of French-American literary and intellectual relations. He has laid out its broad boundaries, demonstrated its complex fascination, and cultivated it intensely himself. He has inspired and directed fellow workers in what is still relatively new territory. His own contribution to the field is a vast one. He has always been deeply interested in the intellectual impact which the New World had upon Europeans, and in reconstructing the history of their developing awareness of America. His first book, *L'Exotisme américain dans la littérature française au XVIe siècle* (1911), was written at Brown University, where there is a remarkable collection of narratives of voyages to this continent. This was followed by *L'Amérique et le rêve exotique dans la littérature française au XVIIe et au XVIIIe siècles* (1913) and by a whole series of other studies centering on Chateaubriand, Volney, Madame d'Houdetot, Jefferson, Du Pont de Nemours, John Adams, Diderot, Lapérouse, Washington, Billardon de Sauvigny, Chamfort, Pascal, Morelly, Samuel Miller; on thinkers, explorers, refugees, books, ideas, and ideals that shuttled constantly between the continents, weaving our modern intellectual world. And there are more studies to come—a volume to be called *Aspects principaux de l'exotisme au dix-neuvième siècle*, and a series of *Études sur l'image de l'Amérique*.

The extent and the importance of Chinard's vast production have, despite numerous awards and honors, never been sufficiently recognized either here or in France. This is because he has worked in areas where three or four of our traditional fields meet and where imaginary lines of demarcation have been drawn and myopically respected by our traditional academic departments. His imposing array of articles, monographs, critical editions, and editions of correspondences will be better known and appreciated as Americans become more and more interested in the intellectual origins of their institutions and ways of life, and in the succession of varying "mirages américains" that other peoples have conceived in the past four and a half centuries. Quantitatively and qualitatively his published work as a *comparatiste* and intellectual historian in this particular field of activity alone is truly remarkable. No future worker in this

interdisciplinary domain can escape indebtedness to him. Chinard's long
career has been marked by a single-minded devotion to his scholarly pur-
suits. Any conversation with him inevitably veers to his work, is filled
with discussion of his many projects, or a spirited account of his latest
discovery. Every summer he goes to Europe, and every fall he returns
with new and exciting materials for future monographs. His study is
cluttered with precious papers in the handwriting of Franklin or Maurice
de Guérin, with old volumes describing voyages to far-off lands, which
throw light not only on the history of exploration but also on the enrich-
ment of the verbal palette of the literary artist. Printer's copy in prepara-
tion, proof in process of correction, his own published volumes, a series of
monographs by his former graduate students, innumerable books on
shelves, on desks, on chairs—and in the midst of these proofs of a prodigious scholarly activity, a thoroughly human and kindly scholar with a
pipe, a twinkle in his eye, and an enthusiasm that has not failed in forty
years.

   In 1929 Professor Chinard was one of the founders of the Institut
Français de Washington, and he has always been a prime mover in this
organization which has published twenty-five or thirty monographs and
collections of documents on French-American relations. The Institut also
sponsored and underwrote the *French American Review*, a quarterly that
appeared under Chinard's editorship from January 1948 through December 1950. In the final number of his distinguished journal, Chinard an-
nounced its suspension in an editorial which he entitled, characteristically,
"Looking Forward." This tribute to our co-worker and friend may fit-
tingly conclude with an excerpt, which is a profession of faith:

   To achieve the understanding so necessary in critical times, it is
   not enough to observe and study, however thoroughly, the French
   and the Americans of today. One must also realize that they
   have a common past and that American history has been since
   the days of the discovery part and parcel of the history of France,
   as much as French history has been part and parcel of the history
   of America.
   The essential purpose of the Institut Français de Washington
   ever since its foundation has been to study and make available
   documents which permit to form a more truthful picture of the
   two peoples, to discover and to analyze also the influences which
   at times may have distorted the "image" of France and the
   "image" of America. Our aim for the future remains unchanged.
   The task is enormous and the field only superficially explored.
University of Oregon

PART THREE

COMPARATIVE LITERATURE AT HOME AND ABROAD*

The International Federation of Modern Languages and Literatures

The sixth triennial congress of the IFMLL at Oxford from September 9-16, 1954 certainly was a social success and all the participants will remember the great hospitality of the University, the Colleges and the City, the delightful excursions to Stratford and Cambridge, and the friendly atmosphere which united colleagues from many countries. The president, Carlo Pellegrini (Florence), did an excellent job with his many allocutions in French; the Oxford organizers, particularly Professors Ewert, Sayce and Moore, were available for all possible requests of the congressists, including a subscription to any British newspaper they cared to read during the week of their sojourn at Oxford.

The overall topic, "Literature, Language and Science," was awkward in that the humanists knew too little about science and the scientists too little about literature. Those who tried to make a pure science out of language and literature brought the confusion to a peak. All this should not obscure the fact that many of the talks which dealt with the general topic only vaguely were excellent. There were two types of sessions, plenary and sectional. The plenary sessions, which were well attended, offered an inquiry into the relations between science and literature from the viewpoint of a scientist by Herbert Dingle, from the University of London, and from the viewpoint of a linguist by A. Ewert, from Oxford. A difficult and somewhat disappointing parallel between literary and scientific history was worked out by Professor Francis Johnson (Stanford). Two other Americans excelled as a kind of team in stressing the existing scientific and technical implications of palaeography (Ruth Dean, Mount Holyoke College) and bibliography (James G. McManaway, Folger Shakespeare Library, Washington, D. C.). The Janus-faced stylistics was, of course, a special topic, viewed from its methodological approach as well as from the viewpoint of its bearing on scientific (G. Temple, Oxford) and poetic (H. Hatzfeld, Washington) literature. Psychoanalysis and literature was the topic selected by W. Rose (London) and Gilbert Mayer (Rennes).

Among the particular sessions, section A, dealing with methods, was the most crowded one; sections B, C, D, dovetailing the general subject according to centuries, provoked less interest. The discussions in the A-section were vivid, since not everybody was as enthusiastic as M. L. Dufrenoy (California at Berkeley) about "The Use of Statistics in Plotting Out Literary Trends," or as E. R. P. Vincent (Cambridge) about

---

* "Comparative Literature in American Universities," a work report from individual institutions all over the country, will henceforth be published every second year.

"Mechanical Aids for the Study of Literary Style." Here arose the really fundamental difference between science and literature, namely the question of value. Along this line, one of the outstanding performances was given by G. Pistorius (Paris), in his "Comparative Method in Literary History and in the Sciences." Closest to the concept of a "science" of literature came D. I. Masson (Liverpool), who following Trubetzkoy's phonostylistics dealt with "Some Problems in Literary Phonaesthetics." In the other sections, S. Dresden (Leiden) and Bernard Weinberg (Northwestern) offered opposite views on the value of the critical method of Sainte-Beuve. The Nestor of the convention, Gustave Charlier (Brussels), aroused the hilarity of outsiders with his dissertation on "La locomotive dans la poésie romantique." Dante was dragged into "science" in a somewhat controversial way by Yvonne Batard (Rennes) and Hiram Peri (Jerusalem). Among truly original problems was the tentative discovery by W. G. Moore (Oxford) of a poetic-psychological method in the French Classics which comes close to a scientific method, and the attack by R. Roedel (St. Gallen) on Manzoni for his lack in scientific interest. This met with sharp counter-attacks on the part of the audience. Goethe, of course, was the best example for "naturwissenschaftliches Denken" in a poet and was presented as such by R. Boeckmann (Heidelberg), and confronted on this level with Paul Valéry by E. Freiherr von Richthofen (Frankfurt).

Count d'Harcourt extended to the assembly the greetings and wishes of the French Academy. Professor Boeckmann brought from the rector of the University of Heidelberg an invitation, which was accepted, for the meeting of 1957. Among the more than two hundred and fifty visitors there were about twenty-five Americans, some of them on sabbatical leave, some vacationing in Europe. For all of them the convention will be a valuable memory.

Among the newly-elected officers of the International Federation of Modern Languages and Literatures are the following: Honorary Presidents: F. Baldensperger, G. Charlier, C. Pellegrini. President: R. W. Zandvoort (Groningen). Vice-Presidents: P. Kohler (Bern), F. C. Roe (Aberdeen), Margaret Gilman (Bryn Mawr), K. Wais (Tübingen). Secretary General: S. C. Aston (Cambridge). Treasurer: Z. L. Zaleski (Paris).

HELMUT A. HATZFELD

Catholic University of America.

The International Association of Comparative Literature, Oxford, 1954

For several years the project has been mooted of bringing together into an International Association the ever increasing phalanx of comparatists. This occurred notably at the meeting at Tübingen in 1950, and again in 1951 at the meeting of the F.I.L.L.M. in Florence. As numerous comparatists were expected, naturally enough, to attend the Oxford F.I.L.L.M. Congress of September, 1954 this moment was chosen to bring into constitutional existence a new international group of which the need was obvious. M. Charles Dédéyan of the Sorbonne who had, as Secretary of the F.I.L.L.M., undertaken a key task in the organisation of the Oxford Congress had, with Professor J. M. Carré, also found time to organise for last September, a series of meetings at which the comparatists could make a review of recent activities in their various fields. The F.I.L.L.M. Congress with its very full syllabus, diversified in addition with social, academic and touristic activities, fortunately contrived to leave a margin of free time. Into this margin was neatly fitted the programme of the simultaneous Congress of the new International Association of Comparative Literature. Following a preliminary meeting for the election of a Provisional Committee, three special sessions on 10, 11 and 15 September were devoted to a report upon the present state of studies in comparative literature in a certain number of countries. These papers were given by an international team of comparatists, each being allotted the task of dealing with the field of comparative literature for which he had evinced particular interest.

At the opening of the first study-session F. C. Roe read a paper on the present state of comparative literature in Great Britain between 1950-54. Comparative literature has one thing in common with the British constitution: neither one or the other can claim official definition but that does not prevent both leading a very real existence! This paper was followed by a clear statement by Mlle A. Van Eupen, who gave an interesting account of the work done by the new Institute of Comparative Literature founded five years ago in Utrecht, and represented by her at the Congress. This Institute has been of great service in furnishing documents and in supplying information to the whole of Holland and is perfectly willing and ready to be of the same service to other countries. The closing paper at this first session was given by Z. L. Zaleski (Paris) who spoke with an emotion that his audience felt on the contemporary contribution made to comparative literature by Poland despite difficult handicaps.

The following day the session opened with a very instructive paper on comparative studies in U.S.S.R., read by Milan Markovitch who holds the Chair of Slavonic studies in the University of Rennes. He was followed by C. Pellegrini (Florence) who had presided with so much competence and grace over the F.I.L.L.M. Conference and who brought a Latin elegance to his account of the present state of his subject in Italy. G. Pistorius made a brief and clear summary of the comparatist's situation in Czechoslovakia. The reports on Rumania and India unfortunately could not be made, S. Munteano and T. P. Wash having found it impossible to attend the Oxford meetings. It is hoped that a publication including the report concerning Rumania will appear later.

The last session of the comparatists comprised, like the first during this Congress, successive literary and administrative meetings. The opening paper on this occasion was given by M. F. Guyard (Nancy) who dealt with recent work on comparative literature in France, a country which was a pioneer and has produced a remarkable and numerous crop of students and likewise has shown, since the last war, a marked increase in the number of Chairs devoted to this subject. Professor Lázaro of Salamanca brought much new information in his review of present studies in Spain. Kurt Wais (Tübingen) who had played an important part in the 1950 meeting at Tübingen, dealt with the present situation in Germany. In the absence of W. P. Friederich, who was to have treated comparative study in the U.S.A., H. Hatzfeld, on the invitation of Charles Dédéyan, gave his impressions of present-day comparative literature in the U.S.A. The closing discourse was made by the illustrious author of a series of fine books on Western Europe, M. Salvador de Madariaga, former Professor of Spanish at Oxford. In an eloquent and moving speech he recalled the noble and urgent task undertaken by comparative literature which was capable of playing a beneficial part in the construction of a united and diverse Europe. At the end of the session a new Committee was constituted with the following personnel:—

Committee of Honour: MM. F. Baldensperger, G. Charlier, T. S. Eliot, S. de Madariaga.

Presidents: MM. J. M. Carré, C. Pellegrini.

Vice-Presidents: H. Hatzfeld (United States),
P. Kruger (Denmark),
F. C. Roe (Great Britain),
K. Wais (Germany).

Members: J. G. Andison (Vancouver),
F. Lázaro (Salamanca),
B. Munteano (Paris),
H. Roddier (Lyon),
J. Roos (Strasbourg).

General Secretaries: W. P. Friederich (America),
M. F. Guyard (Europe).

Treasurer: Z. L. Zaleski.

Assistant Treasurer: Mlle E. Le Hénaff.

The headquarters of the Association in so far as concerns Europe, was based at the Institute of Comparative Literature in the Sorbonne, and for America in the University of North Carolina. The annual subscription was fixed at 100 frs. payable by members abroad in the form of postal coupons. For 1955 or 1956 it was hoped that a Comparatists' Congress would be held in Venice.

F. C. ROE

University of Aberdeen, King's College

Comparative Literature in Japan

The news from Japan indicates a rapidly growing activity in the field of Comparative Literature—a re-evaluation of the position of Japanese Literature not only in relation to the other Asiatic literatures and cultures, but also in its relation to the Western World, to Europe and, more lately, to America. In order to supplement the recent article by Mr. J. K. Yamagiwa in *Yearbook* II, 1953 ("Comparative, General, and World Literature in Japan"), I should like to sum up two reports received from Professor Kenichiro Hayashi and Professor T. Nakamura.

The General Spring Assembly of the Japanese Society of Comparative Literature was held at Tokyo University on May 15, 1954, under the presidency of Professor K. Nakajima. The problem of methodology called forth various attempts at a closer definition of the term, and Mr. Wellek's recent disagreement with the French methods (contained in *Yearbook* II, 1953) caused a particularly lively discussion, with some speakers (*e.g.* Professor Kobayashi) defending the French viewpoint and others (*e.g.* Professor Yoshida) advocating a less orthodox and more elastic mode of procedure.

The Autumn Meeting, held in the Kansai and Kyushu Districts, lasted from October 29 to 31, 1954, and was given to a considerable number of individual papers that demonstrate the wide scope of interest of our Japanese colleagues. The six papers read at the Ritsumeikan University in Kyoto on October 29 dealt with Raymond Radiguet and the recently deceased novelist Tatsuo Hori (by Professor Muramatsu); the influence of Zola in Japanese literature (by Professor Shimamoto); songs for children and English poems (by Professor Kinugasa); the impact of Maupassant on contemporary Japanese literature (by Professor Ōnishi); Edgar Allan Poe and "Undine" (by Professor Masuda); and the various conceptions of the Other World in European Literature (by Professor Nogami). The day closed with yet another lengthy discussion on the question of methodology.

The ten papers read on October 30 at the Kobe Girls' University in Nishinomija near Kobe discussed Edgar Allan Poe and the Japanese pre-war novelist Ryunosuke Akutagawa (by Professor Honda); Ibsen's plays in Japan (by Professor Ochi); Chekhov and Japanese literature of the Meiji Era (by Professor Ōtani); the literary journal Doshisha-Bungaku and European and American literature (by Professor Shigehisa); English and Scottish ballads and old songs in the Orient (by Professor Hara); Japanese influences in modern Chinese children's tales (by Professor Nakamura); the murder of the step-father as a literary theme (by Mrs. Nomizo); Romanticism in the Japanese poet Seihaku Irako (by Professor Mori); "Haïku" and Imagist poetry (by Professor Jelliffe); and the future of Comparative Literature (by Professor Nakajima).

The meeting of the last day, held at the Kyushu University in Fukuoka on October 31, produced six papers which analyzed European Literature in the nineteenth century (by Professor Ōtsuka); the neo-psychological literary movement and Joyce's influence in Japan (by Professor Ōta); the present state of the Department of Comparative Literature at the University of Tokyo (by Professor Shimada); the influences of the Japanese "ukiyoé" on French literature (by Professor Gotô) and a summing up of the present activities in Comparative Literature (by Professor Nakajima).

For us in America it was gratifying to read of the popularity of the *Yearbook* and of the unflagging interest of our Japanese colleagues in what we are trying to do in this country. The *Yearbook* will gladly do its share in promoting ever closer relations not only between our Japanese friends and ourselves, but also between them and the newly established International Association of Comparative Literature.

W.P.F.

PART FOUR

Among the books dealing with the combined arts of Painting, Sculpture, Architecture, Literature, and Music, *The Humanities* by Louise Dudley and Austin Faricy (McGraw-Hill, New York, 1951, xvi+518 pp., illus., 2nd ed.) is the only one I know of that approaches them in a non-historical sequence, much as the social sciences are usually presented. The approach in this volume, however, is entirely aesthetic—there is no attempt to give the student an idea of the social, political, and religious hurricanes that tear in and through the arts from time to time, and no attempt to see art as propaganda. The arts are just the arts—what most well-behaved Americans understand by them. More specifically—as Miss Dudley points out in her preface to a volume containing some of this material in an earlier form, *The Study of Literature* (1928)—the source of the synthesis is Benedetto Croce's *Aesthetic*. As a result, the arts are viewed simply as experience, rather than as interpretation or criticism of life.

Miss Dudley, who has been principally responsible for the book, represents a very fine and humane tradition. A former student of Carleton Brown (under whom she wrote her doctoral dissertation on the Egyptian elements in the *Body and Soul* legend), she has been associated with Stephens College at Columbia, Mo. since 1920. There she undertook to set up a Humanities course in which the material taught would be confined to only what the students "would be expected to remember all their lives." The first edition of the present volume (the music sections of which were written by Austin Faricy) appeared in 1940. Much of the first edition has been rewritten for the second—the rugged contours of the first being softened, sequences rearranged, more discussion questions and bibliographical items added, etc. The main outlines of the book and its prevailing temper, however, remain the same—simple, clear, and reasonable. From Subject and Function, it moves to Medium, then deals with Form and Style, and concludes with Judgment. At all points there are many illustrative details and suggestions for further study. Viewed in terms of its treatment of Comparative Literature, *The Humanities* contributes many insights to the student: the comparison, for instance, between different media in the fine arts and different languages is illuminating. Although the examples and discussions are mostly of English literature, there are many relationships that apply also to works in other languages.

This book is an inspiration to all other teachers to work out their own courses in terms of their own particular situations. My own feeling about

The Humanities, as a course, is that it is not so suitable for students at a metropolitan university (with their more highly differentiated backgrounds and aims) as it is for girls in a junior college. It is a beautiful example, however, of a course developed for a particular purpose; it reflects a very cultured and tempered personality; and it unquestionably cffers for many students the sort of security in aesthetic matters that they desire.

WILLIS WAGER

Boston University

B.

In our American academic life, Italian literature has never been given the place of importance which it so richly deserves. One can hear political, sentimental, and even commercial reasons why the languages and literatures of France and Spain should occupy the positions closest to our natural interest in American and English literature; but relatively few pleas for Italian letters are voiced, and neither American scholars of Italian extraction like Altrocchi, Borgese, Fucilla, La Piana, Luciani, Orsini, Prezzolini and Vittorini, nor American Italophiles with different backgrounds have found it easy to bring about a fairer arrangement in our academic hierarchy of evaluations. This is all the more deplorable because the wealth of Italian literature, the beauty of the Italian language, the welcome presence of innumerable Italian colonies in our midst, and the liveliness of Italo-American relations in political, social and economic matters should certainly facilitate a greater awareness of Italian culture also in our colleges and universities. Yet, in the same casual fashion that they turn to German literature if they are interested in Romanticism, many of our students and younger colleagues turn to Italian literature only if they are interested in the Renaissance. The result—a nodding acquaintance with less than half a dozen Italian authors—is far from inducing them and their later students to that kind of enthusiasm which alone, at some future date, might bring about a juster balance of study. American comparatists who have been among the leaders of those scholars most eager to redress the balance have hitherto been handicapped also by the absence of a first-class history of Italian literature in the English language that could be recommended as an introduction for their students and that would compare favorably with the many histories of French, German or Spanish literature in the English language which do the necessary spade-work in the great task of cultural enlightenment.

This gap has now happily been filled by the beautiful and complete *History of Italian Literature,* written by Ernest Hatch Wilkins, the dean of American Italianists, and published by the Harvard University Press (1954, 523 p. $7.50). Specialists in Italian literature reviewing this book will no doubt hail its excellence, its conciseness, its mature judgment; for us in the field of Comparative Literature who have always been anxious to emphasize Italian literature more than the deplorable dearth of tools permitted, it is enough to state that this is at long last the book we have been waiting for, the source of information that will always be close at hand on our seminar shelves when we are instructing students whose past curriculum prevented them from studying Italian literature in the original. The book contains 52 chapters and ranges from the earliest beginnings (there are five chapters before Dante) to Pirandello and Croce. Though there is a natural emphasis on the Renaissance and again on the period after 1775, other centuries are by no means neglected; as an example of Dr. Wilkins' admirable thoroughness we can, for instance, quote the chapter-headings in the so-called dull period between Tasso and Vico: The Pastoral Play and the *Commedia dell'Arte*; Giordano Bruno; The Drama in the Late Sixteenth Century; Marino and Other Poets; Campanella; Galileo and Other Prose Writers; Early Opera; A Stagnant Interval; Metastasio and Other Arcadians. The main stress, in chapter-headings as well as in individual treatments, is always on the uniqueness of a poet, his biographical data, and the enumeration and evaluation of his works; terms like Baroque, Enlightenment, Realism, Naturalism, Symbolism, etc., if they are to be found at all, are purely incidental. Many chapters begin with a brief paragraph dealing with the historical or cultural background of the period in question, and brief references to Italy's literary relations with Anglo-American authors open up a most welcome vista into the field of Comparative Literature. All quotations are either in English or in Italian accompanied by an English translation; and the "List of English Translations" and the list of "Books in English Dealing with Italian Literature" at the end of the volume (pp. 502-12), arranged according to chapter sequence, is another feature of this work that will be warmly appreciated by the average reader. Other items in the Appendix include a list of minor authors who, for lack of space, could not be discussed in the text proper (of these, Algarotti, Botta, Cesarotti, Dolce, Gioberti, Martelli, Ada Negri, Matilde Serao, Silone and Varchi would seem to have deserved at least a short paragraph each, and Rosmini is mentioned neither here nor in the text). The evolution of literary genres is not stressed in particular, though an excellent Index at the end of the book, in addition to names of authors, contains also coherent references to comedy, tragedy, epic, novel, *novella*, etc. Special praise is due also to the very adequate treatment of Literary Criticism (beginning with Foscolo, Mazzini, de Sanctis, *et al.*) and of Italian Dialect Literature (Sicilian, Roman, Neapolitan, etc.), which, thanks to the Index, can again easily be found and checked.

The non-specialist in Italian literature who uses this book in order to fill a gap in his knowledge of the panorama of European culture is apt to find just two flaws which he, for his own personal sake, might wish to see mended. One is the brevity of the references to concurrent Italian history, art, or music. The novice might wish for a few more foot-notes (used so demonstrably, for instance, in outlining the family-tree of the Medicis on p. 177) in order to learn just a little bit more about the Guelphs and the Ghibellines (p. 17) or the conquest of Naples by Aragón (p. 123), or to have more meat added to such sentences as "Andrea del Sarto continued the tradition of Florentine painting, bringing to it a softly glowing poetic quality; . . . Giorgione and Titian enriched Venice with penetrant characterization and a new luxuriance of color; and in Correggio beauty justified sentimentality" (p. 178-79) or "During the first half of the century Rossini, Bellini, and Donizetti were producing their dozens of operas —among them the Barbiere di Siviglia, Norma, and Lucia di Lammermoor" (p. 388). One can easily sympathize with the predicament of author and publisher in pondering the length of such cultural allusions; yet for once a compromise between too little or too much does not seem to be the best solution. The second flaw is the system of chapter headings, which, arranged according to authors instead of movements, do not permit an easy integration with the other European literatures familiar to the outsider. Though one should beware of pigeon-holing poets and of stultifying their living thought by giving it some shopworn label, it does help when one is able to classify literary works according to some general European trends. Italian literature is at times confusing enough (think, for instance, of the many classical traits in the so-called "romanticists" Leopardi or Monti); and any help Dr. Wilkins could have given us, especially in the literature of the last one hundred years, by using such terms as Naturalism, Impressionism, Symbolism, would have been most welcome. As a consequence of his not doing so, authors like Carducci, Pascoli, Fogazzaro, Pirandello and even d'Annunzio seem to hover in a vacuum. Also our efforts to tackle the same problem from another angle by looking for the foreign roots of these authors are not always successful, for we find a few references to Zola or Mallarmé, but none to Baudelaire, Marx, Nietzsche, or Ibsen. My own field of interest extends from Dante to Alfieri and I believe that Dr. Wilkins has covered that period supremely well and that he has answered practically all the questions his readers might wish to ask him. But if I should ever wish to go on into the nineteenth or twentieth centuries, I would have to engage in thorough additional studies before I would be able to assign to the Italian authors of this period their appropriate place in the history of European literary movements. Dr. Wilkins' suggestion, on p. 501, to use yet another set of terms in lieu of those we are used to (the Foscolian, Manzonian, Mazzinian, Carduccian Periods, etc.) only adds to our confusion.

W.P.F.

C.

A few lines will suffice to inform the reader that *The Triple Stream: Four Centuries of English, French and German Literature, 1531-1930* by Antony Brett-James (Dufour Editions, Philadelphia, 1954, 178 pp.) is not quite what the title seems to indicate. It is not a parellel history of the three literatures with their manifold interrelationships, translations and cross-fertilizations; instead, it is a chronological table, painstakingly arranged by successive years (pp. 2-121), enumerating, in five columns, who was born, who died, and what English, French and German works were produced in every particular year. The information is restricted to author and title; though one naturally could not hope for a brief description of outstanding works, one might legitimately have expected a few brief cross-references to the importance of some of these works in the other two literatures. Beyond North's Plutarch, Chapman's Homer and Schlegel's Shakespeare, there are practically no references at all to translations; important intermediaries like Florio, Bode or Sismondi are missing; the choice of dates is of often dubious accuracy (*e.g.*, 1604 for Marlowe's *Faustus*, 1775 for Goethe's *Faust*). There are exactly two pages of text in which the compiler explains that he eschewed any reference to such categories as Classicism, Romanticism, Realism, etc., because he wanted to show the three literatures as a constant stream which would indicate "the contemporaries of any one given author, the emergence of each literary figure, the year in which some giant quitted the active world of letters, the books that were published one hundred years ago, the date of any writer's centenary or bicentenary of birth or death." Other modest ambitions and feeble justifications for the existence of this book are that "a student of the Romantic Movement in France, when told of the influence upon French poets and novelists of Byron and Sir Walter Scott, can find out when and what those two great writers produced. In fact, the lists of literary works and their authors that follow provide material from which *many deductions* may be drawn."

More important than these chronological and parallel tables with their many unfortunate omissions and strange inclusions (*e.g.* Baden-Powell's *Scouting for Boys*, Clausewitz' *Vom Krieg* and the first Baedeker) are the many rich Indices (pp. 122-178), useful not so much because of all the important English, French and German authors listed with their dates, but because of the individual works arranged in alphabetical order: for almost everything is listed from *Absalom and Achitophel (Dryden), 1681* to *Yeoman of the Guard, The (Gilbert), 1888,* or from *Abbassiden, Die (Platen), 1835* to *Zwischen Wasser und Urwald (Schweitzer), 1920.*

The fact remains, however, that Paul van Tieghem and his many international collaborators have produced a much better and much richer book in the *Répertoire chronologique des littératures modernes* (Paris-Genève, 1935), which is still the basic work (though it stopped in 1900) and which Mr. Brett-James has not replaced.

W.P.F.

D.

It is interesting to note the measure of his own personality which a conscientious editor can impart even to an anthology of world literature. In his editing of Addison Hibbard's *Writers of the Western World* (Houghton Mifflin Company, Boston, 1954. 1239 p.), Horst Frenz leaves the marks of a sensitive and thorough scholar. Hibbard's presentation, though only twelve years earlier, seems like the writing of another era—colorful, ebullient, rambling introductions, first-person justifications of critical positions taken. What Frenz, on the other hand, loses in spontaneity, he gains in academic care in the re-drafting of the old rhetorical introductions and biographical sketches. For example, in the statement on the romantic mood Hibbard wrote, "For decades, critics of literature on the Continent, in England, in America, have *sought to plant the oak tree of romanticism in neat flowerpots.*" Frenz reduces the italicized line to "*attempted* to find ready definitions of romanticism." The critical sections of the book retain adequate interest and literary quality in their own right, but the personality of the new editor is best revealed in his sober, clearcut phrasing.

Certain characteristics of *Writers of the Western World* tend to distinguish it from its competitors in the anthology field. Most noteworthy of these is its organization by literary movement, or, as Hibbard put it, by "temper." Thus, instead of presenting the selections chronologically as most such volumes do, or by *genre* as a few collections attempt, Hibbard and Frenz group their masterpieces in three major categories according to dominant classical, romantic, or realistic moods. Symbolism is presented as a variation of romanticism, while naturalism, impressionism, and expressionism are shown to be developments from the realistic temper. That the seven moods are not mutually discrete is admitted by the editors, who caution the reader against facile compartmentalization, wisely pointing out the romantic characteristics of works such as the *Iliad* which are included under the heading of classicism, and so on. It may nevertheless be argued that any artificial classification is a dangerous technique and that even the naming of the seven tempers tends to obscure their interrelationships. Whether such criticisms have validity or not, there can be little derogation of the scholarly qualities of this collection. The present reviewer finds the seven short essays on the literary movements the most illuminating he has read. Written with flavor and deep appreciation, they carry the authority of definitive statement. No other anthology performs this service so well.

One of the effects of the classification of masterpieces by literary movement is to emphasize the continuity of human expression. Just as Zola in *The Experimental Novel* insisted on the ancient origin of the naturalistic approach, so Hibbard and Frenz point out that there was romanticism in Ovid as well as in Shelley, and impressionism in the Hebrew Psalms as truly as in the tales of Joseph Conrad. Like any valid method, however, this one is subject to certain reservations. The praiseworthy emphasis on continuity does obscure somewhat the dominant manifestations of the several literary moods. To indicate realistic features in Chaucer, for instance, reduces the dynamics of nineteenth century realism, impelled by the scientific, industrial, and social revolutions of that epoch. Conversely, there are long time-gaps in the selections presented in this volume which might make the reader wonder if the given temper had not been sporadic rather than constant in its manifestation. Was there, for example, no outstanding illustration of the realistic "fervor for truth" in the long years of the Renaissance? And would it not have been wise to include a selection from, say, La Bruyère to show the persistence of realism even in a classical age? Or, again, was it good to terminate the illustrations of classicism with Voltaire's Candide cultivating his somewhat unclassical garden? The restrained style of André Gide, for example, might have entitled that controversial Nobel prize winner to a place among the classicists and would thereby have emphasized the continuity of temper professed by the editors.

Of course, no anthology, even of ten times twelve hundred pages, could satisfy the taste of every reviewer. The position of the editors, moreover, is well taken when they state that longer selections from a limited number of writers give a more effective representation than cyclopedic fragments from a great many. It is with understanding diffidence, therefore, that this reader laments the omission of any selections from such distinctive writers as Catullus, Cicero, Petrarch, Machiavelli, Boileau, Lessing, Schiller, Maupassant, Strindberg, and Proust. It seems especially unfortunate that Flaubert, who was represented in the first edition by a chapter from *Madame Bovary*, should have had to give way, presumably for Paul Claudel. Professor Frenz's desire to avoid printing fragments of novels is understandable (although the volume does contain key chapters from *Old Goriot*, *Crime and Punishment*, *Anna Karenina*, *The Magic Mountain*, *L'Assommoir*, and *Ulysses*); but why then resort to the use of Flaubert's *A Simple Heart*, as other anthologists have done. It seems regrettable, too, that Ibsen, who is primarily a realist, should be included only among the romantic symbolists, by *The Master Builder*. Finally, it might be noted that modern Italian literature has contributed only Pirandello to this anthology, that Spain receives no attention after Cervantes, and that contemporary Russian literary expression is revealed only through a pre-Revolution story by Gorki. Weak as Soviet literature undoubtedly is, it might have been possible to find suitable material in the works of Alexey Tolstoy or of Sholokhov.

At the same time that we criticize the editors for their omissions, we must note that Professor Frenz has done some judicious cutting and adding. For Galsworthy, Dreiser, the Goncourt brothers, Yevreinov, and Thomas Hardy, he has substituted Pirandello, Kafka, Chekhov, and Faulkner—surely a mark of wisdom. He has also expanded the selections from Thomas Mann and from several of the older writers. The section from Voltaire's *Candide* is, for example, happily augmented by the inclusion of Chapters XX and XXI, the argument with Martin the Manichean and the voyage to Constantinople, respectively. Frenz has also used his allotted pages more economically than did his predecessor. Careful arrangement of verse selections has permitted the addition of several poems by John Donne and of delightful, single lyrics by Heine, Ben Jonson, and others. This is just another illustration of his editorial devotion.

There are many reasons to recommend *Writers of the Western World* as an instrument of teaching. The material on music and the well chosen reproductions of great paintings are so arranged as to emphasize the interrelationship of art forms. The bibliographies and suggestions for further reading are carefully selected, thoroughly edited, and brought up to date by Frenz (who has, however, dispensed with the annotations supplied by Hibbard). There is a chronological table of authors, a guide to the types of literature, and a good index of authors, titles, and first lines. The translations are at least as good as those of the average collection; some of the recent ones are outstanding. All in all, this is an admirable text for the student of comparative and world literature. More than that, it is a reference volume which will be both a stimulation and a utility for the mature reader.

University of Southern California   PAUL E. HADLEY

. . . AND OF RECENT TRANSLATIONS AND EDITIONS.

I.

In addition to the three great Theban plays of Sophocles, which, in a sense, form a unit, chance has left the world four more plays of that author. These plays, *Electra, Philoctetes, Women of Trachis,* and *Ajax,* have recently been translated by E. F. Watling (Penguin Classics, no. L28, 1953. $.50), who has already translated the Theban plays, previously reviewed in this *Yearbook.* In his cogent introductory analysis of the plays, Mr. Watling reveals the distinctiveness of each of these four plays both in theme and conception. He discusses with great clarity their significant and "original" technical similarity, their use of a third actor. Yet, possibly excepting *Electra,* each of these four plays deviates from Aristotle's norm-tragedy (and from its mates) in such a way as to give it a strangely rich interest. *Ajax* is strongly anti-climactic, the *Women of Trachis* has a disturbing disunity of theme, and *Philoctetes* is suggestively but artificially resolved. These various peculiarities are well brought out by Mr. Watling's translation itself.

This translation achieves, it seems to me, what any translation of Greek drama must achieve: it frequently rises to the level of real poetry. This is evident in the translations of choral lyrics, occasionally into rhymed verse (the choral lament over Philoctetes' plight, pp. 185-7), more often into clear blank verse (the chorus' address to Electra, just before Orestes and Pylades enter with the urn, pp. 100-102; the great praise of and lament to Salamis by the sailors in *Ajax,* pp. 38-9; the announcement of the arrival of Heracles by the women of Trachis, pp. 150-51). This achievement also appears in the convincing portrayal (in prose) of deeply emotional scenes. Thus the crazed Ajax, the despairing Electra, and the physically agonized Heracles and Philoctetes are all "real" and moving characters to the reader. And for those who feel that E. V. Rieu's translation of Homer is excessively colloquial, the dignified but modern English of Watling will be agreeable. When he does employ unusual language, it is to fine effect: Heracles calls the shirt of Nessus a "death-trap"; the messenger in *Ajax*, announcing the return of Teucer thus describes Teucer's near escape from death by stoning:

> And it went so far,
> Hands flew to hilts and blades were ripped from scabbards.
> Till, *in the nick of time*, the intervention
> Of elder voices settled the dispute. (p. 42, my underlining.)

A sampling, too, of Watling's characteristic translation of a speech by Philoctetes (his pathetic lament when he is left alone with the sailors of Neoptolemus, and thinks he will be left to perish on Lemnos) may help to focus both the beauty and a criticism of Watling's translation:

> My stony house, my cave,
> Sun-hot, ice-cold, to be
> My dwelling place for ever,
> And now my grave.
> Home of my misery,
> How shall I live, where turn
> For my provisioning?
> The birds above my head
> Are free as the winds that sing,
> And my strength fled. (p. 199)

This attractive passage is not sufficiently faithful to the Greek. A certain pathos of the original is lightened in this English verse. The short, rhymed, iambic lines of the English preclude a "sentimental," "lamenting" quality which is clear in the Greek text. The exclamatory laments ("o talas," and "omoi moi moi") are absent from the English. The emphasized futurity of two verbs in the original is lost in the English, and with it a certain quality of hopelessness in time marked in Philoctetes' feeling. And, in this same passage, the problem of translating difficult lines has been evaded. The lines of the original in which Philoctetes describes the foul misery of his cave, and those in which he states his hopelessness, in complex syntax, have been freely and weakly read by Watling. These criticisms are intended not to be pedantic, though even if they were only that, a damaging number of them could be collected. Rather, they are criticisms of Watling's "inaccuracy" in the widest sense. Frequently, in these translations, fidelity to the spirit of the original is lost through infidelity to the details of the original. Sophocles' drama is rich in "local texture." A review of this translation must at least suggest the question whether translation, in order to remain such, must not be a precise, though vital interpretation. Anyone who feels that it must will harbor certain limited reservations about Watling's treatment of these four plays.

FREDERIC WILL, JR.

Pennsylvania State University

II.

The Bible and Plato's Dialogues, those chronic inseparables in the cultural experience of the Western world, have once again been submitted to a closely comparable treatment. Through the joint and several labors of many hands they are being garbed anew in English, with twin aims: maximal clarity of language for the contemporary reader, and the closest fidelity to the texts, in the light of the latest and most critical scholarship. Over the birth of these newer versions has presided that jealous god of these latter times whose name is Semantics, a deity who demands for sacrifice upon his altar many traditional aesthetic values, but promises in return to free us from the "noise" and distractions of loosely associated feelings and thoughts aroused in the mind of the modern reader by the older versions, and thus to quicken our perception of the essential meanings of their great originals. All this is to be done at little or no aesthetic cost, as measured in terms of contemporary taste. Greatly daring for the sake of concreteness, I should name as the major prophets of this movement Edgar Goodspeed, who led the revolt against King James, and Ivor Richards, who with apologies revolted against the king of Platonic translators, Benjamin Jowett.

The appearance of two new Penguin Classics, *Plato: The Last Days of Socrates (The Apology, Crito, Phaedo)* translated and with an introduction by Hugh Tredennick (No. 37, 1954, $ .50) and *Plato: The Symposium,* a new translation by W. Hamilton (No. 24, 1951, $ .50), is a welcome event, for they offer to the general public and to students on the college level fresh translations, with appropriately elementary introductions and notes, of some of the most memorable and widely read of the Platonic dialogues. I hope it will not be considered an ungrateful or inhospitable act to submit the newcomers to some gentle questioning as to their relation to the program of translation theory that we were just now considering, and the success with which they have carried out those parts of it they have chosen to adopt.

Be it said at once that neither of our translators is in any sense a literal and thoroughgoing disciple of Ivor Richards; they have allowed themselves no comparable liberties of selective emphasis, omission, and condensation, as indeed would have been far less defensible in rendering the short *Apology* and *Crito,* though the longer *Phaedo* and *Symposium* might well have tempted a true Richardian. Nor have they, like Richards in his version of the *Republic,* limited their vocabularies on principle to the simplest and most familiar English words. They have, in fact, permitted themselves to employ polysyllabic abstract vocables rather more often than the Platonic text requires, and certainly more often than Jowett, with a resulting loss in human warmth and dramatic immediacy. Even so, both have on occasion employed techniques consistent with what Richards has called for, and with mixed effect. Thus those recurrent interjections and epithets with which Plato has diversified and enlivened his conversations are modernized, so that Jowett's "Nay, my good friend," becomes "No, my good fellow," and the exclamation of astonishment "By Heracles!" appears as "Good God!" Similarly, passing allusions to Athenian institutions and usages are often either omitted or replaced by their quasi-equivalents in our own culture. Thus Mr. Hamilton's reader is spared Plato's reference to the Athenian political subdivisions called demes, and in one passage, "barbarians" become "Persians"; Tredennick generalizes the Orphic Mysteries into "religious initiations." This method achieves some gain of pace, but with a loss of perspective, especially to a reader concerned with social and cultural history, and at the risk of introducing serious confusions, of which I shall presently cite an extreme example.

As to scholarship, in the severer sense, my study of the two translators has convinced me that they have spared no pains in turning to account the results of philological inquiry accruing in the period since Jowett published his third revised edition of the Dialogues in 1891.

Raising now the question of literary style, we find it illuminating to learn from Mr. Tredennick's preface that his translation was prepared and presented to the radio listeners of the B. B. C.'s famous Third Program. One feels how well adapted ("influenced" might be the better word) is his transparent and rapid diction, with its occasionally added breaks and interjections, to the specific demands of a good radio script. Such qualities, indeed, are by no means lost on the written page, and are well suited to a book designed to carry a casual reader over the threshold of Platonism. But to my reading, they entail the defect that Mr. Tredennick's version, when set beside Jowett's, runs a little abstract and thin. Mr. Hamilton's seems to me in its main features at the least fully equal in literary excellence to that of Tredennick; if the latter has more rapidity, the former may claim on occasion a more plastic and rounded style.

The promised instance of the method of modernizing Platonic allusions, at its confusing worst, is to be found in Tredennick's *Crito* (pp. 64-5). Here in the original text Socrates is declaring, on behalf of the personified laws of Athens, that he as a citizen of Athens may no more properly disobey her injunctions than a slave may retaliate a blow from his master. Tredennick has replaced the words "slave" and "master" by their near-equivalents in contemporary free societies, "servant" and "employer." As a consequence, the unhappy reader is being invited to draw the monstrous conclusion that in fifth century Athens, ordinary free citizens were expected to endure, without retaliation or demur, such physical chastisement as their employers might choose to bestow. Such extreme conclusions are rare; they do, however, serve to illustrate the sort of risk that is run by those who have set their feet on the dangerous path of modernizing an ancient author.

It is to praise Mr. Tredennick's precision of scholarship by the method of faint damns to cite as the only example I have been able to discover of what may reasonably be styled a mistranslation, the following, from the *Phaedo* (p. 153). As a careful reading of the text makes clear, Socrates is talking about the *promises* that Crito and his other friends may make to him now as to their behavior after his death. Mr. Tredennick's version, "even if you don't agree with me now," misses the point, and in view of the actual state of agreement prevailing between Socrates and his companions, seems irrelevant and disruptive of the sense.

It remains to consider what Mr. Hamilton has done in his far more difficult enterprise of conveying across the cultural barrier an honest and yet, to a contemporary heterosexual reader, acceptable and even inspiring image of Plato's dramatic depiction of Greek Eros in the *Symposium.* This problem, it may be parenthetically remarked, is no new one and, contrary to frequent report, had already been met by Jowett with a candor the more notable in view of the high reserve of his mid-Victorian outlook. Jowett's introduction to the *Symposium* contains no attempt to conceal, and despite an obvious distaste, a very minimum of misrepresentation, and his translation is even more scrupulous in its honesty.

Hamilton has conducted himself with dignity and discretion: he has woven no fig-leaf screens, and has struck no posture of shocked dismay. His introduction will prepare a contemporary reader to make the necessary distinctions between *us* and *them*, and further shows, as best may be within its narrow space, that beneath and within those distinctions, identical issues and alternatives reassert themselves. The reader is thus saved the painful futility of choosing between accepting the unacceptable and condemning as immoral one of the most truly moral of great books.

As to the translation, Mr. Hamilton is, as has been said, an accomplished scholar, his renderings of difficult or disputed passages giving evidence of critical intelligence and acquaintance with the literature. As with Tredennick, one might raise an occasional question; thus, we hear (p. 91) of the lover's going "in search of a beautiful environment for his children," which suggests a conscientious father's exploration of the suburbs, while the meaning is that the lover is in search of a fair and good friend whose beauty will assist him to bring to birth the noble thoughts with which his soul is pregnant.

To teachers standing at the crossroads where the arrows point, one way, "To Jowett's Aesthetic Intensity and the Grand Manner," and, in the other, "To Modern Convenience and Streamlined Efficiency," I may venture a suggestion: given a student level of "literacy" incapable of reading Victorian prose with ease and understanding, versions such as those of Tredennick and Hamilton seem clearly indicated. For students of somewhat higher reading skill, I should myself be tempted to stick to Jowett, with indication of those semi-occasional passages in which Jowett's departure from Plato's ascertainable sense makes a genuinely important difference, and to supplement this with the requirement that at least one dialogue should be read in a recent version, as a means of deepening semantic insight into the problems and opportunities presented to the translator. For this purpose, Tredennick and Hamilton would again be invaluable.*

I will conclude on a note of hope. The four volume revision of the Jowett translation published last year by the Clarendon Press, under the editorial direction of Allen and Dale, has left untouched the essential structure and style of the earlier edition, while correcting all discoverable errors and reworking those passages where Jowett's English sat so loosely to the Greek original as to leave doubt as to the precise sense. On the day when this edition becomes available in small packages and at a popular price, the problem of suiting the tastes and needs of our maturer undergraduates will be greatly eased.

RONALD B. LEVINSON

University of Maine

III.

A people, a nation, is judged best by what it reads and re-reads, by what it hears and likes to hear again and again. For the more than 300 million Hindus that is the Bhagavad Gītā which now has been made available to everyone as a Mentor Book under the title of *The Song of God, Bhagavad-Gita*, translated by Swami Prabhavananda and Christopher Isherwood, with an introduction by Aldous Huxley (The New American Library, New York, 1954, $ .35). We shall call it henceforth simply Gītā, "The Song."

There are dozens of translations of the Gītā into English, the early Charles Wilkins one of 1785 known to Emerson, Sir Edwin Arnold's fine poetic version ("The Song Celestial"), the theosophical one of Annie Besant (1895), the critical one of Franklin Edgerton (1944), the genially prefaced one of S. Radhakrishnan (1948). But none can be bought for such a low price as the Mentor one which renders the original Sanskrit verses in a mixed style.

The significance of this is patent. Thousands of non-Hindus the world over have studied the Gītā in the past; now it is anybody's guess how many more thousands will not only read but be inspired by it. This represents one of the *étapes* of the successful invasion of Hinduism into the Western world. For, like the Bible, it is no ordinary scripture. It has, moreover, something the Bible has not: A philosophy of life based on a metaphysics which appeals to reason rather than pure faith. Aldous Huxley presents the Gītā as a work of the Perennial Philosophy. This is a true estimate, but it has features which other works in this category lack: It is an epic story, it is a dialogue, it is mystical, it is religious, it is psychological, it appeals to reason. Above all, the Gītā is and will for a very long time

---

* I regret having been unable to examine the recent translation of the *Euthyphro, Apology, Crito, Phaedo,* and *Gorgias,* by W. D. Woodhead, in which that remarkable Canadian scholar has, I am told, produced a good translation into plain English.

be *actuelle* by virtue of its main ethico-philosophical problem which everyone sometime or other will come face to face with, that is, doing a deed
that clashes with one's better judgment before it has been implicated in
universal philosophical principles.   Hence, as a piece of world literature
which must not be omitted in a comparative literature course, it is more
than a composition some two thousand or more years old, or a part of one
of the greatest of epics, the Mahābhārata, or the most important text of
Krishnaism, which is a religion of *bhakti*, devotion, or an early text of the
philosophical Sāṅkhya-Yoga system, or yet a conglomeration of ideas from
Vedāntic and other sources.

The story in brief is, and the present translators tell it vividly and
condensed, that in the great fratricidal war between the Pāndavas and
Kauravas the hero and leader of the former, Arjuna, is dismayed over
the prospect of killing his relatives and friends and, what is worse to a
Hindu, his teachers, and takes his charioteer into confidence.   But that
one was God Krishna himself in disguise who forthwith instructs and
persuades him that both from duty accruing to his station in life and
from a cosmic point of view involving history as well as theophany and
true self-realization, he must fight, which he does.

To guard against the almost instinctive Western reaction toward such
counsel, the book has two appendices, written by the translators, one on
"The Cosmology of the Gita," the other on "The Gita and War," showing
concisely the plausibility and reasonableness of Krishna's discourse and
request.   To say that the Gītā finds an "easy" way out of the most crucial
situation by an appeal to emotion or a mystical identification with the
divine would be falsifying the facts in the case.   For it leaves uncon-
sidered the close metaphysical logic and the typical presuppositions of
Hinduism—whether it be taken as an ethnic religion without a known
founder, or a social complex based on time-honored practices in the land
of Hind.   Those two appendices are, therefore, necessary parts of any
presentation of the Gītā to a Western public.   In fact, any Gītā translation without a commentary of some length would be worthless.

The Gītā is difficult to translate into English because English gram-
matical and sentence structure, unlike the German, is never very close to
the Sanskrit.   While this is a problem, the far greater difficulty is that
of rendering the sense accurately in a world of thought dominated, as ours
is, by concepts of evolution, progress, sense-realism, atomic individualism.
Hence, we cannot quarrel much with the translation of certain words and
passages, or the translation as a whole.   If it is based, as this one is, on
the full understanding of one versed and reared in Hindu traditions, we can
assume—and the assumption is borne out by the performance—that the
best efforts have been put forth to preserve the original meaning without
offending the rules of Western aestheticism.

Let no one think that the problems surrounding the Gītā are few or
solved.   A tremendous literature has accumulated in India and in Europe
centering on every topic, linguistic, historical, philosophical.   The most

acute problem is that of the unity of the whole. The Mentor translation assumes the essential unity of the poem, which is in accordance with Hindu tradition, but not with the findings of some Western scholars, such as Richard Garbe and his pupil, Rudolf Otto. They speak of a truly epic *Urgītā*, a Khrishnaization of the same, a superimposition of doctrinal material, a Vedaization, a Vedāntization and what not. The devout Hindu regards such higher textual criticism as close to blasphemy. The reader should, therefore, be apprised of the fact that the Mentor rendering hews to the orthodoxy and makes no concessions to these scholarly views. Moreover, all ancient texts of the Hindus require glossaries. The Gītā forms no exception. The translator, Swami Prabhavananda, mentions three classical commentaries and a modern one which he has drawn upon. Himself a swami of the Vedānta order, he cannot conceal his leanings.

As a first introduction to the Gītā to be read quickly by the beginner, the translator has performed a useful task, provided it is kept in mind that there is considerable affective toning by the views and teachings of the Ramakrishna Order, by Isherwoodian idiosyncrasies, and the syncretism of an Aldous Huxley whose introduction is bound to influence the reader powerfully in the direction of overlooking essential differences in Hinduism, Buddhism, Judaism, Christianity, and Islam. Not that any of these need particular censure. But for effective use in a comparative literary way much more of a critical apparatus is needed than is supplied here, besides the full translation or transliteration of all names and epithets, and indications of where the verses begin.

Enough, however, is presented here to make the general reader realize that for a Westerner to understand the sacred literature of India he requires more than a superficial acquaintance with Indian philosophy. This will, however, not prove a deterrent from further study. For we are aware that the Western mind now, and at long last, realizes that without philosophy even religion may lose its vitality. The solution of the problem of the Gītā, thus, has a momentous appeal to any and every searching mind, because it is a reasonable and a practical one at the same time, more fully adequate to its many-sidedness and depth, psychological and cosmic.

KURT F. LEIDECKER

Mary Washington College of the
University of Virginia

IV.

I may be wrong and I am not sure that I haven't lost count, but I have a distinct impression that the twentieth century has already brought forth more translations of Dante into English than any other, and I have the further impression that they are appearing with an accelerating tempo. Testimony surely to the vitality of the interest in Dante and perhaps also in a way to the difficulty of satisfying all tastes in the matter of translation. Some affirm that "if it isn't *terza rima* it isn't Dante";

others while conceding that *terza rima* is alien to English yet insist that a verse translation is essential if the impact of the original is to be conveyed; still others argue for prose as giving us the best chance to get Dante's content at least and incidentally saving us from the danger of mistranslating the untranslatable—the music of the original. Professor H. R. Huse in his Dante Alighieri, *The Divine Comedy* (Rinehart Edition 72, 1954, $ .95) has elected the way of prose.

It is good prose, too, and remarkably faithful to the original. It does not have the archaisms or the tortured sentence structure of the Carlyle-Wicksteed (which I have always thought excellent as a "trot" and execrable as a translation). Professor Huse's prose will stand on its own feet and that, I think, is all to the good. Sometimes to be sure the well known verses sound rather flat: "that day we read no farther" (Inf. V, 138), or "What favor for me is this?" (Purg. xxiii, 42); but this is the inevitable hazard of prose and generally speaking the tone is dignified without being pedantic, literal without being awkward. I think I would like it even better than I do if it were not set up in *terzine*. I suppose the notion is to make for easy reference to the original; in my own case when my eye sees a *terzina* I expect a *terzina* and, finding no such poetic rhythm in a pattern where I would expect it, I felt a sense of disappointment. If the prose were set as prose I think I should probably find it reads quite smoothly and no doubt with a prose rhythm of its own.

The edition is primarily pedagogical in purpose and Professor Huse has some new devices that may be found appealing. He breaks up the conventional argument usually put at the head of each canto and feeds the items into the text at strategic moments. Some teachers will appreciate the pedagogical utility of this method, others may feel that it is an intrusion on the flow of the text. Likewise Professor Huse inserts many brief footnotes into the text; e.g., Francesca says "The city (Ravenna) where I was born . . .", the "Ravenna" being Professor Huse's insertion. Again, it is convenient but it does break the flow of the text. Sometimes the information is a little sparse; "A Gallehaut (pander) was the book . . ." does not give quite the gloss on Gallehaut that one could wish. On the other hand there is enough material given in notes and arguments, however unorthodox the arrangement, to make for intelligent reading of the text. There are some good diagrams (no edition of the Comedy should be without them) and a modest but useful introduction by the author. A good job done conscientiously and with imagination.

                                                        T. G. BERGIN
Yale University

V.

Croce offers to all translators the discouraging choice of faithful ugliness or faithless beauty, just as the Italian proverb in the same disagreeable spirit admonishes, *"Traduttore, traditore"* (Translator, traitor). Yet unless critics ever insist on the cliché that "something is lost in translation," Marianne Moore deserves pure, unqualified praise for *The Fables of La Fontaine* (New York, The Viking Press, 1954). She has in no way betrayed the French, nor has she been bound by Croce's alternatives. Fidelity and beauty, letter and spirit of the original work are here, not to be merely acknowledged as duties performed, but vaunted as opulent merits.

Miss Moore is a first-rate poet, one who might serve as a model for the cardinal principle proposed by Rolfe Humphries: "For our century, the job of translation must be entrusted only to those who have themselves some creative experience of the art over which they are engaged."[1] And when W. H. Auden urged her to this task some eight years ago, he undoubtedly realized that no practicing poet is more aptly skilled and experienced.

Like La Fontaine, Miss Moore herself writes highly civilized poems about animals. Not a panting naturist in the manner of Robert Frost, she none the less probes nature more deeply by force of sharp objectivist images. Hers is an aesthetic pantheism, with a toad or an ostrich if not actual lions scrupulously kept in the ivory towers—queer animals, plastic and dimensional as rococo still-life, yet vitalized by the same capricious ironies that enliven the creatures of La Fontaine. Thus the beasts of the fables pass uncorrupted into her own collectors cage—"shallow-brained timorous frogs," "chameleons of no consequence," "a vigilant vulture," "demoralized doves," "a careworn lion, all bones and pained in each paw." Her sophisticated whimsy, a fastidious choice of words, and (drawing on her self-analysis) "an exaggerated tendency to visualize" make this the first English version with characters that are graphically alive and true to their French originals, whether oysters:

> Oysters close like a vise
> But one lay apart, for sun to inundate
> As it drank soft air from the sea,
> Swelling in and out with a sense of luxury—
> The morsel a gourmet would call ultra-delicate.   (VIII:9)

Or elephants:

> A mite of a rat was mocking an elephant
> As it moved slowly by, majestically aslant,
> Valued from antiquity,
> Towering in draped solemnity
> While bearing along in majesty
> A queen of the Levant—
> With her dog, her cat, her sycophant.   (VIII:15)

Miss Moore's articulation of the fables is authentic beyond mere verbal accuracy.

Nor has any English translator before reproduced the ornate prosody of the French. Enriched by strident rhymes and irregular metrics, La Fontaine's novel stanzas have heretofore defied duplication; and tiresome jingles have been born of the myriad efforts to render the fables in simpli-

---

[1] Rolfe Humphries, "Translations in Revival," *New World Writing: First Mentor Selection* (New York, 1952), p. 81.

fied English verse. Here the creative works of Miss Moore again have a special relevance, for ever since *Poems* (1921) her versification has been much like La Fontaine's. She is one of the few American poets today whose lines are rich in rhyme. She has acquired distinction, too, for strophes which, like his, are bizarre and original yet functional and tight. Still more important, her measures are ordered more by syllabic than by accentual count, a factor favorable to translating any French *vers*, particularly these. Finally, with all this technical fitness as a poetess, she has in the role of translator followed as a governing principle for rhythm and syntax the practice of Ezra Pound, i.e., "the natural order of words, subject, predicate, object; the active voice where possible; a ban on dead words, rhymes synonymous with gusto" (p.x). Approximation of the original rhythms has been her aim and achievement throughout.

"Dear Connoisseur, give ear," the fabulist wrote to Monsieur de Barillon (VIII:4). Read the fables aloud. Hear them as they were heard in the salons, where the shy La Fontaine introduced Monsieur Gaches as his lector. They are above all else poems—exquisite, eloquent miniatures of classic wisdom and wit. Their author, contrary to current debate, was primarily a poet—not a storyteller, nor a dramatist. His poetry has been faithfully preserved in this translation. Delicately, and hence accurately, Miss Moore has delivered to English readers the subtle excellence—the elegance—of a modest virtuosity, to which the original fables owe their long survival.

ROBERT ALAN CHARLES

Richmond Professional Institute of the
College of William and Mary

VI.

Bayard Quincy Morgan, Professor Emeritus of German at Stanford University, has translated Johann Wolfgang von Goethe, *Faust: Part One*, into English prose for The Library of Liberal Arts (No. 33, New York, [1954] $.75). His preface, except for two agreeably brief paragraphs on the composition of *Faust* (both parts) and its cosmic-human theme, explains why he has presented us with an English prose version of a text so frequently translated as *Faust I*. Although "the basic meaning and message of the work are still in violent dispute," the fact that "all" commentators agree that the message is important has persuaded the translator "that the time is ripe for a version which should endeavor to focus the reader's attention exclusively, or as nearly as the English language will permit, upon the meaning of the text." This is surely a most laudable aim, to translate without distorting the sense of the text translated, and I suspect that Mr. Morgan has come as near to achieving it successfully as is possible within his self-imposed limitations of a prose translation. (Twice, however, he lapses into verse: for *Zueignung*, which he regards, as he indicates in a note, as "not strictly a part of the drama," and for the song of Margarete that begins "There was a king in Thulë / Kept troth unto the grave, / Whom the one he loved so truly / A golden goblet gave." Other songs, however, are rendered into prose, e.g., "There once was a rat in the cellar that lived on nothing but fat and butter, and had fed so much that he had a potbelly like Dr. Luther. The cook put out poison, and now the world tightened around him as if he had love in his belly.")

But it may well be asked whether a verse translation necessarily conveys the "meaning" of a text any less well than a prose one. Mr. Morgan, as one who has "tried his hand at verse translation," categorically asserts that verse means a sacrifice of sense, adding "particularly if rhyme is involved." He is undoubtedly right in stating that "no translation can retain the rhyme and rhythm of an original work without some distortion of the sense," and in observing that "it is a law for the translator into English that the danger of distortion is markedly increased by such poetic devices as short lines, feminine rhymes, and triple or multiple rhymes." He does not, however, consider the alternative of a verse translation not retaining the rhymes and rhythms of the original text, although it is theoretically conceivable that such a translation might both be faithful to the thought of the original and possess intrinsic beauty of language. In the case of Goethe's *Faust*, I suspect, such a verse translation might convey the meaning of the original even more effectively than Mr. Morgan's admirably accurate prose, if only because an increasing or decreasing of metrical regularity (not to consider the practicability of radical changes in rhythmic patterns) could be used to mark differences in mood, tone or tempo that regularized prose must ignore, although such differences convey emphasis—and hence "meaning"—in the German text.

As Mr. Morgan points out in his preface, every translator of a poetic text must choose at times between alternate meanings of a given word in the original and thus sacrifice some of the ambiguity characteristic of poetic language. His comments on why he translates as he does "was träumet ihr auf eurer Dichterhöhe," "Du darfst auch da nur frei erscheinen" and "ein dunkler Ehrenmann" reveal both the sureness of his knowledge of Goethe's language and his conscientious desire to convey the essential meaning of each sentence or sentence-unit in the dramatic context in which it stands. His prose translation itself shows that he has consistently made his translator's choices wisely and conservatively, and within the limits of prose he has achieved a greater range of levels of diction—more successfully, perhaps, above the colloquial levels—than all but the best verse translators of *Faust*. The principles which he follows and the skill which he possesses might well be utilized in the translation of other German verse dramas; they are, I believe, particularly well suited for producing readable and dignified translations of works in which one level of diction and one verse form are maintained uninterruptedly, or almost uninterruptedly, throughout.

Harvard University   STUART ATKINS

VII.

Theories vary as to a translator's function and as to the art of translation from foreign poetry; but today, perhaps in part because of increasing awareness of the density and variety of meanings in the poetry of our own time, there seems at last to be a growing belief that the translator should try to bring his readers into as precise and immediate a relationship as possible with the particularities of his original text. With this belief there arises of necessity a demand for prose instead of verse as the translator's medium.

The greatest objection urged against prose for translation from a work in verse is that with its employment the poetic form is lost. But in most verse translations the original poetic form is also in great part lost, except for possible retention of a general rhythmic pattern and rhyme-scheme; for versifiers are not poets, and merely to put the *Commedia*, say, into English *terza rima* can hardly be seriously regarded as retaining the essential form of Dante's poem. The most useful accomplishment here is perhaps in most cases that of keeping the logic of expression within a general printed form for the eye; and this can be accomplished as well in prose as in verse.

No one concerned would willingly lose beautiful adaptations into English verse from great lyric poetry of other languages (for example, the adaptations of Landor and Rossetti from Sappho, Beardsley from Catullus, Pound from *The Seafarer*, Fitzgerald from Omar Khayyam, Rossetti from Villon, to cite a few of the better poems); but most of these are far from precise translations and are memorable in great part because of the poetic talent of the translators themselves. Attempts in verse are all but doomed from the start if the aim is really to show what the original writer said. Demands of fixed rhythm alone destroy precision in meaning, and rhyme usually makes completely impossible a close reproduction of sense. In the densely connotative language of lyric poetry, such problems multiply.

The idea of employing bilingual texts on opposite pages, with careful and sensitive prose translation from the original verses affords translators unusual opportunities for adapting their techniques to a cross-reference pattern of reading. By this method a reader who can pronounce the original verses with some assurance and who has a little background in the foreign grammar and vocabulary can be brought remarkably close to both the form and the meaning of foreign poetry. This advantage has long been enjoyed in varying degrees with many Greek and Latin master-pieces through the Guillaume Budé and the Loeb series for French and English readers. It is encouraging to see at last the gradual appearance of texts of this sort for poetry in the modern tongues.

Professor William Aggeler and his publishers have now offered such a text complete for one of the most famous volumes of French poetry,

Baudelaire's *Les Fleurs du Mal.** The prose translation (on the right-hand pages opposite the original) has a notable visual advantage over the translations in the Loeb and Budé series in that it follows the printed verse-patterns of the French text. Thus, for the eye, the form is much the same as in the original poems; and the logic of expression has been carefully adapted to the visual form. Such a work might seem of little use to anyone familiar with the foreign tongue concerned; but a close analysis of Professor Aggeler's translation can be of great interest even to specialists and can provide many unusual insights into Baudelaire's poems.

With the ideal translator—one who combined superior knowledge with natural gifts for expression and an intuitive sense of poetic meaning—this sort of translation might in itself afford light amounting almost to radiance. But the combination required for such performance is rarely found. In general, Professor Aggeler's translation is quite euphonious and shows excellent linguistic knowledge, but sometimes suggests a lack of imagination and at critical moments misses essential poetic relationships between words. It blurs poetic meaning by omissions or dilutions in vivid metaphor. It employs inversions in syntax that weaken dramatic ideas and images. It reveals a certain insentience to the differing effects of singular and plural nouns. It sometimes fails to take advantage of interrelations between cognates in the two languages, and seems on occasion almost deliberately to avoid using the precise expression that would keep the poetic sense intact among various words or images. Yet, in a close reading one is probably most conscious of these limitations for the very reason that the translator has not, like so many others, allowed himself to abscond from his original text. In general he follows Baudelaire so carefully that deviations are evident.

There are excellent passages in Professor Aggeler's translation that link a reader very successfully with Baudelaire's poetry; e.g., the stanza from *Confession* whose verses offer so memorable a view of Paris by moonlight:

Il était tard; ainsi qu'une médaille neuve
La pleine lune s'étalait,
Et la solennité de la nuit, comme un fleuve,
Sur Paris dormant ruisselait.

It was late; like a newly struck medal
The full moon spread its rays,
And the solemnity of the night streamed
Like a river over sleeping Paris.

Stanzas from *Le chat* show a similar skill:

Quand mes yeux, vers ce chat que j'aime,
Tirés comme par un aimant,

When my gaze, drawn as by a magnet,
Turns in a docile way

---

* Charles Baudelaire, *The Flowers of Evil*. Translated from the French by William Aggeler. [Definitive French text from Crépet and Blin (1950). Foreword by Y.-G. Le Dantec. Introduction, Commentaries and Notes by the translator.] Fresno, California: Academy Library Guild, 1954. Pp. xxviii-570. $6. [$4.80 to educators.]

Se retournent docilement	Toward that cat whom I love,
Et que je regarde en moi-même,	And when I look within myself,
Je vois avec étonnement	I see with amazement
Le feu de ses prunelles pâles,	The fire of her pale pupils,
Clairs fanaux, vivantes opales,	Clear signal-lights, living opals,
Qui me contemplent fixement.	That contemplate me fixedly.

Here, with a possible exception of the third line, the precision and clarity of diction are admirable, and the translation is faithful in meaning and is in itself a pleasure to read.

In the ensuing remarks I have no intention of belittling the very considerable accomplishment of Professor Aggeler; for he and his publisher have done valuable service in providing a complete, attractive, and remarkably useful bilingual text of a monumental work in French poetry. A rather close examination of the book has been a rich experience—so rich that I have thought of asking students to obtain copies for their own discoveries in detailed analysis. The observations below are intended to suggest that even more can be done than has been accomplished in the present translation and to indicate by implication, with examples in point, what seem to me some of the further obligations of the ideal prose translator for bilingual texts of this sort.

It is obvious that the translator should be thoroughly acquainted with the languages concerned in his work, and that he should be so full of his subject as to sense the basic stresses and strains in his author's mind. Thus, in the first verse of Baudelaire's *Au lecteur* it seems an error to translate *sottise* "folly" and *lésine* "avarice" (as Professor Aggeler has done in rare examples of this sort of lapse); for to me it is significant that in *Les Fleurs du Mal* Baudelaire begins with *stupidity*, and that his stress is on the pettiness in "la ménagerie infâme de nos vices"—on *stinginess*, not avarice, since Baudelaire did not see the souls of his contemporaries as generally bold enough for sins of strength.

A versifying translator invariably alters his text by omitting some elements and adding others as he tries to satisfy the exacting demands of rhythm and rhyme; but there would seem to be no justification for this in a prose version intended for a bilingual text. To translate "La Haine est un ivrogne *au fond d'*une taverne" (*Le tonneau de la Haine*) "Hatred is a drunkard in a tavern" sacrifices an essential part of the brooding sense in the original metaphor with its stress on the habitual drunkard's withdrawal into the depths of his tavern and his vice. On the other hand, to translate "Celui-là, lecteur, est un sage" (*Vers pour le portrait de M. Honoré Daumier*) "He is a sage, *gentle* reader" introduces an Anglicism that contrasts rather sharply with Baudelaire's own "Hypocrite lecteur—mon semblable—mon frére!"*

A recurrent problem for translators is that of the singular and plural forms of words. At times it is hard to keep the number of a foreign text;

---

* This famous concluding verse from *Au lecteur* is translated "Hypocritish reader . . ."!

yet the effect of one or the other form may be subtly different, and changes of this sort can ruin the effect of vivid image or metaphor. Baudelaire's "Le tombeau, confident de mon rêve infini" (*Remords posthume*) recalls the strange power of Catullus's "Nox est perpetua una dormienda" with its implication of unbroken sleep; but the impression is greatly weakened in the translation "The tomb, confident of my infinite *dreams.*" In *Le guignon*, Baudelaire intensifies a simile from Longfellow by putting its subject in the singular:

> Mon cœur, comme un tambour voilé,
> Va battant des marches funèbres.

The rare immediacy in the figure of a heart beating like a muffled drum for funeral marches is lost in the generalizing effect of a plural substantive:

> My heart, like muffled *drums,*
> Goes beating funeral marches.

Here the rendition seems almost wilfully to attenuate the shock of powerful imagery.

A translator is often forced unavoidably to change the order of words and phrases in turning expressions from one language to another; and Professor Aggeler has shown unusual skill on occasion in rearrangements of this sort. But unnecessary change can be costly, as in the translation from the last lines of *Les petites vieilles*:

Où serez-vous demain, Èves octogénaires,	Octogenarian Eves, upon whom rests
Sur qui pèse la griffe effroyable de Dieu?	God's terrible claw, where will you be tomorrow?

The ultimate impression in the original is the visual image of God's claw in the sky. This claw that *weighs upon* the old women is probably the most vivid image in the poem, and it is certainly the most terrifying. With altered syntax much of its power is lost. There is similar loss of the dramatic situation of the word *fright* at the very end of *Le revenant*:

Comme d'autres par la tendresse,	I wish to hold sway over
Sur ta vie et sur ta jeunesse,	Your life and youth by fear
Moi, je veux régner par l'effroi.	As others do by tenderness.

Serious inadequacies in translation are likely to result from omission of concrete reference, from failure to see the exquisite relations in image-structure, or from not looking deeply enough into the roots of words. For example, in *Hymne à la Beauté* Baudelaire develops the metaphor of a door opened by Beauty upon the Infinite:

> Que tu viennes du ciel ou de l'enfer, qu'importe,
> O Beauté! monstre énorme, effrayant, ingénu!
> Si ton œil, ton souris, ton pied, m'ouvrent *la porte*
> D'un Infini que j'aime et n'ai jamais connu?

The translator may have felt that Baudelaire was using awkward imagery here (with an eye or a smile opening a door); but much is lost with omission of the concrete image in the last two lines:

> If your regard, your smile, your foot, open for me
> An Infinite I love but have not ever known?

Baudelaire was seeking not a glimpse through a window, but "la porte d'un

Infini"; and the symbol of the opening door seems too full of suggestion for easy sacrifice.

In *La Beauté* Baudelaire employs his most vivid imagery in the last stanza, where Beauty tells of the power of her eyes over poets:

> Car j'ai, pour *fasciner* ces dociles amants,
> De purs miroirs qui font toutes choses plus belles:
> Mes yeux, mes larges yeux aux clartés éternelles!

To translate *fasciner* here as *enchant* is to emphasize the power of song rather than that of eyes and to destroy the integrity of the metaphorical and dramatic structure in the poem, whose whole final movement is directed toward Beauty's wide eyes and their eternal lights.

Metaphors often live deep within the etymologies of words, and successful translators must develop sensitiveness to imaginative impulses radiating through these ancient roots of poetry. When a word so involved has no cognate in the language of the translation, the translator is often at a loss. How would one turn into French the vast poetry of Joyce's apparently simple phrase, "Dark ages clasp the daisy roots"? The etymology of *daisy* whirls the image into the macrocosm and shows time, far back, in a weird contrast of light and dark, clasping the roots of our great sun. The French *marguerite* has no equivalent poetry to offer here.

Such problems are relatively rare for translators from French to English because of the great number of cognate words that have kept the same or closely related meanings in the two languages. It is, then, all the more strange that translators seem on occasion deliberately to seek other synonyms when the cognate may be not only a literal equivalent, but even the only one that can carry the rich poetic sense of the original. One is not likely to forget the "strange and fatal myth" of Baudelaire's lonely swan, wandering in a Parisian gutter and longing for the beautiful lake where it was born. It came to mind when I saw the word *onduleux* translated *sinuous* from the following verses of *Les bijoux*:

> Les yeux fixés sur moi, comme un tigre dompté,
> D'un air vague et rêveur elle essayait des poses,
> Et la candeur unie à la lubricité
> Donnait un charme neuf à ses métamorphoses;
>
> Et son bras et sa jambe, et sa cuisse et ses reins,
> Polis comme de l'huile, *onduleux* comme un cygne,
> Passaient devant mes yeux clairvoyants et sereins. . . .

Is it not likely that the poet's serene, clairvoyant eyes saw the wave for the swan in the etymology of his lovely epithet?

It would be unjust to leave an unfavorable impression of a valuable work; and I should like to cite one last quotation (from *Le serpent qui danse*) to show how successfully Baudelaire's strange accent can be caught in English prose and how precisely careful translation can follow the meaning of his verse:

Et ton corps se penche et s'allonge
  Comme un fin vaisseau
Qui roule bord sur bord et plonge
  Ses vergues dans l'eau.
	And your body stretches and leans
	  Like a slender ship
	That rolls from side to side and dips
	  Its yards in the sea.

Comme un flot grossi par la fonte	Like a stream swollen by the thaw
Des glaciers grondants,	Of rumbling glaciers,
Quand l'eau de ta bouche remonte	When the water of your mouth rises
Au bord de tes dents,	To the edge of your teeth,
Je crois boire un vin de Bohême,	It seems I drink Bohemian wine,
Amer et vainqueur,	Bitter and conquering,
Un ciel liquide qui parsème	A liquid sky that scatters
D'étoiles mon coeur!	Stars in my heart!

Professor Aggeler's translation of *Les Fleurs du Mal* will repay careful reading by Baudelaire specialists and by others who can enjoy the poet's own language with the skill of native readers. It will be a most welcome aid to those of fair reading competence who still need some help in the language. For those who read French only with difficulty or to whom it is a completely alien tongue the translation will afford an unusually close approach to the ideas and particular expressions in the complete masterpiece of one of the greatest French poets. Its publication is an important event and one may hope a milestone in the printing of great modern poetry with conscientious prose translations in complete bilingual texts.

ALFRED G. ENGSTROM

The University of North Carolina

VIII.

New English translations of the plays of Anton Chekhov have come out with great regularity in the half-century since the plays were written. The frequency of these fresh editions attests not only our continuing interest in the playwright, but also a rather constant dissatisfaction over the quality of the translations themselves. Even in Russian Chekhov's dramas are often extremely elusive; the task of rendering them into English with a minimum of distortion is arduous and often discouraging.

Chekhov's dialogue is deceptively simple. For the most part it is ordinary conversation, free of declamation, elaborate imagery, or effects of purely verbal beauty. Designed to induce actors to behave on the stage as naturally as possible, Chekhov's speech is carefully modulated and largely devoid of ornamentation. On the other hand, since his style aims at instilling a poetic quality into that which is ostensibly commonplace, his choice of words is precise and delicate. A successful translator of his plays must be a gifted person indeed. In striving to preserve the restraint of the original Russian, he must avoid timid literalism, such as that of Constance Garnett, who often turned out English lines which were merely flat and dull. Conversely, he must resist the temptation to use excessively vivid English in his efforts to convey the emotional significance of the Russian lines. Above all, he must be content with the realization that the two languages are so remote from one another that a great deal is bound to be lost in even the best translation.

The two present volumes translated by Elisaveta Fen (*Three Plays: The Cherry Orchard; Three Sisters; Ivanov*, The Penguin Classics, no. L19,

1951, $. 65 and *The Seagull and Other Plays: The Seagull; Uncle Vania; The Bear; The Proposal; A Jubilee*, The Penguin Classics, no. L38, 1954, $ .50) make available in very inexpensive editions, all of Chekhov's major plays and three of his most popular one-act farces. The translation may very well be the best that has yet been done, for its chief distinction is the modesty, accuracy, and conversational ring of its language. Unlike many of its predecessors, it will not force actors to a display of emotion in excess of that which the author intended. Readers will likewise discover much of the same quiet suppleness and suggestiveness that is to be found in the Russian. Miss Fen is deeply familiar with the characters, their problems, and their motivations, and this knowledge has given her the freedom to produce an English version which is precise and, at the same time, idiomatic and graceful.

A brief comparison with two other translations will illustrate the virtue of her method, which is essentially one of understatement. In *The Three Sisters*, a line of Olga contains the expression *"radost zavolnovalas v moei dushe."* Bernard Guilbert Guerney translates this as "joy began to riot in my soul," while Constance Garnett writes, "joy stirred in my heart." Both translations are essentially correct, yet each seems self-consciously poetic and stilted. Miss Fen, in contrast, renders the line simply, "I felt so moved and so happy." Her translation is looser than the other two, but it captures the spirit of the original Russian much more accurately than they. It is subdued, yet colloquial and perfectly articulate, and should be amply flexible for any actress interpreting the role.

This is not to say that Miss Fen's translation is flawless. Occasionally there appear such lines as the following: "They say the fire's getting less fierce." Even allowing for the fact that the plays have been translated throughout into British idiom and will therefore sound a little strange to Americans, expressions like this seem intrinsically awkward. More serious errors, moreover, arise where Miss Fen has attempted to edit the plays. It is fortunate that she has not repeated the mistake of Garnett, who deleted whole passages, nor has she tampered with their structure in the manner of Guerney, who reduced the number of acts in *The Three Sisters* from four to three. And it is possible that she has improved the opening line of *The Three Sisters* by changing it from a declaration to a question. But in placing stage directions where none existed in the original, she has, in at least one instance in the same play, attributed entire lines to the wrong characters.

These flaws, and they are few indeed, are the result of over-zealousness rather than of negligence. Both volumes are notable for their meticulous attention to detail and for their attempt to make the plays as clear as possible for the reader. The long and useful biographical introductions which accompany both volumes also indicate the carefulness with which this edition has been prepared.

DEMING BROWN

Northwestern University

IX.

As the translator, Herman Salinger, says, *Twentieth Century German Verse: A Selection* (Princeton University Press, 1952, $2.50) "does not pretend to be a grand tour of German poetry in our century." And yet this slim volume of forty-three poems from Isolde Kurz (born 1853) to Hans Egon Holthusen (born 1913) provides, in its excellent selection of the originals and in its imaginative English versions a clear insight into contemporary German verse.

Salinger gives us no detailed accounting for his selection of poets or of their works; he simply states that he felt "these poems yearned to be reborn in English." One can wish for no better criterion of choice, for if a poem, no matter how great or how "important" did not appeal in this way to a translator, the result would be a waste of effort and paper, and, surely more serious, a distorted view of the original creation. As it is, the English reader is able to feel that these are significant examples. And the reader of German (through the originals on the opposite pages) can appreciate the skill and imagination of the translator without wishing, more than once or twice, for a more felicitous rendition of a word or phrase.

No harm whatsoever is done by the fact that certain poems have been previously translated; indeed, advantage is gained from having improved translations, and especially from having a consistent interpretation or commentary furnished by a single gifted translator of these varied examples of recent poetry.

It is hardly necessary to say that the famous German lyricists Rilke, Hofmannsthal, George, Trakl, Werfel, Weinheber are well represented by characteristic poems, affording a good understanding of aspects of their work. Nor does one look in vain for younger figures like Albrecht Haushofer, Ulrich Becher, and Hans Egon Holthusen.

Perhaps of particular interest are the poems of writers known best—both in the United States and in Germany—for their prose fiction. I refer especially to Binding's "Love Song" with its clarity and strictness of form, even when dealing with passion and love; to Hesse's splendid eight poems with their nature tones and their themes of unity with nature, their evocation of feelings of youth, their stress on moral responsibility, and their somewhat nostalgic realization of the transitoriness of life; to Carossa's "Star-Song" evoking a note of maturity, inner confidence, and faith in eternal values; to the expression of the firm faith and trust of Ina Seidel's "Marriage;" to Wiechert's "A Child Cried at Night," for its appeal of simple life, fundamental emotions, and responsibility to others. I should also like to single out for particular mention the moving ballad, "Ghost," by Agnes Miegel, who, although not in the forefront of the development of contemporary German poetry, is nevertheless the best modern writer of ballads—a form which has far more vigor in German than in English today.

Observable most clearly, perhaps, in Schnitzler's "Encouragement," serving as an epigraph to the collection, and in Holthusen's "Sacrifice" and "It Was My Blood" (the last two of the volume), but yet pervading the entire selection, are the tones of a sturdy and positive individualism combined with a lofty idealism and a feeling of responsibility for and to one's fellow man.

ROBERT T. ITTNER

The University of Akron

PART FIVE

BIBLIOGRAPHY OF COMPARATIVE LITERATURE

PREFACE

The happy possibility of being able to spend a year in Australia, as Fulbright Professor of Comparative Literature at the University of Melbourne (with additional lectures at the Universities of Adelaide, Brisbane, Perth, Sydney and Tasmania), called for a small reduction in the usual scope of this Bibliography. Next year's issue will amply make up for this unavoidable curtailment.

In view of my absence from Chapel Hill till February 1956, Professor Horst Frenz (himself just back from a guest-professorship at the University of Hamburg) has kindly agreed to check the galley-proofs and the page-proofs not only of this Bibliography, but of the entire *Yearbook IV*.

Foremost among the individual contributors to whom I am deeply indebted for help unstintingly given are Professors Francis M. Rogers, Dean of the Harvard Graduate School (for Portuguese items), Gleb Struve, University of California at Berkeley (Slavic items), Claudio Isopescu, University of Rome (Italian and Rumanian items) and Calvin Brown, University of Georgia (Literature and Music).

Among the group-bibliographers who have generously agreed to put their findings at our disposal, there are again two:

The Prose Literature Group in the MLA (C.L. I):
American Literature: H. B. Rouse (Mt. Union—and chairman and editor).
English literature: R. C. Boys (Michigan), R. M. Kain (Louisville), J. P. Kirby (Randolph-Macon).
French literature: I. Putter (Berkeley).
German literature: Lienhard Bergel (Queens).
Hungarian literature: J. Remenyi (Western Reserve).
Italian literature: D. Vittorini (Pennsylvania).
Polish literature: Manfred Kridl (Columbia).
Russian literature: Gleb Struve (Berkeley).
Scandinavian literature: P. M. Mitchell (Kansas).
Spanish literature: J. E. Englekirk (Tulane), J. López-Morillas (Brown), and

The Franco-German Group in the MLA (C.L. VII):
Konrad Bieber (Connecticut College for Women).
Marianne Bonwit (Berkeley).

Joseph M. Carrière (Virginia).
Oscar A. Haac (Emory).
Ludwig W. Kahn (N.Y. City College).
E. A. MacCormick (Harvard).
Wolfgang Paulsen (Connecticut—and chairman and editor).
A. G. Reichenberger (Pennsylvania).
H. H. H. Remak (Indiana).

I am also happy to be able to announce that from 1956 on the Anglo-Franco-American bibliographers of Group V are likewise going to join our efforts to present to our colleagues at home and abroad an increasingly complete and useful bibliography of the international interrelationships of literature.

The following pages are again doubly numbered, and in cross-references pages 1-701 refer to the Baldensperger-Friederich *Bibliography of Comparative Literature*, pages 702-760 to the supplement in *Yearbook I*, pages 761-822 to *Yearbook II*, pages 823-906 to *Yearbook III* and pages 907 ff. to *Yearbook IV*. Starred forms indicate a correction or a supplementation of a previously given item.

Melbourne   W. P. F.
March/May 1955

List of Abbreviations

A	Apollon. St. Petersburg.
Aatseel	Bulletin of the American Association of Teachers of Slavic and East European Languages. Philadelphia.
AC	L'Antiquité classique. Wetteren.
Acme	Annali della Facoltà di filosofia e lettere dell' Università di Milano.
ACUM	Annales du centre universitaire méditerranéen de Nice.
AFR	Anglo-French Review. London & Paris.
AGR	American-German Review. Philadelphia.
AHR	American Historical Review. New York.
AJPh	American Journal of Philology. Baltimore.
AL	American Literature. Durham, North Carolina.
AM	Atlantic Monthly. Boston.
AQ	American Quarterly. Philadelphia.
AR	Archivum Romanicum. Firenze.
A & R	Atene e Roma. Bullettino della Società italiana per la diffusione degli studi classici. Firenze.
Archiv	Archiv für das Studium der neueren Sprachen & Litteraturen. Braunschweig.
ASEER	American Slavonic and East European Review. New York.
ASR	American-Scandinavian Review. New York.
AUA	Annals of the Ukrainian Academy of Arts and Sciences in the United States. New York.
B	Brazda, Sarajevo.
BA	Books Abroad, Norman, Oklahoma.
BAGB	Bulletin de l'Association Guillaume Budé. Paris.
BDB	Börsenblatt für den deutschen Buchhandel. Leipzig.
BH	Bulletin Hispanique. Bordeaux.
BHR	Bibliothèque d'Humanisme et Renaissance. Genève.
BI	Bulletin Italien. Bordeaux.
BNYPL	Bulletin of the New York Public Library. New York.
BRL	Bulletin of the John Rylands Library. Manchester.
BSS (or BHS)	Bulletin of Spanish (or: Hispanic) Studies. Liverpool.
BSSL	Bulletin de la Société des sciences et des lettres de Łodz.
BURS	Bibliothèque Universelle et Revue Suisse. Genève.
C	Critique. Paris.
CA	Cuadernos Americanos. Mexico.
CB	Classical Bulletin. Chicago.
CE	College English. Chicago.
CJ	Classical Journal. Chicago.
CL	Comparative Literature. Eugene, Oregon.
C & M	Classica et Medievalia. København.
CMF	Časopis pro moderni filologii. Prague.
Conv.	Convivium, Rivista di lettere, filosofia e storia, Università Catt. del Sacro Cuore. Milano-Torino.
CP	Classical Philology. Chicago.
CQ	Classical Quarterly. London.
CS	Cahiers du Sud. Marseilles.
CW	Classical Weekly. Lancaster, Pennsylvania.
DAN	Doklady Akademii Nauk SSSR. Moscow.
DJ	Dziś i Jutro. Warsaw.

DLZ	Deutsche Literaturzeitung. Leipzig.
DN	Družba Narodov. Moscow.
DVLG	Deutsche Vierteljahrsschrift für Literaturwissenschaft und Geistesgeschichte. Halle.
EA	Etudes anglaises. Paris.
EC	Etudes Classiques. Namur.
EG	Etudes Germaniques. Paris.
EI	Etudes italiennes. Bordeaux.
EL	Ezik i literatura. Sofia.
ELH	English Literary History. Baltimore.
E & S	Essays & Studies by Members of the English Association. Oxford.
ESn	Englische Studien. Leipzig.
ESs	English Studies. Groningen.
FAR	French-American Review. Washington.
FD	Fanfulla della Domenica. Roma.
F & F	Forschungen und Fortschritte. Berlin.
FM	Filosofska Mis'l. Sofia.
FR	French Review. New York.
FS	French Studies. Oxford.
Gxvi	God šestnadcatyj. Almanach. Moscow.
GD	Giornale dantesco. Firenze.
GLAIU	Gledališki list Akademije za igralsko umetnost. Ljubljana.
GLL	German Life and Letters. Oxford.
GLSNG-L	Gledališki list Slovenskega narodnega gledališča v Ljubljane. Ljubljana.
GLSNG-M	Gledališki list Slovenskega narodnega gledališča v Mariboru. Maribor.
GQ	German Quarterly. Lancaster, Pennsylvania.
G & R	Greece and Rome. Oxford.
GR	Germanic Review. New York.
GRM	Germanisch-romanische Monatsschrift. Heidelberg.
GSLI	Giornale storico della letteratura italiana. Torino.
Hi	Hid. Novi Sad.
Hisp.	Hispania. Stanford (1918 ff.); also Paris, 1918-22.
HK	Hrvatsko Kolo. Zagreb.
HLQ	Huntington Library Quarterly. San Marino, California.
Ho	Hochland. Monatsschrift für alle Gebiete des Wissens. München.
H & R	Humanisme et Renaissance. Paris.
HR	Hispanic Review. Philadelphia.
HSPhL	Harvard Studies and Notes in Philology and Literature. Cambridge, Mass.
IAN	Izvestija Akademii Nauk. Moscow.
IAN, OLJA	Izvestija Akademii Nauk SSSR, Otdelenie literury i jazyka. Moscow.
IAN, OON	Izvestija Akademii Nauk SSSR, Ordelenie obščestvennyx nauk. Moscow.
IAN, ORJaSL	Izvestija Otdelenija russkogo jazyka i slovesnosti Akademii Nauk. Moscow.
IANUz	Izvestija Akademii Nauk Uzbekistanskoj SSR. Taškent.
ICS	L'Italia che scrive. Roma.
ILGU	Izvestija Leningradskogo Gosudarstvennogo Universiteta. Leningrad.
IRJaSl	Institut Russkogo Jazyka i Slovesnosti Pri Akademii Nauk SSSR.

IS	Italian Studies. London.
Ital.	Italica. Chicago.
IVGPI	Izvestija Voronežskogo gosudarstennogo pedagogičeskogo instituta. Voronež.
Iz	Izvor. Zagreb.
JAAC	Journal of Aesthetics and Art Criticism, Cleveland, Ohio.
JAF	Journal of American Folklore. Lancaster, Pennsylvania.
JaiL	Jazyk i Literatura. Leningrad.
JAOS	Journal of the American Oriental Society. Baltimore.
JbDG	Jahrbuch der Dante Gesellschaft. Leipzig.
JbShG	Jahrbuch der Shakespeare Gesellschaft. Weimar.
JEGP	Journal of English and Germanic Philology. Urbana, Illinois.
JHI	Journal of the History of Ideas. New York.
JIFM	Journal of the International Folk Music Council. Cambridge, England.
JS	Journal des Savants. Paris.
JWI	Journal of the Warburg and Courtauld Institute. London.
K	Književnost. Belgrade.
KB	Komunist. Belgrade.
KiR	Kniga i Revoljucija. Leningrad.
KN	Krasnaja Nov'. Moscow.
KnN	Književne novine. Belgrade.
KP	Kulturní Politika. Prague.
KR	Kenyon Review. Gambier, Ohio.
Kž	Kulturni Zivot. Belgrade.
LDL	Letopis Doma Literatorov. Petrograd.
LE	Literarisches Echo. Berlin.
Lett. mod.	Letterature moderne. Milano.
LF	Listy filologické. Prague.
LG	Literaturnaja Gazeta. Moscow.
LiM	Literatura i Marksizm. Moscow.
LitM	Literaturnaja Mysl. Petrograd.
LK	Literaturnyj Kritik. Leningrad.
LM	Les Langues Modernes. Paris.
LMS	Ljetopis matice srpske. Novi Sad.
LN	Literaturnoe Nasledstvo. Moscow.
LNI	La Nuova Italia. Perugia.
LQHR	London Quarterly and Holborn Review.
LT	Levende Talen. Bruxelles.
LvSk	Literatura v skole. Moscow.
LZ	Literaturnye Zapiski. St. Petersburg.
MA	Medium Aevum. Oxford.
MDU	Monatshefte für deutschen Unterricht. Madison, Wisconsin.
Me	Meander, Warsaw.
MF	Mercure de France. Paris.
MG	Mołodaja Gvardija. Moscow.
Ml	Mladost. Belgrade.
MlR	Mladinska Revija. Ljubljana.
MLF	Modern Language Forum. Los Angeles.
MLJ	Modern Language Journal. Menasha, Wisconsin.
MLN	Modern Language Notes. Baltimore.
MLQ	Modern Language Quarterly. Seattle.
MLR	Modern Language Review. London.
MP	Modern Philology. Chicago.
MS	Mediaeval Studies. Toronto.

NAnt	Nuova Antologia di Scienze, Lettere ed Arti. **Roma.**
NaR	Naša Reč. Paris.
NBLU	Naučnyj Bjulleten' Leningradskogo Universiteta. Leningrad.
NCF	Nineteenth Century Fiction. Los Angeles.
NEQ	New England Quarterly. Baltimore.
NG	Neue Gesellschaft. Berlin.
NISGU	Naučnye Izvestija Smolenskogo Gosudarstvennogo Universiteta. Smolensk.
NJK	Nastava Jezika i Književnosti u srednoj školi. Belgrade.
NL	Nouvelles Littéraires. Paris.
NM	Neuphilologische Monatsschrift. Leipzig.
NO	Nova Obzorja. Maribor.
NoM	Novyj Mir. Moscow.
Nož	Nový Život. Svaz. čsl. spisovatelů. Prague.
NP	Neophilologus. Groningen.
N & Q	Notes and Queries. London.
NR	Neue Rundschau. Berlin.
NRF	Nouvelle Revue Française. Paris.
NRFH	Nueva Revista de Filología Hispánica. México.
NS	Novi Svet. Ljubljana.
NSp	Die neueren Sprachen. Marburg.
NSR	Neue Schweizer Rundschau. Zürich.
NTBB	Nordisk Tidskrift för Bok- och Biblioteksväsen. Stockholm.
NTIPI	Naučnye Trudy Industrial'no-Pedagogičeskogo Instituta. Moscow.
NW	Neue Welt. Berlin.
Nž	Naša Žena. Ljubljana.
Nžu	Novyj Žurnal. New York.
O	Oktjabr'. Moscow.
Op	Opyty. New York.
Os	Osvit. Belgrade.
P	Polonistyka. Warsaw.
PAPS	Proceedings of the American Philosophical Society. Philadelphia.
PAU-AN	Polska Akademia Umiejętnosci. Archivum Neophilologicum. Warsaw.
PBA	Proceedings of the British Academy. London.
PBSA	Papers of the Bibliographical Society of America. New York.
PCA	Proceedings of the Classical Association. Cambridge, England.
PEGS	Publications of the English Goethe Society. London.
PiR	Pečat' i Revoljucija. Moscow.
PiS	Puškin i ego sovremenniki. Leningrad.
PL	Poet Lore. Philadelphia.
PMLA	Publications of the Modern Language Association. New York.
Po	Polet. Belgrade.
PPL	Prace Polonistyczne. Lódz.
PPW	Prace Polonistyczne. Wroclaw.
PQ	Philological Quarterly. Iowa.
PR	Partisan Review. New York.
PS	Pamiętnik Slowianski. Cracow.
PWTN-A	Prace Wrocławskiego towarzystwa naukowego. Seria A. Wrocław.
PZ	Przeglad Zachodni. Poznań.
PZM	Pod Znamenem Marksizma. Moscow.

QQ	Queen's Quarterly. Kingston, Ontario.
R	Republika. Zagreb.
RA	Revue Archéologique. Paris.
RBPh	Revue Belge de Philologie et d'Histoire. Bruxelles.
RCC	Revue des Cours et Conférences. Paris.
RCLI	Rassegna critica della letteratura italiana. Roma.
RdF	Revue de France. Paris.
RDM	Revue des Deux Mondes. Paris.
REA	Revue des Etudes Anciennes. Paris.
REG	Revue des Etudes grecques. Paris.
REH	Revue des Etudes hongroises. Paris.
REL	Revue des Etudes Latines. Paris.
RELV	Revue de l'Enseignement des langues vivantes. Le Havre.
RES	Review of English Studies. London.
RF	Romanische Forschungen. Erlangen.
RFC	Rivista di Filologia Classica. Torino.
RFE	Revista de Filología Española. Madrid.
RFH	Revista de Filología Hispánica. Buenos Aires.
RH	Revue Hispanique. Paris.
RHLF (or RHL)	Revue d'Histoire littéraire de la France. Paris.
RHPhC	Revue d'histoire de la philosophie et d'histoire générale de la civilisation. Lille.
RI	Rivista d'Italia. Roma.
RIA	Revista Iberoamericana. México.
RIL	Rendiconti dell'Instituto lombardo. Milano.
RiSL	Rossija i Slavjanstvo. Paris.
RLC	Revue de Littérature comparée. Paris.
RLM	Rivista di Letterature moderne. Firenze.
RLR	Revue des Langues romanes. Montpellier.
RM	Russkaja Mysl'. Before 1918: Moscow-Petrograd; after 1918: Sofia, Prague, Berlin, Paris.
RMM	Revue de Métaphysique et de Morale. Paris.
RP	Revue de Paris.
RPh	Romance Philology. Berkeley, California.
RR	Romanic Review. New York.
RS	Ricerche Slavistiche. Napoli.
RuB	Russkoe Bogatstvo. St. Petersburg.
RyF	Razón y Fe. Madrid.
SAB	Shakespeare Association Bulletin. New York.
SAQ	South Atlantic Quarterly. Durham, North Carolina.
SAU	Sprawozdania Akademii Umiejętnosci. Cracow.
SBAW	Sitzungsberichte der Bayrischen Akademie der Wissenschaften. München.
SEER	Slavonic and East European Review. London.
SF	Socialistički Front. Zagreb.
SFQ	Southern Folklore Quarterly. Gainesville, Florida.
SIFC	Studi italiani di filologia classica. Firenze.
SL	Soviet Literature. Moscow.
Sla	Slavia. Prague.
SlP	Slovenski poročevalec. Ljubljana.
SloP	Slovanský přehled. Prague.
SlPo	Slovenské pohl'ady. Turčiansky Svätý Martin.
SlR	Slavistična Revija. Ljubljana.
SN	Sovetskaja Nauka. Moscow.
SO	Sibirskie Ogni. Irkutsk
SoZ	Sovremennye Zapiski. Paris.
SP	Studies in Philology. Chapel Hill.
Spec	Speculum. Cambridge, Mass.
SQ	Shakespeare Quarterly. Washington.
SRL	Saturday Review of Literature. New York.

SS	Scandinavian Studies. Lawrence, Kansas.
SV	Slovesná Věda. Prague.
SVL	Studien zur vergleichenden Literaturgeschichte. Berlin.
SZ	Sovremennye Zapiski. Paris.
SZ47	Sekspirovskij Sbornik, 1947. Moscow.
T	Teatr. Moscow.
TAPhA	Transactions and Proceedings of the American Philological Association. Lancaster, Pennsylvania.
TB	Tvorba. Bratislava.
TBGU	Trudy Belorusskogo Gosudarstvennogo Universiteta. Minsk.
TLS	Times Literary Supplement. London.
TNT-FF	Towarzystwo Naukowe w Toruniu. Prace Wydziału Filologiczno-Filozoficznego. Toruń.
TODRL	Trudy Otdela drevnerusskoj literatury, Akademija Nauk SSSR. Moscow-Leningrad.
Tov	Tovariš. Ljubljana.
TTPI	Trudy Tbiliskogo Gosudarstvennogo Pedagogičeskogo Instituta im. Puškina. Tiflis.
TVIIJ	Trudy Voennogo Instituta Innostrannykh Jazykov. Leningrad.
Tw	Twórczość. Cracow.
UCPP	University of California Publications in Modern Philology. Los Angeles.
UKCR	University of Kansas City Review.
UQ	Ukrainian Quarterly. New York.
UTQ	University of Toronto Quarterly.
UZII	Učenye Zapiski Instituta Istorii. Moscow.
UZLU	Učenye Zapiski Leningradskogo Universiteta. Leningrad-Saratov.
UZLU-FN	Učenye Zapiski Leningradskogo Universiteta, Serija Filologičeskix Nauk. Leningrad-Saratov.
UZMPI	Učenye Zapiski Moskovskogo Gosudarstvennogo Pedagogičeskogo Instituta im. Potemkina. Moscow.
UZSGU	Učenye Zapiski Saratovskogo Gosudarstvennogo Universiteta. Saratov.
UZTI	Učenye Zapiski Tixookeanskogo Instituta. Vladivostok.
UZUPI	Učenye Zapiski Ural'skogo Pedagogičeskogo i Učitel'skogo Instituta im. Puškina. Sverdlovsk.
VE	Vestnik Evropy. St. Petersburg.
Ver	Versty. Paris.
VJ	Voprosy Jazykoznanija. Moscow.
VLU	Vestnik Leningradskogo Universiteta. Leningrad.
VND	Vprašanja naših dni. Ljubljana.
VNFH	Vjesnik Narodnog Fronta Hrvatske. Zagreb.
Vozr	Vozrождenie. Paris (Before 1936, daily; 1936-40, weekly. Since 1948, bimonthly).
VPD	Vremennik Puškinskogo Doma. Moscow-Leningrad.
VR	Volja Rossii. Prague.
VZ	Vostočnye Zapiski. Moscow.
WSJ	Wiener Slavistisches Jahrbuch. Wien.
XF	Xudožestvennyj Fol'klor. Moscow.
XL	Xudozestvennaja Literatura. Moscow.
Yb	Yearbook of Comparative and General Literature. Chapel Hill.

YFS	Yale French Studies. New Haven, **Connecticut**.
Z	Zora. Sarajevo.
ZDA	Zeitschrift für deutsches Altertum und deutsche Literatur. Leipzig.
ZDMG	Zeitschrift der deutschen morgenländischen Gesellschaft. Leipzig.
ZDP	Zeitschrift für deutsche Philologie. Halle.
ZFEU (or **ZEFU**)	Zeitschrift für französischen und englischen Unterricht. Berlin.
žMNP	Žurnal Ministerstva Narodnogo Prosveščenija. St. Petersburg.
ZRNI	Zapiski Russkogo Naučnogo Instituta. Belgrade.
ZRP	Zeitschrift für romanische Philologie. Halle.
ZSP	Zeitschrift für slavische Philologie. Leipzig.
Zv	Zvezda. Leningrad.
ZVL	Zeitschrift für vergleichende Literaturgeschichte. Berlin.
ZvV	Zvezda Vostoka. Taškent.

Other Abbreviations: C.R.: Compte rendu; Jb: Jahrbuch; n.d.: no date; Zs: Zeitschrift; Zt: Zeitung.

Bibliography

A. GENERALITIES, INTERMEDIARIES, THEMATOLOGY, LITERARY GENRES

III. LITERATURE AND ARTS AND SCIENCES.

Dance, Fine Arts, Gardens, History, Music, Philosophy

Agrawala, V. S. Sanskrit Literature dealing with Art, Architecture and Sculpture. Journal of United Provinces Hist. Society, 17, 1944, 6-12.

Atkinson, Margaret. Musical Form in Some Romantic Writings. MLR, 44, 1949.

Becker, A. Gestalt und Gehalt in Wort und Ton. GRM, 34, 1953, 13-28.

Benz, R. Die Welt der Dichter und die Musik. Düsseldorf, 1949. 300 p. [General introductory considerations, and specific discussions of Wackenroder, Hoffmann, Klopstock, Herder, Brentano, Novalis, Hölderlin, Schiller, Fichte, Kleist, Jean Paul, Goethe and Nietzsche.]

Bontempelli, M. La poesía contra la história. Sur, 225, 1953, 131-36.

Brown, C. S. Tones into Words: Musical Compositions as Subjects of Poetry. U. of Georgia P., 1953. [A study of some 300 poems, in various languages, dealing with specifically identified compositions. The history of such attempts, together with the techniques, types of approach, etc. and detailed analysis of three ambitious examples.]

Buford, A. H. History and Biography: the Renaissance Distinction. Festschrift G. C. Taylor. Chapel Hill, 1952, 100-12.

Burd, V. A. Another Light on the Writing of Modern Painters. PMLA, Sept. 1953.

Capone Braga, G. La filosofia francese e italiana del settecento. Arezzo, 1920.

Carpenter, Nan C. Musicians in Early University Drama. N&Q, 195, 1950.

Cassirer, E. The Philosophy of the Enlightenment. Princeton U.P., 1951.

Chaix, Marie-Antoinette. La correspondance des arts dans la poésie contemporaine. Paris, 1919.

Citoleux, M. La poésie philosophique au XIXe siècle. Paris, 1906.

Croce, B. Filosofia, poesia, storia. Milano, 1951.

Eissfeldt, O. Geschichtsschreibung im Alten Testament. Krit. Bericht über die neueste Literatur dazu. Berlin, 1948.

Fontaine, L. Le théâtre et la philosophie au XVIIIe siècle. Paris, n.d.

Fraenkel, H. Dichtung und Philosophie des frühen Griechentums. Amer. Philol. Assoc. New York, 1951. 680 p.

Franke, O. Der Sinn der chinesischen Geschichtsschreibung. Sinolog. Arbeiten, 3, 1945.

Gailly, L. Philosophes et philosophie dans la comédie grecque. Diss. Liége. RBPh, 25, 1946-47.

Ganay, E. de. Poésies et jardins au XVIIIe siècle. RP, 38, 1931, 414-32.

García Morente, M. Ideas para una filosofía de la história de España. Rev. Nacional de Educación, 2, 1942.

Gilbert, Katharine E. Aesthetic Studies: Architecture and Poetry. Duke U.P., 1953. 145 p.

Giovannini, G. Methods in the Study of Literature in its Relation to the Other Fine Arts. JAAC, 8, 1950. [Cautions against comparatism based on the metaphors of the critic.]

Hard, F. Some Interrelations between the Literary and the Plastic Arts in the 16th and 17th Centuries. College Art Journal, 10, 1951.

Hatzfeld, H. Literature through Art: A New Approach to French Literature. Oxford U.P. 1951. (Cf. CL, 4, 1952). [Radical attempt to break away from the one-sided ideological concept of literature; suggests complementation through art.]

Hautecoeur, L. Littérature et peinture en France du XVIIe au XXe siècle. Paris, 1942.

Heissig, W. Zum Umfang der mongolischen Geschichtsliteratur. Monumenta Sinica, 10, 1945.

——— Die mongolische Geschichtsschreibung im 18. und 19. Jahrhundert. Saeculum, 3, 1952.

Herding, O. Geschichtsschreibung und Geschichtsdenken im Mittelalter. Theolog. Quartalschrift, 130, 1950.

Herrero-García, M. Contribución de la literatura a la historia del arte. RFE, 1944.

Herter, H. Vom dionysischen Tanz zum komischen Spiel. Die Anfänge der attischen Komödie. Iserlohn, Westf., 1947.

Hourticq, L. L'art et la littérature. Paris, 1946. [Comparative treatise on aesthetics.]

Hutton, J. Some English Poems in Praise of Music. In: English Miscellany, ed. M. Praz. Roma, 1951, 1-64.

Kressler. Die japanische Literatur im Spiegel der Geschichte. Mitteilungen der dt. Ges. f. Natur- und Völkerkunde Ostasiens, 16, 1928.

Lacroix, B. M. The Notion of History in Early Mediaeval Historians. MS, 10, 1948.

Lanson, G. Origines et premières manifestations de l'esprit philosophique dans la littérature française de 1675 à 1748. RCC, 16-18, 1907-10.

Larroumet, G. Etudes de littérature et d'art. Paris, 1896.

Lenhart, C. The Influence of Music on American Poetry. Diss. Illinois. Georgia U.P., 1953. [From the beginnings to 1900.]

Lifšic, M. Voprosy iskusstva i filosofii. Moscow, 1935. 320 p.

Löwith, K. Meaning in History: the Theological Implications of the Philosophy of History. Chicago U.P. 1949.

Maritain, J. Creative Intuition in Art and Poetry. New York, 1953. 455 p.

*Maury, P. Arts et littérature comparés: Etat présent de la question. Paris, 1933. [Condensed presentation of historical problems concerning mutual elucidation.]

Meylan, P. Les écrivains et la musique. Etudes de musique et de littératures comparées. 2 vols. Lausanne, 1944-51. [Baudelaire, Debussy, Mann, Proust, Mallarmé, Valéry, Cocteau, Wagner et al.]

Misra, S. B. Contribution of Hindu Literature to Indian History. Patna, 1934.

Montigny, R. Das Verhältnis zwischen Literatur und Musik im französischen Schrifttum. Antares (Baden), Sept. 1953.

Morel, J. M. Théorie des jardins ou l'art des jardins de la nature. Paris, 1774.

Motherwell, R. (ed) The Dada Painters and Poets: An Anthology. New York, 1951.

Munro, T. The Arts and their Interrelations. A Survey of the Arts and an Outline of Comparative Aesthetics. New York, 1950.

Neuman, A. R. The Evolution of the Concept Gesamtkunstwerk in German Romanticism. Diss. Michigan, 1951.

Orozco Díaz, E. El huerto de Melibea: Para el estudio del tema del jardín en la poesía del siglo XV. Arbor, 19, 1951, 47-60.

Owings, M. A. The Arts in the Middle English Romances. New York, 1952. 204 p.

Peysner, N. English and German Art, and their Interrelations. GLL, 2, 1938.

Pittfield, T. B. Present-Day Composers and Poets. Musical Opinion, 75, 1952.

Praz, M. (ed) English Miscellany: A Symposium of History, Literature, and the Arts. Vol. 3. Roma, 1952. 284 p. (Cf. CL, 1953.)

Priddin, D. The Art of the Dance in French Literature. London, 1952.

Pypin, A. Izučenie russkoj narodnosti. Istoriko-literaturnyj obzor. VE, 1881-82.

—— Novejšie issledovanija russkoj narodnosti. VE, 2-11, 1883.

Quadri, G. La filosofia degli Arabi nel suo fiore. 2 vols. Firenze, 1939.

Quinn, A. H. Literature and the Allied Arts. In: The Literature of the American People. New York, 1951, 534-66. [Rather general account of similar movements and tendencies, with some considerations of paintings, operas, etc. based on literary works. Musical relationships largely confined to ballads and other folksongs.]

Read, H. Parallels in English Painting and Poetry. In: Defense of Shelley and Other Essays. London, 1936.

Remenyi, J. Art and Twentieth Century European Literature. College Art Journal, 11, 1951, 20-26.

Rogerson, B. Ut musica poesis: The Parallel of Music and Poetry in Eighteenth Century Criticism. Diss. Princeton, 1946.

Rousseau, J.-J. Discours sur les sciences et les arts. 1755.

Rummens, J. Bibliographie des principaux ouvrages concernant la philosophie de la Renaissance italienne, 1930-50.

Rev. internat. de philosophie, 5, 1951, 200-28.

Sachs, C. The Commonwealth of Art: Style in the Arts, Music and the Dance. New York, 1946. [Regrettable omission of literature within its impressive synthesis.]

Salerno, L. Seventeenth-Century English Literature on Painting. JWI, 14, 1951, 234-58.

Sánchez Alonso, B. Historia de la historiografía española. 3 vols. Madrid, 1941-52.

Schläger, G. Ueber Musik und Strophenbau der französischen Romanzen. Halle, 1900. 46 p.

Schloezer, B. de. Musique et poésie. Cahiers du Sud, 32, 1945, 481-86. [Offers a highly improbable theory of sound-meaning common to both arts.]

Schueller, H. M. The Use and Decorum of Music as Described in British Literature, 1700-1800. JHI, 13, 1952, 73-93. [Eighteenth-century ideas on music as it affects the individual, and society in general; these lead to a dichotomy between the use and the abuse of music.]

Sirén, O. China and the Gardens of Europe in the Eighteenth Century. New York, 1951.

Souriau, E. La correspondance des arts. Eléments d'esthétique comparée. Paris, 1947. [Comparative study of literature and the arts of design, with Greek, Latin, and French examples.]

Spencer, H. Literary Style and Music. New York, 1951.

Spire, A. Musique et poésie. Cahiers du Sud, 28, 1941, 196-206. [Underlines fundamental differences.]

Staiger, E. Dichtung und Musik in der Romantik. Universitas, 4, 1949.

Stein, L. Appreciation: Painting, Poetry and Prose. New York, 1947. [Pedagogical approach.]

Sternfeld, F. W. The Musical and Rhythmical Sources of Poetry. English Institute Essays, Columbia U.P., 1952, 126-45.

Stevens, W. The Relations between Poetry and Painting. New York, 1951.

Stobaugh, Margaret H. La música en la novela mexicana de 1810 a 1910. México, 1952. 136 p.

Taruschio, L. Nuova stilistica, ovvero dell' elemento musicale in letteratura. Macerata, 1936. [Impact of melody and rhythm on style, and their investigation.]

Taylor, J. F. A. et al. An Introduction to Literature and the Fine Arts. East Lansing, Mich., 1950.

Thompson, D. B. Ancient Gardens in Greece and Italy. Archeology 4, 1951, 41-47.

Venturini, M. La filosofia dell' umanesimo. Torino, 1949.

Wais, K. Symbiose der Künste. Stuttgart, 1936. [Critical-bibliographical presentation of problem.]

Walzel, O. Wechselseitige Erhellung der Künste. Berlin, 1917.

Wehrli, F. Die Geschichtsschreibung im Lichte der antiken Theorie. Festschrift E. Howald. Zürich, 1947.

Welland, D. S. R. (ed). The Pre-Raphaelites in Literature and Art. London, 1953. 215 p.

Willey, B. Poetry and Philosophy. BBC Listener, 2.II.1950.

Wimsatt, W. K. & T. M. Greene. Is a General Theory of the Arts of a Practical Value in the Study of Literature? JAAC, 8, 1950, 213-28. [Stresses dependence of criticism on general aesthetics and vice versa.]

Yoshida, M. Word Music in English Poetry. Ibid. 11, 1953, 151-59.

Science and Technology
especially Astronomy, Book-Printing,
Darwinism and Psychology
(Freudianism)

Anselmo, A. Bibliografia das bibliografias portuguesas. Lisboa, 1923.

———— Bibliografia das obras impresas em Portugal no século XVI. Lisboa, 1926.

Borisov, E. Frejd i ego učenie o poétičeskom tvorčestve. Vestnik Vospitanija, 7, 1914, 17-46.

Borovskij, V. Stravnitel'naja psixologija i frejdizm. PZM, 9, 1927, 214-22.

Bretnor, R. (ed). Modern Science Fiction: Its Meaning and its Future. New York, 1953.

Brjusov, V. Naučnaja poézija. RM, 6, 1909, 155-67.

Büchler, E. Die Anfänge des Buchdrucks in der Schweiz. Bern, 1951. 210 p.

Cargill, O. Science and the Literary Imagination in the United States. CE, 13, 1951.

Cortez Pinto, A. Da famosa arte da imprimissão: Da imprensa em Portugal às cruzadas d'além-mar. Lisboa, 1948.

Derleth, A. Contemporary Science-Fiction. CE, 13, 1952, 187-94. [An interesting, informative account of present-day tendencies with a useful bibliography.]

Donnelly, Mabel C. Freud and Literary Criticims. CE, 15, 1953, 155-58.

Dworkin, M. S. Poetry and the Machine. Personalist, 32, 1951.

Freud: see also Marxism 12, 702, 762.

Fuerst, N. & S. I. Mintz. Relations of Literature and Science: Selected Bibliographies Symposium, 1951 ff.

Grigor'ev, I. Psixoanaliz kak metod issledovanija xudožestvennoj literatury. KN, 7, 1925, 224-40.

Heffening, W. Ueber Buch- und Druckwesen in der alten Türkei. ZDMG, 100, 1950.

King, D. L'influence des sciences physiologiques sur la littérature française de 1670 à 1870. Paris, 1929.

Kocher, P. H. Science and Religion in Elizabethan England. San Marino, Calif. 1953.

McDonnell, T. P. The Cult of Science Fiction. Catholic World, 178, 1953, 15-18.

Miller, Minnie M. Science and Philosophy as Precursors of the English Influence in France: A Study of the Choix des anciens journaux. PMLA, 45, 1930, 856-96.

Palau y Dulcet, A. De los orígines de la imprenta en España. Barcelona, 1952. 13 p.

Robertson, J. K. Science in Literature. QQ, 58, 1951.

Šaginjan, M. Literatura i nauka. O, 10, 1946, 179-84.

Salter, A. The Case against Psychoanalysis. New York, 1952.

Shapiro, K. Poets and psychologists. Poetry, 80, 1952, 166-84.

Thorndike, L. Mediaeval Magic and Science in the Seventeenth Century. Speculum, 28, 1953, 692-704.

Varia. Bibliografia Geral Portuguesa: Século XV. Acad. das Ciências de Lisboa, 2 vols. 1941-42.

Voronskij, A. Frejdizm i iskusstvo. KN, 7, 1925, 241-62.

Weisinger, H. English Treatment of the Relationship between the Rise of Science and the Renaissance, 1740-1840. Annals of Science, 7, 1951.

White, E. A. Science and Religion in American Thought. Stanford, 1952.

Individual Poets, Artists, Composers, Scholars and Scientists

Amari, G. Il concetto di storia in Sant' AGOSTINO. Roma, 1951. 212 p.

Evans, H. La pathologie de Louis Lambert: BALZAC aliéniste. RHL, 50, 1950.

Maurice-Amour, L. Balzac et la musique. MF, 308, 1950.

Tielrooy, J. Maurice BARRÈS et les beaux-arts. MF, Aug, 1953.

Hamilton, K. M. William BLAKE and the Religion of Art. Dalhousie Rev., 29, 1949.

Schrade, L. Music in the Philosophy of BOETHIUS. Musical Quart., 33, 1947.

Merton, E. S. Science and the Imagination in Sir Thomas BROWNE. New York, 1949.

Horowitz, I. L. The Renaissance Philosophy of Giordano BRUNO. New York, 1952.

Michel, P. H. Giordano Bruno et le système de Copernic d'après la Cène des Cendres (1584). In: Pensée humaniste et tradition chrétienne, ed. by J. Bédarida. Paris, 1950.

Zawadzki, W. Giordano Bruno—wyznawacz Kopernika. Tw, 6, 1950.

Farinelli, A. Apuntes sobre CALDERÓN y la música en Alemania. Cultura española, 1, 1907.

Hesse, E. W. Calderón and Velázquez. Hispania, 35, 1952, 74-82. [Parallels well seen, but not their aesthetic implications.]

Silva, L. P. da. A Astronomia dos Lusíadas (CAMOENS). Coimbra, 1915.

Filler, L. Parrington and CARLYLE: Cross Currents in History and Belles-Lettres. Antioch Rev., 12, 1952, 203-16.

Hanke, L. Bartolomé de las CASAS, Historian. Gainesville, 1952.

Del Arco y Garay, R. La música y la danza en las obras de CERVANTES. Revista de Ideas Estéticas, 35, 1951, 253-70.

Diego, G. Cervantes y la música. In: Anales Cervantinos, Madrid, 1951, 5-40.

Hatzfeld, H. Artistic Parallels in Cervantes and Velázquez. Festschrift Menéndez Pidal, 3, Madrid, 1952, 265-

97. [Concerned with impressionism, interior, feminine beauty, national grandeur.]

Querol, M. Cervantes y la música. RFE, 32, 1948.

Salazar, A. Más sobre la música en Cervantes. NRFH, 5, 1951.

Bald, R. C. Sir William CHAMBERS and the Chinese Garden. JHI, 11, 1950.

Engel-Janosi, F. CHATEAUBRIAND as an Historical Writer. Catholic Hist. Rev. 1948.

Edinger, W. CICEROS Stellung zur Kunst (Dichtkunst, Bildkunst, Musik) in seinen rhetorischen Schriften. Diss. Innsbruck, 1951.

Bate, W. J. COLERIDGE on the Function of Art. In: Perspectives of Criticism, ed. by H. Levin. Harvard U.P., 1950.

Kwiat, J. J. Stephen CRANE and Painting. AQ, 4, 1952, 331-38. [Crane knew a number of painters well, was interested in their work, and used their problems in his fiction. His technique, especially in description, shows some parallels to that of impressionistic painting.]

Palgen, R. DANTES Sternglaube. Heidelberg, 1948.

Blass, A. Die Geschichtsauffassung Daniel DEFOES. Heidelberg, 1931.

Carpentier, J. DIDEROT et la science de son temps. Rev. du mois, 16, 1913, 537-52.

Langen, A. Die Technik der Bildbeschreibung in Diderots Salons. RF, 61, 1948, 324-87. [Art and art criticism as sources for creative prose.]

Prod'homme, J. G. Diderot et la musique. Zs. internat. Musikges., 15, 1913-14, 156-82.

Kwiat, J. J. DREISER and the Graphic Arts. AQ, 3, 1951, 127-41.

—— Dreiser's The Genius and Everett Shinn, the Ash-Can Painter. PMLA, 67, 1952, 15-31. [Dreiser closely followed Shinn as his model for the art career of E. Witla with respect to the incidents of Shinn's career as artist and to the principles of the early 20th century realistic school of art whose theories paralleled those of Dreiser in fiction.]

Newman, F. B. EMERSON and Buonarroti. NEQ, 25, 1952, 524-35.

Martínez, O. Juan del ENCINA: el músico poeta. La Habana, 1951.

Oliver, A. R. The ENCYCLOPEDISTS as Critics of Music. New York, 1947. 227 p.

Tiersot, J. Gluck and the Encyclopedists. Musical Quart., 16, 1930, 336-57.

Clagett, M. The Mediaeval Latin Translations from the Arabic of the Elements of EUCLID, with Special Emphasis on the Versions of Adelard of Bath. Isis, 44, 1953, 16-42.

Brogan, H. O. Fiction and Philosophy in the Education of Tom Jones, Tristram Shandy, and Richard Feverel (FIELDING et al) CE, 14, 1952. [Shows a continuing tradition of educational theory and a rebellion against an over-systematized concept of education.]

Chaumeix, A. Un précurseur de la littérature scientifique (FONTENELLE). Rev. hebdomadaire, Oct. 1910, 512-31.

Battaglia, F. Il concetto di storia nel GENTILE. Firenze, n.d.

Abert, H. GOETHE und die Musik. Stuttgart, 1922. 127 p.

Andrade, E. N. Goethe as a Natural Philosopher. Nature, 164, 1949.

Basserman, D. Goethe als Naturforscher. Berlin, 1947.

Behre, Ellinor H. Goethe and Anatomy. In: Goethe after Two Centuries, ed. by C. Hammer. Baton Rouge, La, 1952, 91-94.

Benn, G. Goethe und die Naturwissenschaften. Zürich, 1949.

Benz, R. Goethe und die romantische Kunst. München, 1949.

Brasch, H. D. Goethe as a Scientist. Australian Journal of Science, 12, 1949, 1-5.

Fischer, H. Goethes Naturwissenschaft. Zürich, 1950.

Fischer, T. Goethes Verhältnis zur Baukunst. München, 1948.

Gadamer, H. G. Goethe und die Philosophie. Leipzig, 1947.

García, A. Goethe frente a la historia. América (Quito), 25, 1950, 30-51. [Goethe and philosophic thought since the Renaissance.]

Gebhardt, M. Goethe als Physiker. Ein Weg zum unbekannten Goethe. Berlin, 1932. 171 p.

Greenhill, J. Goethe's Attitude Towards Music and Contemporary Composers. Proc. Australian Goethe Soc., 1950, 18-26.

Gruenthal, E. & F. Strauss. Abhandlungen zu Goethes Naturwissenschaft. Bern, 1949.

Guttmann, A. Musik in Goethes Wirken und Werken. Berlin, 1949.

Hartner, W. Goethe and the Natural Sciences. In: Goethe and the Modern Age, ed. by A. Bergstraesser. Chicago, 1950.

Henel, H. Goethe und die Naturwissenschaft. JEGP, 48, 1949.

Hetzer, T. Goethe und die bildende Kunst. Leipzig, 1948.

Hocquette, M. Les fantaisies botaniques de Goethe. Lille, 1946.

Kantor, J. R. Goethe's Place in Modern Science. In: Goethe Bicentennial Studies, ed. by H. Meessen. Bloomington, 1950.

Kisch, B. Der Naturforscher Goethe. New York, 1950.

Klages, L. Goethe als Seelenforscher. Zürich, 1949.

Lawson, D. E. Goethe as Philosopher. In: Southern Illinois Goethe Celebration, ed. H. A. Hartwig. Carbondale, Ill., 1952, 15-17.

Lindegren, C. C. Goethe the Biologist. Ibid.

Meinecke, F. Goethe und die Geschichte. In: Die Entstehung des Historismus. München, 1949.

Michéa, R. Les travaux scientifiques de Goethe. Paris, 1943.

Moser, H. J. Goethe und die Musik. Leipzig, 1949.

Nettl, P. Goethe und Mozart, eine Betrachtung. Eblingen, 1949.

Popov, S. Gete v russkoj muzyke. LN, 4-6, 1932, 881-908.

———— Russkaja muzyka na teksty Gete. Bibliografičeskij ukazatel'. LN, 3-6, 1932, 1033-40.

Reich, W. Goethe und die Musik. Zürich, 1949.

Sauerlander, Annemarie. Goethe's Relation to Music. In: Festschrift T. B. Hewitt. Buffalo, 1952, 39-55.

Schuh, W. Goethe-Vertonungen. Ein Verzeichnis. Zürich, 1952. 95 p.

Semper, M. Die geologischen Studien Goethes. Leipzig, 1914.

Stelzer, O. Goethe und die bildende Kunst. Braunschweig, 1949.

Sternfeld, F. W. Goethe and Music: A List of Parodies. BNYPL, 54, 1950 ff.

Willoughby, L. A. Goethe, the Natural Philosopher. In: Goethe After Two Centuries, ed. by C. Hammer. Baton Rouge, La, 1952, 3-19.

Winter, P. Goethe erlebt Kirchenmusik in Italien. Hamburg, 1949.

Wolff, E. B. On Goethe's Reputation as a Scientist in 19th Century England. GLL, 6, 1953, 92-102.

Baskin, V. GOGOL' v muzyke. RM, 5, 1909, 178-89.

Baženov, N. Bolezn' i smert' Gogolja. RM, 1-2, 1902.

Berkov, V. Gogol on Music. (In Russian). Moscow, 1952.

Durylin, S. Gogol' ob iskusstve. Voprosy Filosofii, 3, 1952, 65-79.

Montagu-Nathan, M. Gogol and Music. Monthly Mus. Record, 82, 1952, 92-98.

Šambinago, S. Gogol' i Goja (Goya). RM, 12, 1909, 1-19.

Strakhovsky, L. The Historianism of Gogol. ASEER, 12, 1953, 360-70.

Angus-Butterworth, L. M. GOLDSMITH as Historian. SAQ, 48, 1949.

Montolíu, M. de. El sentido arquitectónico y musical en la obra de GÓNGORA. Bol. Real Acad. Española, 1948, 69-88. [Works out symmetrical types, sonnets in bouquet form, in rocket form, etc.]

Finlay, I. F. Music in GOTFRID's Tristan. Music & Letters, 33, 1952, 50-54.

Elwert, W. T. Geschichtsauffassung und Erzählungstechnik in den historischen Romanen F. D. GUERRAZZIS. Suppl. ZRP, 84, 1935. [Double introduction to unknown art of Guerrazzi.]

O'Flaherty, J. C. Unity and Language: A Study in the Philosophy of J. G. HAMANN. Chapel Hill, 1952.

McCormick, J. HEMINGWAY and History. Western Rev., 17, 1953, 87-98. [He is seen as among the more self-conscious contemporary social historians in fiction whose major theme is that of responsibility.]

Lefebvre, G. Les historiens naturalistes. Les adversaires du rationalisme: HERDER, Vico, Rousseau. Année propédeutique, 3-4, 1952.

Debruges, Suzanne. L'oeuvre de H. HESSE et la psychanalyse. EG, 7, 1953, 252-61. [Psychoanalytical studies assisted Hesse in understanding and presenting the totality of the human personality, but he discarded psychoanalysis after it had served its function. In the later phase of his work he emphasizes the conscious, rather than the subconscious, elements in man.]

Thalmann, Marianne. E. T. A. HOFF-MANS Wirklichkeitsmärchen. JEGP, 51, 1952, 473-91. [Demonstrates in detail the threads linking the art of Hoffmann with the opera bouffa, the Viennese popular opera of the 18th century, and particularly with Mozart.]

Wellesz, E. HOFMANNSTHAL and Strauss. Music & Letters, 33, 1952, 239-42.

Moore, R. E. HOGARTH's Literary Relationships. Minnesota U.P. 1953. 202 p.

Drees, Thea. HÖLDERLINs Bild von der Geschichte. Die Pforte, 1, 1948.

Hoffmeister, J. Hölderlin und die Philosophie. Leipzig, 1944. 172 p.

Labordus, L. W. De astronomische mythen in de griekse literatuur van HOMERos tot Aratos. Amsterdam, 1945.

Haight, Elizabeth H. HORACE on Art: Ut pictura poesis. CJ, 47, 1952.

Clark, H. H. The Role of Science in the Thought of W. D. HOWELLS. Transactions Wisconsin Acad. of Sciences, 42, 1953, 263-303.

Bombaci, A. La dottrina storiografica di IBN HALDUN. Annali Scuola Normale Sup. Pisa, 15, 1946, 159-85.

Marçais, G. Les idées d'Ibn Khaldoûn sur l'histoire. Bull. des Etudes arabes, Jan. 1941.

Hall, V. JOYCE's Use of Da Ponte and Mozart's Don Giovanni. PMLA, 66, 1951, 78-84. Don Giovanni, both text and music, as a running motif in Bloom's mind in Joyce's Ulysses.

Reichert, H. W. The Basic Concepts in the Philosophy of Gottfried KELLER. Chapel Hill, 1949.

Beaver, J. LANIER's Use of Science 'for Poetic Imagery. AL, 24, 1953, 520-33.

Glicksberg, C. I. D. H. LAWRENCE and Science. Scientific Monthly, 73, 1951.

Wais, K. D. H. Lawrence, Valéry, Rilke in ihrer Auseinandersetzung mit den bildenden Künsten. GRM, Oct. 1952, 301-24.

Errante, V. LENAU e i Canti dei Giunchi. Bologna, 1922. [The influence of music on poetry analyzed.]

Anderson, I. E. LEONARDO y Freud. Sur (Buenos-Aires), 217-18, 1952, 64-66.

Cecchi, E. Leonardo e Baudelaire. Corriere della Sera (Milano), 29.II.1952.

Frattini, A. Filosofia e poesia in Leonardo. Responsabilità del Sapere, 30, 1952, 324-36.

Jaspers, K. Lionardo als Philosoph. Bern, 1953. 80 p.

Mautner, F. H. LICHTENBERG as an Interpreter of Hogarth. MLQ, 13, 1952, 65-80.

Solari, A. Lo storicismo di LIVIO. Rendiconti Accad. dei Lincei, Roma, 6, 1951, 213-17.

Kunstmann, J. G. LUTHER's Frau Musica. Lutheran Scholar, 8, 1951, 128-30.

Munro, T. The Afternoon of a Faun and the Interrelation of the Arts. JAAC, 10, 1951, 95-111 & Revue d'Esthétique, 5, 1952. [Development and relations: MALLARMÉ's poem, Manet's illustrations, Debussy's tone-poem, and Diaghlieff's ballet.]

Beerli, C. A. Le peintre-poète Nicolas MANUEL et l'évolution sociale de son temps. Genève, 1953, 352 p.

Simone, J. F. de. MANZONI and the Fine Arts. Italica 28, 1951, 270-78.

Parr, J. Tamburlaine's Malady and other Essays on Astrology in Elizabethan Drama. (MARLOWE). Alabama U.P. 1953. 158 p.

Ribner, I. The Idea of History in Marlowe's Tamburlaine. ELH, 20, 1953, 251-66.

Hammer, W. MELANCHTHON, Inspirer of the Study of Astronomy. Popular Astronomy, 59, 1951-52, 308-19.

Carpenter, Nan C. The Place of Music in L'Allegro and Il Penseroso (MILTON). UTQ, 22, 1953, 354-67.

Finney, Gretchen. A Musical Background for Lycidas. HLQ, 15, 1952, 325-50.

Myers, R. M. Handel and Milton. Tulane Studies in English, 3, 1952, 93-124.

Olshausen, W. Hardenbergs Beziehungen zur Naturwissenschaft seiner Zeit (NOVALIS). Leipzig, 1905.

Salet, P. OMAR KHAYYAM, savant et philosophe. Paris, 1927.

Livingstone, L. ORTEGA Y GASSET's Philosophy of Art. PMLA, 67, 1952, 609-54.

Acosta, T. PALMA y la historia. CA, 67, 1953, 211-13. [On his poetic interpretation of history.]

Pease, O. A. PARKMAN's History: the Historian as Literary Artist. Yale U.P. 1953, 86 p.

Lamprecht, F. Zur Theorie der humanistischen Geschichtsschreibung: Mensch und Geschichte bei Francesco **PATRIZI**. Zürich, 1950.

Broos, H. J. M. **PLATO** and Art: A New Analysis of the Philebus. Mnemosyne (Leiden), 4, 1951, 113-28.

Bury, R. G. Plato and History. CQ, 45, 1951, 86-93.

Murley, C. Plato and the Arts. CB, 27, 1950, 13-14.

Bonaparte, Marie. Edgar **POE**, étude psychanalytique. Paris, 1933.

Pruette, Lorine. A Psychoanalytic Study of E. A. Poe. Am. Journal of Psychology, 31, 1920.

Hay, D. **POLYDORE VERGIL**, Renaissance Historian and Man of Letters. London, 1952. (Cf. Erasmus, 1953.)

Hier, Florence. La musique dans l'oeuvre de Marcel **PROUST**. Columbia U.P. 1933. [Points out how music interprets eternity as well as time.]

Beljaev, M. Otraženie jubileja Puškina v izobrazitel'nom iskusstve. **PUŠKIN** Vremennik, 6, 1941, 497-523.

Ejges, I. Musyka v žizni i tvorčestve Puškina. Moscow, 1937, 287 p.

Glumov, A. Muzykal'nyj mir Puškina. Moscow, 1950. [His relation to music and folk music of his time.]

Ljackij, E. Puškin-povestvovatel' v Istorii Pugačevskogo bunta. In: Puškinskij Sbornik, Russkij Naučnyj Institut, Praha, 1929, 265-96 (With French résumé).

Vernadskij, G. Puškin kak istorik. Učenye Zapiski Russkoj Učebnoj Kollegii, Praha, 2, 1924, 61-79.

Zibel', E. Puškinskie romansy sovetskix kompozitorov. Puškin Vremennik, 6, 1941, 523-25.

Carpenter, Nan C. **RABELAIS** and Music. Chapel Hill, 1954, 149 p. [Musical analysis also helvs to establish authenticity of Book Five.]

Lapp, J. C. Three Attitudes toward Astrology: Rabelais, Montaigne, and Pontus de Tyard. PMLA, 64, 1949.

Mérigot, L. Rabelais et l'alchimie. Cahiers d'Hermès, 1, 1947.

Courthion, P. **RAMUZ** et Cézanne. Cahiers de la Quinzaine, ed. by M. Péguy, 17, Paris, 1926,189-200. [Not more than a causerie.]

Faller, M. Johann F. **REICHARDT** und die Anfänge der musikalischen Journalistik. Kassel, 1929, 101 p.

Blanckenhagen, P. H. von. Picasso and

RILKE: La famille des saltimbanques. Measure, 1, 1950, 165-85.

Closs, A. The Influence of Art on Rilke's Poetic Vision. RLM, 2, 1951.

Jansen, B. Het relief Hermes-Euridice-Orpheus en Rilke's gedicht Orpheus-Euridice-Hermes. NP, 22, 1948.

Kohlschmidt, W. Rilke e Rodin. RLM, 2, 1951.

Rilke, Clara (ed) Rilkes Briefe über Cézanne. Wiesbaden, 1952. 54 p. [The letters are from the year 1907 and were taken from two quite inaccessible volumes. The fateful meeting with Cézanne was for him "volle Bestätigung und Bezug." In penetrating descriptions of certain paintings Rilke reveals deep insight into the essence of the Kunstding.]

Graaf, D. A. de. Arthur **RIMBAUD** en de muziek. Mens en Melodie, 7, 1952, 252-57.

Comettant, O. De l'influence de la musique sur le style littéraire. In: J. J. **ROUSSEAU** jugé par les Français d'aujourd'hui. Paris, 1890, 404-12.

Jansen, A. Jean-Jacques Rousseau als Musiker. Berlin, 1884. 482 p.

Masson, P. M. Les idées de Rousseau sur la musique. Revue musicale 8, 1912.

Pochon, A. J.-J. Rousseau musicien et la critique; essai de mise au point. Montreux, 1940, 53 p.

Pougin, A. Jean-Jacques Rousseau musicien. Paris, 1901, 141 p.

Neumann, A. R. Philipp Otto **RUNGE** and Music. GR, 27, 1952, 165-72.

Girard, R. L'histoire dans l'oeuvre de **SAINT-JEAN PERSE**. RR, 44, 1953, 47-55.

Nevins, A. **SANDBURG** as Historian. Illinois Hist. Soc. Jour., 45, 1953, 337-72.

Boase, T. S. R. Illustrations of **SHAKE-SPEARE**'s Plays in the 17th and 18th Centuries. JWI, 10, 1947.

Flatter, R. Sigmund Freud on Shakespeare. SQ, 2, 1951.

Jones, E. A Psychoanalytic Study of Hamlet. In: Essays in Applied Psychoanalysis. London, 1923.

Parr, J. Shakespeare's Artistic Use of Astrology. In: Tamburlaine's Malady and Other Essays. Alabama U.P., 1953, 57-69.

Stearns, M. W. Hamlet and Freud. CE, 10, 1949.

Stoll, E. E. A Freudian Detective's Shakespeare. MP, 48, 1950.

Withington, R. Why Put Freud into Hamlet? CE, 10, 1949.

Banerjee, J. The Philosophy of SHELLEY. Calcutta Review, 30-31, 1929.

McCullough, J. W. Robert SOUTHEY's Theories and Concepts of History. Diss. U. of N. Carolina, 1952.

Gottfried, R. The Pictorial Element in SPENSER's Poetry. ELH, 19, 1952, 203-13.

Streicher, S. SPITTELER und Boecklin. 2 vols. Zürich, 1927.

Magnani, L. STENDHAL e la musica della felicità. Rass. musicale, 22, 1952, 97-112.

Uppvall, A. J. STRINDBERG in the Light of Psychoanalysis. SS, 21, 1949.

Benson, A. B. SWEDENBORG as a Scientist. Bull. Amer. Swedish Inst, 6, 1951, 16-30.

Colli, L. La musicalità e il colore nella Gerusalemme. Napoli, 1936. [Study of an important aspect of TASSO's style.]

Watson, J. A. THACKERAY and Music. Monthly Musical Record, 82, 1952, 60-66.

Anrich, Elsmarie. Gross göttlich Ordnung. THOMAS VON AQUIN, Paracelsus, Novalis und die Astrologie. Tübingen, 1951, 111 p.

Stock, L. Die Geschichtsauffassung bei THUKYDIDES und Sallust. Diss., Freiburg i. Br., 1946.

Annenkov, P. Istoričeskie i éstetičeskie voprosy v romane gr. L.N.Tolstogo "Vojna i mir." (TOLSTOY). VE, 2, 1868, 774-95.

Jovanović, M. O moralnom metodu Lava Tolstoja. LMS, 1951, 469-77.

Kareev, N. Istoričeskaja filosofija v romane gr. L.N. Tolstogo "Vojna i mir." VE, 7, 1887, 227-69.

Rubinštejn, M. Filosofija istorii v romane L.N. Tolstogo "Vojna i mir." RM, 7, 1911, 78-103.

Jedlicka, G. Paul VALERY und die bildenden Künste. Festschrift T. Spoerri. Zürich, 1950.

Seznec, J. Literary Inspiration in VAN GOGH. Magazine of Art, 43, 1950, 282-88.

Moser, H. J. Didonis novissima verba in der Musik. Ein Beitrag zum Nachleben VERGILs. Gymn, 58, 1951, 322-26.

Alexander, I. W. VOLTAIRE and Metaphysics. Philosophy, 19, 1944, 19-48.

Libby, Margaret S. The Attitude of Voltaire to Magic and the Sciences. New York, 1935. 299 p.

Pellissier, G. Voltaire philosophe. Paris, 1908. 304 p.

Saunders, R. M. Voltaire's View of the Meaning of History. UTQ, 22, 1953, 44-54.

Straeten, E. van der. Voltaire musicien. Paris, 1878. 299 p.

Wade, I. O. Voltaire's Micromégas: A Study in the Fusion of Science, Myth, and Art. Princeton U.P., 1950.

Beaver, J. Walt WHITMAN—Poet of Science. New York, 1951.

Bergman, H. Whitman on Beethoven and Music. MLN, 66, 1951, 556-57. [Excerpts from an unpublished article by Mrs. A. W. Moore on "Walt Whitman and music: Personal reminiscences." Mrs. Moore often played the "Appassionata" for Whitman, who heard it as a struggle between the old and the new. "The Poet is overcome, the Present triumphant, the Future assured!"]

Roaten, D. WÖLFFLIN's Principles Applied to Lope's Fuente ovejuna. Bull. of the Comediantes, 4, 1952.

———— & Sánchez Escribano, F. Wölfflin's Principles in Spanish Drama 1500-1700. New York, 1952. 200 p.

Read, H. WORDSWORTH's Philosophical Faith. Sewanee Rev., 58, 1950.

Glicksberg, C. I. William Butler YEATS and the Hatred of Science. Prairie Schooner, 28, 1953, 29-36.

García de Franca, M. ZOLA y Rodin. Dos formas de una misma idea. La Habana, 1946. [Stress on everyday work, love, woman, solitude, suffering.]

Arens, H. Stefan ZWEIG und die Musik. Musica, 6, 1952, 59-62.

B. ORIENT, ANTIQUITY, JUDAISM, ISLAM

I. THE ORIENT.

Generalities

(See also genres—e.g. The Japanese drama, Vietnam prose, Moroccan poetry, etc.)

Anderson, G. L. The Study of Oriental

Languages and Literatures in American Colleges and Universities. Yb, 3, 1954, 35-43.

Baranowski, B.   The Knowledge of the Orient in Poland before the 18th Century. (In Polish.) Lodz, 1950.

Braden, C. S.   The Novelist Discovers the Orient. Far Eastern Quarterly, 7, 1947-48.

Cansinos-Assens, R.   Los orientalismos en nuestra literatura.   In: Los témas literarios y su interpretación. Madrid, n.d.

Christy, A. E. (ed.).   The Asian Legacy and American Life. New York, 1945.

Dinet, E. & Ben Ibrahim, S.   L'Orient vu de l'Occident. Paris, n.d.

Ebersolt, J.   Orient et Occident.   Recherches sur les influences byzantines et orientales en France pendant les Croisades. Paris, 1929.

Fano, G.   Teasofia orientale e filosofia greca. Bibl. di cultura, 33. Firenze, 1949, 230 p.

Fernández y Gonzáles, F.   Influencia de las lenguas y letras orientales en la cultura de los pueblos de la Peninsula Ibérica. Discurso ante la Real Academia Española. Madrid, 1894.

Ferry, F. de.   Trois cents ans de livres français sur l'Extrême-Orient (1651-1951.) France-Asie, 8, 1952.

Filliozat, J.   L'humanisme européen et les civilisations d'Extrême-Asie: La découverte spirituelle de l'Extrême-Asie par l'humanisme européen. BAGB, Oct., 1953, 80-96.

Grottanelli, V. L.   Asiatic Influences on Somali Culture. Ethnos, 12, 1947.

Jannaccone, S.   Polemiche nella letteratura cristiana contro le religioni d'Oriente. Aevum, 1948.

Machabey, A.   Lyrique orientale et lyrique occidentale du haut moyen âge. Romania, 74, 1953.

Nyberg, H. S.   Das Studium des Orients und die europäische Kultur. ZDMG, 103, 1953.

Oliver, E. S.   The Orient and American Literature. Korean Survey, 2, 1953, 10-13.

Peeters, P.   Orient et Byzance. Le tréfonds oriental de l'hagiographie byzantine. Bruxelles, 1950. 236 p.

Potanin, G.   Vostočnye osnovy russkogo bylinnogo éposa. VE, 3-5, 1896.

Sacy, S. de.   La Renaissance orientale. MF, April, 1951.

Saunders, J. J.   The Orient and the Graeco-Roman World before Islam. History, 25, 1940.

Shubart, W.   Europa und die Seele des Ostens. Pfullingen, 1951. 350 p.

Schurhammer, G.   Die zeitgenössischen Quellen zur Geschichte Portugiesisch-Asiens und seiner Nachbarländer (Ostafrika, Abessinien, Arabien, Persien, Vorder-und Hinterindien, Malaiischer Archipel, Philippinen, China und Japan) zur Zeit des Hl. Franz Xaver (1538-52). Leipzig, 1932.

Tustes, A.   Les sources orientales des légendes poétiques. Esprit français, 10, 1933.

Wais, K.   Zur Berührung der altorientalischen und europäischen Erzählungsdichtung: Ulikummi, Hrungnin, Armilus und Verwandte.   In: Edda, Skalden, Saga: Festschrift F. Genzmer. Heidelberg, 1952.

Whymant, A. N. J.   The Study and Translation of Far Eastern Poetry. Japan Mag., 13, 1922.

China, Japan, Korea, Siam, Siberia, Tibet, Vietnam

Anon.   La langue poétique viêtnamienne au XVIe siècle et l'influence chinoise. France-Asie, 7, 1951.

────── Pogled na kitajsko književnost in umjetnost. Tov., 6, 1950.

Appleton, W. W.   A Cycle of Cathay: the Chinese Vogue in England during the Seventeenth and Eighteenth Centuries. Columbia U.P., 1951. (Cf. CL, 1952).

Azevedo, N. de.   O Chi-Klng [of Confucius] e os Cancioneiros Medievais. In: A arte literária na idade média. Porto, 1947.

Baty, T.   The Literary Introduction of Japan to Europe. Monumenta Nipponica, 7, 1951.

Blyth, R. H.   Zen in English Literature and Oriental Classics. Tokyo, 1948.

Bodde, D.   Chinese Ideas in the West. Washington, 1948.

Brion, M.   La sagesse nous vient de la Chine. NL, 24.III.1949.

Brüning, A.   Der Einfluss Chinas und Japans auf die europäische Kunst. Velhagen & Klasings Monatshefte, 15, 1900.

Chatley, H.   The Origin and Diffusion of Chinese Culture. Asiatic Review, 44, 1948, 417-22.

Čivrny, L. Heroic Korea in the Culture of Czechoslovakia. (In Czech). Nový Život, 7, 1952.

Cranmer-Byng, L. The Vision of Asia. An Interpretation of Chinese Art and Culture. London, 1949.

Ferrand, G. Relations de voyages et textes géographiques arabes, persanes et turcs relatifs à l'Extrême-Orient du XIIe au XVIIIe siècles. 2 vols. Paris, 1913-14.

Figueiredo, F. de. De re japonica: Evoluçao do japonismo literário português desde Fernão Mendes Pinto a Wenceslau de Morais. Vasco da Gama, 1, 1925-26, 202-19.

Gaspardonne, E. Les lettres chinoises au Japon. Paris, 1933.

Gulyam, G. Navoj and our Era. IANUz, 5, 1948. [In Uzbek, with résumé in Russian.]

Hallberg, I. L'Extrême Orient dans la littérature et la cartographie de l'Occident des XIIIe, XIVe, et XVe siècles. Gotenborg, 1906.

Hightower, J. R. Chinese Literature in the Context of World Literature. CL, 5, 1953, 117-24.

Hoffmann, H. Die Qarluq in der tibetischen Literatur. Oriens, 3, 1950, 190-208.

Keene, D. Japanese Literature: An Introduction for Western Readers. London, 1953.

Liu Wu-chi. The Original Orphan of China. CL, 5, 1953, 193-212.

Matsuo, K. (et al.) L'influence de la littérature nippone sur les lettres étrangères. In: Histoire de la littérature japonaise des temps archaïques à 1935. Paris, 1935, 180-84.

Maverick, L. A. China, a Model for Europe. I. China's Economy and Government admired by Seventeenth and Eighteenth Century Europeans. II. Despotism in China, a Translation of François Quesnay's Le despotisme de la Chine, Paris, 1767. San Antonio (Texas), 1946.

Miller, R. A. Some Japanese Influences on Chinese Classical Scholarship of the Ch'ing Period. JAOS, 72, 1952.

Nykl, A. R. Los primeros mártires del Japón. HR, 10, 1942, 160-63.

Pelliot, P. L'origine des relations de la France avec la Chine: Le premier voyage de "L'Amphitrite" en Chine. Paris, 1930.

Potanin, G. Mongol'skoe skazanie o Gésér-Xane. Po voprosu o proisxoždenii russkix bylin. VE, 9, 1890, 121-58.

Rose, E. Die Romantik und China. Geistige Arbeit, 5, 1938.

*——— China und die Spätromantik. Mitt. d. Akad. z. Wissenschaft, Erforschung & z. Pflege des Deutschtums, 15, 1940.

——— China as a Symbol of Reaction in Germany, 1830-80. CL, 3, 1951.

Rothbart, W. Der Einfluss der japanischen Dichtkunst auf die deutsche. Ost-Asien, 10, 1907-08.

Sakanishi, S. (et al.) A List of Translations of Japanese Drama into English, French and German. Washington, 1935.

Sirén, O. China and the Gardens of Europe in the Eighteenth Century. New York, 1951.

Teele, R. E. Through a Glass Darkly: A Study of English Translations of Chinese Poetry. Ann Arbor, 1949.

Têng, Ssu-Yu. Chinese Influence on the Western Examination System. Harvard Journal of Asiatic Studies, 7, 1943.

Tixonov, N. Nizami i Navoj. DN, 15, 1947.

Venne, P. China und die Chinesen in der neuren englischen und amerikanischen Literatur. Zürich, 1951.

Xamidov, X. On the Question of Navoj's Influence on the Literatures of the Oriental Peoples. IANUz, 5, 1948. [In Uzbek, with Russian résumé.]

Yamagiwa, J. K. Comparative, General and World Literature in Japan. Yb, 2, 1953, 28-39.

Australia, Burma, India, Indonesia, Philippines

Aquarone, J.-B. L'aventure portugaise dans les mers de l'Inde. BAGB, 3, 1953. [One of a series by different authors entitled L'humanisme européen et les civilisations d'Extrême-Asie; la découverte spirituelle de l'Extrême-Asie par l'humanisme européen.]

Awasthi, G. C. Views of Scholars regarding the Vedas. Journal Ganganatha Jha Research Institute, 6, 1949, 151-55.

Baião, O. (ed.) Itinerários de Índia a Portugal por terra. Coimbra, 1923.

Bamboat, Zénobie. Les voyageurs français

dans l'Inde aux XVIIe et XVIIIe siècles. Société de l'histoire des colonies fr., Paris, 1933. 197 p.

Bigandet, P. Legend of the Burmese Buddha, called Gaudama. Journal of the Indian Archipelago, 6—8, 1852-54.

Boxer, C. R. Fidalgos in the Far East, 1550-1770: Facts and Fancy in the History of Macao. The Hague, 1948.

Brochado, C. Que significa a Índia para os Portugueses. Lisboa, 1954.

Ch'en, K. S. A Study of the Svagata Story in the "Divyāvadāna" in its Sanskrit, Pali, Tibetan, and Chinese Versions. Harvard Journal of Asiatic Studies, 9, 1947, 207-314.

Connor, J. P. The Ramayana in Burma. Journal Burma Research Soc., 15, 1925.

Coomaraswamy, A. K. Recollection, Indian and Platonic. JAOS, Suppl., 64, 1944.

Dhani Nivat, Siamese Versions of the Panji Romance. In: India Antiqua. Festschrift Vogel, Leiden, 1947, 95-101.

Gray, B. Indian Influences on the Culture of South-East Asia. Asiatic Review, 48, 1952.

Harkare, G. R. Sanskrit under Mohammedan Patronage. Islamic Culture, 26, 1952.

Hümmerich, F. Quellen und Untersuchungen zur Fahrt der ersten Deutschen nach dem portugiesischen Indien 1505/6. München, 1918.

Jhaveri, K. M. Buddhism in Gujarati Literature. In: B. C. Law Volume, pt. 2. Poona, 1946.

Kunstmann, F. Die Fahrt der ersten Deutschen nach dem portugiesischen Indien. München, 1861.

—— Die Kenntniss Indiens im fünfzehnten Jahrhundert. München, 1863.

Kya, Ba & G. H. Luce. A Dictionary of Burmese Authors in Translation. Journal Burma Research Soc., 10, 1920.

Lubac, H. de & H. Bernard-Maître. L'humanisme européen et les civilisations d'Extrême-Asie: La découverte du bouddhisme. BAGB, Oct., 1953, 97-112.

Mayrhofer, M. Die Indus-Kulturen und ihre westlichen Beziehungen. Saeculum, 2, 1951, 300-05.

Medhi, K. R. The Brajavali Literature in

Assam. Journal of Assam Research Society, 9, 1942, 57-72.

Melzer, F. Indische Weisheit und christliche Erkenntnis. Tübingen, 1948. 266 p.

Muharjo, A. Hindu Indian Influence on Indonesian Civilization. New Review (Calcutta), Sept., 1949.

Ronkel, P. S. van. The Ramayana in Malay. Acta Orientalia, 7, 1929.

Sarkar, H. B. Indian Influences on the Literature of Java and Bali. Calcutta, 1934.

Schwab, R. Connaissance de l'Inde (Note bibliographique). MF, Dec., 1951.

Solov'ev, V. Buddijskoe nastroenie v poézii. VE, 5-6, 1894.

Sutherland, B. On Australian Literature. Meanjin, 9 (Melbourne), 1950, 45-49.

—— An American Looks at Australian Literature. Ibid. 11, 1952, 152-56.

Winstedt, R. The Malay Version of the Ramayana. In: B. C. Law Volume, pt. 2, Poona, 1946.

Yabes, L. Y. The Filipino Essay in English (1910-41). Philippine Social Science and Humanities Review, 15, 1950.

Yule, H. & A. C. Burnell. Hobson-Jobson: A Glossary of Colloquial Anglo-Indian Words and Phrases, and of Kindred Terms, Etymological, Historical, Geographical and Discursive. London, 1903.

The Islam (especially Arabia)

Alonso, M. A. Humayn traducido el latin por Ibn Dâwûd y Domingo Gondisalvo. Al-Andalus, 16, 1951.

Alverny, M. T. d'. L'introduction d'Avicenne en Orient. In: Millénaire d'Avicienne. La Revue du Caire, June, 1951.

—— & G. Vajda. Marc de Tolède, traducteur d'Ibn Tûmart. Al-Andalus, 16, 1951.

Asín Palacios, M. L'Espagne et l'Islam. In: La mission de l'Espagne, Paris, 1941, 268-87.

Ballard, J. (ed.) L'Islam et l'Occident. Paris, 1947. 394 p.

Bannerth, E. Islam in Modern Urdu Poetry. Anthropos, 37-40, 1942-45.

Casimiro, A. Lisboa Mourisca, 1147-1947. Vila Nova de Famalicão, 1947.

Chaplyn, Marjorie A. Le roman mauresque en France de Zayde au Dernier Abencérage. Nemours, 1928. 173 p.

Cohen, G. Le problème des origines arabes de la poésie provençale médiévale. Acad. Roy. de Belgique, Bull. Classe des Lettres, 32, 1946.

Comfort, W. W. The Moors in Spanish Popular Poetry before 1600. Haverford Essays, (Pa.), 1909, 273-303.

—————— The Saracens in Christian Poetry. Dublin Rev., July, 1911.

Deferrari, H. A. The Sentimental Moor in Spanish Literature before 1600. Philadelphia, 1927.

Denomy, A. J. Concerning the Accessibility of Arabic Influences to the Earliest Provençal Troubadours. MS, 15, 1953.

Domingues, G. História luso-árabe: Episódios e figuras meridionais. Lisboa, 1945.

Dulsey, B. & E. H. Mueller. Some Common Spanish 'al-' Nouns of Arabic Origin. Hisp., 36, 1953, 319-20.

Emrich, D. B. M. The Avicenna Legend. Diss. Harvard, 1937.

*Gabrieli, F. Les Mille et Une Nuits dans la culture européenne. Cahiers de l'Est, 6, 1949, 72-85.

Ganz, P. F. The Cancionerillo mozárabe and the Origin of the Middle-High German Frauenlied. MLR, 1953.

García-Gómez, E. Poesía arabigo-andaluza. Breve sintesis histórica. Madrid, 1952.

Goichon, Amélie M. La philosophie d'Avicenne et son influence en Europe médiévale. Paris, 1951. 158 p. (Cf. Universitas, 1954.)

Jodogne, O. Encore sur l'origine arabe de la poésie provençale. Lettres romanes, 4, 1950, 237-38.

Kračkovskij, I. Russkij perevod Korana v rukopisi XVIII veka. In: Festschrift Orlov, Leningrad, 219-26.

Le Gentil, P. Le virelai et le villancico: Le problème des origines arabes. Institut Français au Portugal, 9, Paris, 1954.

Lévi-Provençal, E. Poésie arabe d'Espagne et poésie d'Europe médiévale. In: Islam d'Occident, Etudes d'histoire médiévale. Paris, 1948.

López-Estrada, F. Dos tratados de los siglos XVI y XVII sobre los mozárabes. Al-Andalus, 16, 1951, 331-61.

—————— Miguel Asín Palacios. Yb, 2, 1953, 48-49.

MacDonald, D. B. A Bibliographical and

Literary Study of the First Appearance of the Arabian Nights in Europe. Library Quarterly, 2, 1932.

Massignon, L. Avicenne et les influences orientales. In: Millénaire d'Avicenne. Revue du Caire, June, 1951.

Menéndez Pidal, R. El habla de la España mozárabe y los orígenes del español. In: El idioma español en sus primeros tiempos. Buenos Aires, 1942, 9-16.

Moody, E. A. Galileo and Avempace: The Dynamics of the Leaning Tower Experiment. JHI, 12, 1951.

Murari, R. Il De causis e la sua fortuna nel Medio Evo. GSLI, 34, 1899.

Nimer, M. Influências orientais na língua portuguêsa: Os vocábulos árabes, arabizados, persas e turcos. São Paulo, 1943.

Nikitine, B. La littérature des Musulmans en U.R.S.S. Revue des Etudes Islamiques, 3, 1934.

Nykl, A. R. Notes on Palmer's Translation of the Qur'ân. JAOS, 56, 1936, 77-84.

—————— Las inscripciones árabes de la Alhambra y del Generalife. Al-Andalus, 4, 1936, 174-94.

—————— Algunas inscripciones árabes de Portugal. Ibid. 5, 1940, 399-411.

—————— As inscrições árabes no Museu Etnológico do Dr. José Leite de Vasconcelos. Ethnos, 2, 1942.

—————— Arabic Inscriptions in Portugal. In: Ars Islamica, 11, 1946, 167-83.

—————— Hispano-Arabic Poets in 1001 Nights. In: Festschrift Archer M. Huntington, Wellesley, 1952, 477-90.

Ottolenghi, R. Un lontano precursore di Dante: Ben Gabirol. Lugano, 1910.

Petrov, D. Odna iz ispano-arabskix problem. Zapiski Kollegii Vostokovedenija . . . Akademii Nauk SSSR, 2, 1926, 73-90.

Pires de Lima, J. A. Mouros, Judeus e Negros na história de Portugal. Porto, 1940.

Ryckmans, J. L'Arabie chez les auteurs classiques, d'Hérodote à Agatharchide de Cnide. RBPh, 1948.

Schack, W. & Sarah. 1001 Nights in the Yiddish Theater: From Goldfaden to Thomashefsky. Commentary, 12, 1951.

Smith, H. L. The Phonology of Arabic Loan Words in Old Spanish. Diss. U. of Minnesota, 1953.

Sommerfeld, M. Die Reisebeschreibungen

der deutschen Jerusalempilger im ausgehenden Mittelalter. DVLG, 2. 1924, 816-51.

Spitzer, L. The Mozarabic Lyric and Theodor Frings' Theories. CL, 4, 1952.

Stern, S. M. Hispano-Arabic Poetry. Atlante, 2, 1954.

Zardoya, Concha. España en su história. Cristianos, moros y judios. Ateneo, 27, 1951.

Armenia, Babylon, Persia, Turkey

Anon. Die Firdusi-Feier in Berlin. ZDMG, 88, 1934.

Altheim, F. Zarathustra und Alexander der Grosse. Parola del Passato (Napoli), 6, 1951, 321-37 & Gymnasium, 58, 1951.

Arberry, A. J. (ed.) The Legacy of Persia. Oxford U.P., 1953. 421 p.

Bataillon, M. Nouvelles recherches sur le Viaje de Turquía [published 1557, attributed to Cristóbal de Villalón and to Dr. Angrés Laguna]. RPh, 5, 1951.

Bertels, E. E. Literature in Persian in Central Asia. (In Russian). Sovetskoie Vostokovedeniie, 5, 1948, 199-228.

Burian, O. Interest of the English in Turkey as Reflected in English Literature of the Renaissance. Oriens, 5, 1952, 209-29.

Gail, Marzieh. Persia and the Victorians. London, 1951.

Ghani, M. A. Pre-Mughal Persian in Hindustan. Allahabad, 1942.

Grafenauer, I. The Theme of the Turks before Vienna in Slovene Folksongs, 1529-1683. (In Slovene, résumé in German). SIR, 1951.

Knight, F. J. Cumaean Gates: A Reference of the Sixth Aeneid to Initiation Pattern. Oxford, 1936. [Parallels between Grail-Quest and Gilgamesh-Epic.]

Macler, F. Arménie et Chah-Nameh. Journal Asiatique, 228, 1936.

Nicholson, R. A. Sanā't, of Ghazni: A Persian Forerunner of Dante. Transactions of the Bombay Branch of the Royal Asiatic Society, 1943 and Towyn-on-Sea (Wales), 1944.

Orbeli, I. (et al.). Ferdousi, 934-1934. Leningrad, 1937. 220 p.

Pypin, A. Iranskie istočniki russkoj byliny. VE, 6, 1892, 702-42.

Rice, W. G. Turk, Moor and Persian in English Literature from 1550 to 1660. Diss. Harvard, 1926.

Ringbom, L. I. Graltempel und Paradies. Beziehungen zwischen Iran und Europa im Mittelalter. Stockholm, 1951.

Rossi, E. La fonte turca della novella poetica albanese 'Erveheja' di Muhamet Çami (secolo XVIII-XIX) e il tema di 'Florence de Rome' e di 'Crescentia.' Oriente Moderno, 28, 1948, 143-53.

Schaeder, H. H. Firdusi und die Deutschen. ZDMG, 88, 1934.

Schwartz, J. Les conquérants perses et la littérature égyptienne. Bull. de l'Institut fr. d'Archéologie orientale (Cairo), 48, 1948-49.

Spencer, T. Turks and Trojans in the Renaissance. MLR, 47, 1952, 330-33.

Vajpeyl, A. Persian Influence on Hindi. Calcutta, 1936.

Wendel, C. Das griechische Buchwesen unter babylonischem Einfluss. F&F, 1949.

Yohannan, J. D. Persian Poetry in America: A Two Hundred Year History. Iran Review, 1, 1949, 41-49.

—— The Persian Poetry Fad in England, 1700-1825. CL, 4, 1952.

Africa

(See also Thematology: Negro, 129-30, 710-11, 774, 832)

Anon. Le patrimoine littéraire marocain. Voix Nationale, 22.IV.1940.

Amin H'assoûna, M. L'influence intellectuelle de l'expédition française en Egypte, Al-Kitab (Cairo), March, 1951.

Beccari, C. Notizia e saggi di opere e documenti inediti riguardanti la storia di Etiopia durante i secoli XVI, XVII e XVIII. Roma, 1903.

Collins, H. R. His Image in Ebony: the African in British Fiction during the Age of Imperialism. Diss. U. of Illinois, 1952.

Derchain, P. J. Les Grecs et les dieux égyptiens en Grèce, dans les îles de la mer Égée et les cités ioniennes à l'époque hellénistique. Diss. Liége, RBPh, 1950.

Faria e Maia, C. de. As viagens dos portugueses na África e na Ásia: Relação cronológica das suas principais viagens terrestres, antigas e modernas. Bol. Sociedade de Geografia de Lisboa, 51, 1933.

Flores Morales, A. Africa a través del pensamiento español. Madrid, 1949.

Glanville, S. R. K. The Growth and Nature of Egyptology. Cambridge U.P., 1947.

James, G. M. Did the Greeks Confiscate the Legacy of the African Continent? New York, 1953.

Lebel, R. Le Maroc dans la littérature française depuis le Protectorat. Legionnaire Marocain, 1.VII.1942.

—— L'exotisme marocain dans quelques romans anglais contemporains. Aquedal, April, 1943, 76-78.

Littmann, E. Abessinische und semitische Poesie. ZDMG, 84, 1930.

Mendonça, R. A influência africana no Português do Brasil. Porto, 1948.

Moussa, S. Intellectual Currents in Egypt. Middle Eastern Affairs, 2, 1951, 267-72.

Palumbo, A. L'africanità nei primi apologeti. Nuovo Didaskaleion (Catania), 1947.

Pirenne, J. Religion égyptienne et philosophie grecque. Journal of Juristic Papyrology, 4, 1950.

Schwartz, J. Les conquérants perses et la littérature egyptienne. Bull. de l'Inst. d'archéologie orientale, 48, 1949.

Senghor, L. S. L'âme africaine et la poésie. ACUM, 3, 1948-50.

Tailliart, C. L'Algérie dans la littérature française. Essai de bibliographie méthodique et raisonnée jusqu'en l'année 1924. Paris, 1925. 466 p.

Vel'tman, S. Kolonial'nye siluéty (Afrika i riffy vo francuzskoj xudožestvennoj literature). Novyj Vostok, 13-14, 1926, 364-81.

Walle, B. van de. La transmission des textes littéraires egyptiens. Bruxelles, 1948.

Western Authors and Works Influenced by the East

Suolahti, J. On the Persian Sources Used by the Byzantine Historian AGATH-IAS. Studia Orientalia, 13 (Helsinki), 1947.

Pizzagalli, A. M. Influssi buddhistici nella leggenda di ALESSANDRO. Rendiconti dell'Instituto Lombardo, 76, 1942-43.

Cabaniss, A. Paulus ALVARUS of Muslim Cordova. Church Hist., 22, 1953, 99-112.

Reis, E. Duarte BARBOSA: pioneiro revelador dos costumes das Índias. Macau, 1948.

Frandon, Ida-Marie. L'Orient de Maurice BARRÈS, une étude de genèse, Le Pays lorrain (Nancy), July, 1951.

—— L'Orient de Maurice Barrès. Genève, 1952. 491 p. [Analysis of Barrès's conceptions of the "east" (from Moslem Spain to China, via Italy, Greece, Egypt and Asia Minor, particularly Persia) and of their sources and development. Stresses influence of Madame de Noailles. Deals with Barrès as traveler, reader, philosopher and mystic. Capital contribution to Barrès bibliography.]

Baldensperger, F. Un roman exotique de Mme. le Prince de BEAUMONT. RLC, 26, 1952.

Brazao, E. Em demanda do Cataio: A viagem de BENTO DE GOES à China (1603-07). Lisboa, 1954.

Starkie, Enid. Pétrus BOREL en Algérie. Oxford, 1950.

Moran, Berna. Sir Thomas BROWNE's Reading on the Turks. N&Q, 197, 1952, 380-82, 403-06.

Brosig, Ernestine. China in den Romanen Pearl S. BUCKs und Nora Walns. Diss. Wien, 1952.

Martineau, A. BUSSY et l'Inde française (1720-85). Paris, 1935. 458 p.

Cidade, H. CAMOES e a India. Ocidente, 42, 1952, 225-28.

Machado, R. A flora da India nos Lusiadas. Lisboa, 1947.

Basson, Fernande. CHATEAUBRIAND et la Terre-Sainte. Diss. Paris, 1953.

Duchemin, M. Veritas filia temporis. Chateaubriand à l'Alhambra en 1807. BAGB, June, 1952.

Gautier, J. M. Chateaubriand et l'Inde. RLC, 28, 1954, 198-202.

Folkierski, W. DANTE et l'Islam. IXe Congrès des Sciences Historiques, Paris, 1950.

Gabrieli, F. New Light on Dante and Islam. Diogenes, Spring 1954, 61-73.

Silverstein, T. Dante and the Legend of the Micraj. The Problem of islamic Influence on the Christian Literature of the Otherworld. Jour. of Near Eastern Studies, 11, 1953.

Brittain, Mary Z. DOUGHTY's Mirror of Arabia. Moslem World, 37, 1947, 42-48.

Chidambaram, S. EMERSON and Eastern Values. Aryan Path, Nov., 1951.

Oliver, E. S. The Asia in Emerson's Mind. Korean Survey, May, 1953.

Gilbert, P. Souvenirs de l'Egypte dans l'Hélène d'Euripide. AC, 1949.

Ricard, R. FEIJÓO et la Chine. Lettres Romanes, 1952.

Heuzey, J. Sources inédites de La Tentation de Saint Antoine. (FLAUBERT). RHLF, Jan., 1953.

Bernard-Maître, H. Saint FRANÇOIS XAVIER, orientaliste. Etudes, Dec., 1952, 303-15.

Costa, J. António GALVAO, o "Apóstulo das Molucas." Lisboa, 1943.

Duff, A. B. Lettres persanes du comte de GOBINEAU. RLC, 26, 1952.

Eilers, W. GOETHE und das Morgenland. Proc. Australian Goethe Soc., 1951, 38-57.

Dupuy, A. Les GONCOURT et la leçon du voyage en Alger, 1849. RHLF, April, 1953.

Spies, O. Das GRIMMsche Märchen Bruder Lustig in arabischer Überlieferung. Rheinisches Jb.f. Volkskunde, 2, 1951.

—— Orientalische Stoffe in den Kinder- und Hausmärchen der Brüder Grimm. Walldorf (Hessen), 1952.

Robert, M. Lafcadio HEARN. vol. I: Europe, America; II. Asia. Tokyo, 1951.

Baumgartner, W. HERODOTS babylonische und assyrische Nachrichten. Symbolae Hrozny, 3, Praha, 1949-50, 69-106.

Meulenaere, H. de. Herodotos en Egypte. Diss. Louvain. RBPh, 25, 1946-47.

Schwartz, J. Hérodote et l'Egypte. RA, 37, 1951, 143-50.

Dussaud, R. Les antécédents orientaux à la Théogonie d'HÉSIODE. Annuaire de l'Institut de Philol. & d'Hist. orientales (Bruxelles), 9, 1949.

Albright, W. F. Some Oriental Glosses on the HOMERic Problem. American Journal of Archeology, 1950, 162-76.

Feldman, A. Indians and the Iliad. CJ, 43, 1947.

Struve, V. Epos Gomera i krug skazanij o care Petu bastise. JaiL, 4, 1929, 111-22.

Agostinho, J. (transl. & ed.) História da navegação do holandês João Hugo de Linschoot, às Indias Orientais (Fragmentos vertidos para português da 2.ª edição francesa, 1619) Bol. do Instituto Histórico da Ilha Terceira, 1, 1943, 145-68. [Jan HUYGEN VAN LINSCHOTEN was in Portuguese India in the 1580's. His book was published in Dutch, Amsterdam, 1595-96.]

Menges, K. H. The Oriental Elements in the Vocabulary of the Oldest Russian Epos, The IGOR' Tale. With a Preface by Roman Jakobson. New York, 1951.

Orlov, A. Deva-lebed' v Slove o polku Igoreve. TODRL, 3, 1936, 27-36.

Morales Souviron, F. Cartas de Washington IRVING desde la Alhambra. Clavileño, May, 1952.

Santos, V. O missionário quinhentista Fr. JOAO DOS SANTOS e o seu livro Etiópia Oriental. Lisboa, 1951.

Ricard, R. Ibero Africana. Un arabisant syro-portugais du XVIII siècle: Fr. JOAO DE SOUSA. Hesperis, Archives Berbères et Bull. de l'Inst. des Hautes Etudes Marocaines, 36, 1949.

Cordeiro, Ramo, G. Anotações ligeiras à tradução de JOHNSON da "Viagem à Abissínia," do Padre Jerónimo Lobo. Memórias da Acad. das Ciências de Lisboa. Classe de Letras, 4, 1941, 449-61.

Liebert, H. W. Dr. Johnson's First Book: An account of the variant issues of the first edition of A Voyage to Abyssinia, with a facsimile of their titlepages. Yale U. Library Gazette, 25, 1950.

Szczesniak, B. The Origin of the Chinese Language according to Athanasius KIRCHER's Theory. JAOS, 72, 1952, 21-29.

Guillemin, H. LAMARTINE et son voyage en Orient. Dialogues, April, 1952.

Prichard, Katharine. LAWRENCE in Australia. Meanjin, 9 (Melbourne), 1950, 252-59.

Falshaw, Gladys. LECONTE DE LISLE et l'Inde. Paris, 1923.

Merkel, R. LEIBNITZ und China. Berlin, 1952.

Alvar, M. Romances de LOPE DE VEGA vivos en la tradición oral Marroqui. RF, 63, 1951.

Herculano de Carvalho, J. G. C. O Vocabulário exótico na Histoire des Indes (1553). Biblos, 27, 1952. [About Nicolas de Grouchy's French translation of Fernão LÓPES DE CASTANHEDA, Historia do Descobrimento e Conquista da India pelos Portugueses, Book 1. Lisboa, 1551.]

Figueras, T. G. Españoles en Africa en el siglo XVI: Luis del MÁRMOL

CARVAJAL. Archivos del Instituto de Estudios Africanos, 1.

Ayres, C. Fernão **MENDES PINTO**: Subsidios para a sua biographia e para o estudo da sua obra. Hist. da Acad. Real das Sciencias de Lisboa, N.S. 10 (pt. 1), 1905.

—— Fernão Mendes Pinto e o Japão. Ibid. pt. 2, 1906.

Collis, M. The Grand Peregrination: Being the Life and Adventures of Fernão Mendes Pinto. London, 1949 & Porto, 1951.

Freitas, J. A. de. Subsidios para a Bibliographia portugueza relativa a o estudo da lingua japoneza e para a biographia de Fernão Mendes Pinto. O Instituto (Coimbra), 1905.

Gown, H. H. Five Foreigners in Japan. (Fernão Mendes Pinto, St. Francis Xavier, Will Adams, Ranald Mac-Donald, Townsend Harris). New York, 1936.

Morais, W. de. Fernão Mendes Pinto no Japão. Lisboa, 1942.

Nykl, A. R. Mais observações sôbre as línguas citadas na "Peregrinaçam" de Fernão Mendes Pinto. Petrus Nonius, 4 (Lisboa), 1942.

Rosbroeck, G. L. van. Persian Letters before **MONTESQUIEU**. New York, 1932, 147 p.

Shackleton, R. The Moslem Chronology of the Lettres Persanes. FS, Jan., 1954.

Caland, W. Roberto de' **NOBILI** and the Sanskrit Language and Literature. Acta Orientalia, 3, 1924.

Goldammer, K. **NOVALIS** und die Welt des Ostens. Stuttgart, 1948.

Ficalho, Conde de. García da **ORTA** e o seu tempo. Lisboa, 1886. [About the author of the Coloquios dos simples, e drogas he cousas medicinais da India. Goa, 1563. This is one of the first western books printed in India. It contains a dedicatory ode written by Camões, his first published work.]

Pighi, G. B. Motivi vedici nel **PASCOLI**. Convivium, 1948.

Pérez Bustamente, C. El Pontifice **PAULO V** y la expulsión de los moriscos. Bol. Real Acad. Hist., 129, 1951, 219-33.

Fernández Duro, C. Viajes del Infante D. **PEDRO DE PORTUGAL** en el siglo XV con indicación de los de una religiosa española [Etheria] por las regiones orientales mil años antes.

Real Sociedad Geográfica, 45, Madrid, 1903.

Rossi, E. La fonte turca della novella cornice dei Mille e un Giorno di **PÉTIS DE LA CROIX**. Oriente Moderno, 29, 1949, 28-33.

Rodinson, M. Sur un passage de **PÉTRARQUE** concernant la littérature arabe. Bull. des Etudes arabes, May, 1951.

Cortesão, A. Primeira embaixada europeia à China: O boticário e embaixador Tome **PIRES** e a sua "Suma Oriental." Lisboa, 1945.

Bidez, J. Eos ou **PLATON** et l'Orient. Bruxelles, 1945.

Herriott, J. H. Folklore from Marco **POLO**: Japan. California Folklore Quart., 4, 1945.

Thouvenot, R. Défense de **POLYBE**. Hesperis, 35, 1948.

Cunha Rivara, J. H. Viagem de Francisco **PYRARD DE LAVAL**. 2 vols. Nova Goa, 1858-62. Reprinted Porto, 1944. [The narrative of a journey by a Frenchman at the beginning of the 17th century, 1st published in French, Paris, 1611. He included Portuguese India in his travels.]

Gallagher, L. (ed.) China in the Sixteenth Century. The Journals of Matthew **RICCI**, 1583-1610. New York, 1953, 616 p.

Vásquez de Parga, L. Juan **RUIZ** entre Islam y Occidente. Clavileño, March, 1951.

Le Breton, A. V. L'exotisme dans le roman; Bernardin de **SAINT-PIERRE**. In: Le roman français au XVIIIe siècle. Paris, 1925, 355-96.

Litovčenko, E. Z. **ŠEVČENKO** o kazaxskom narode. UZUPI, 1, 1948.

Falkowna, Maryla. Indian Elements in **SŁOWACKI's** Thought. Słowacki Centenary Volume. London, 1951.

Maver, G. Da Napoli a Zante: Osservazioni marginali sul "Viaggio in Oriente" di J. Słowacki. Ibid.

Dowden, W. S. The Source of the Metempsychosis Motif in **SOUTHEY's** Thalaba. (Koran). MLN, 66, 1951.

Furnas, J. C. Voyage to Windward. The Life of Robert Louis **STEVENSON**. London, 1953. 478 p. [More useful as biography than as a study of Stevenson as historical novelist.]

—— The Road of the Loving Heart.

Robert Louis Stevenson in Samoa.
AM, 188, 1951.
McGaw, Sister Martha M. Stevenson in
Hawaii. Honolulu, 1950.
Baney, M. M. Some Reflections of Life
in North Africa in the Writings of
TERTULLIAN. Patristic Studies, 80.
Washington, 1948. 164 p.
Vachot, C. James THOMSON et l'Orient.
RLC, July, 1953.
Muir, Marcie. Anthony TROLLOPE in
Australia. Adelaide, 1949. 105 p.
Do-Dinh, P. Paul VALÉRY et la Chine.
France-Asie, 4, 1949.
Spinelli, V. (transl. & ed.). Ludovico de
VARTHEMA, Itinerário. (Primeira
tradução portuguesa). Lisboa, 1949.
[The narrative of a journey by an
Italian at the beginning of the 16th
century, 1st published in Italian,
Rome, 1510. He included Portuguese
India in his travels.]
André, J. VIRGILE et les Indiens. REL,
1949.
Gaulmier, J. L'idéologue VOLNEY

d'après des documents inédits. Con-
tribution à l'histoire de l'orientalisme
en France. Beyrouth, 1951.
Fan, T. C. Chinese Fables and anti-WAL-
POLE Journalism. RES, 25, 1949.
Lach, D. F. The Sinophilism of Christian
WOLFF. JHI, 14, 1953, 561-74.
Campbell, J. Heinrich ZIMMER (1890-
1943). PR, 20, 1953, 441-51. [The
source for Thomas Mann's Die ver-
tauschten Köpfe is Zimmer's interpretation of a collection of Indian
stories: "Twenty-five Tales of a
Ghost in a Corpse." The influence of
India on the brothel scene in Ulysses.]
Teller, Gertrude E. Virata or The Eyes
of the Undying Brother and Stefan
ZWEIG's Thought. GR, 27, 1952, 31-
40. [The author examines the importance of Hindu philosophy for Zweig's
novel and studies the ensuing problems of the relationship between
Eastern and Western thought, as it
is reflected in the story.]

C. ASPECTS OF WESTERN CULTURE

III. INTERNATIONAL LITERARY RE-
LATIONS. COLLECTIVE AND
RECIPROCAL INFLUENCES.

Continents and Nations

Brooks, van Wyck. The Confident Years:
1885-1915. New York, 1953. 627 p.
[This fifth and concluding volume in
Mr. Brooks' series of observations
about AMERICAn letters contains
much useful information concerning
the relation of American prose fic-
tion to European movements.]
Brunner, E. Geistige Hindernisse und
Brücken zwischen Amerika und Eu-
ropa. NSR, 8, 1951, 482-95.
Galantière, L. (ed.). America and the
Mind of Europe. N.Y. Public Library
Bull., 1952.
Gohdes, C. The Foreign Book in the
United States. Yb, 3, 1954, 51-53.
Rosenberg, R. The "Great Books" in
(American) General Education. Ibid,
20-35.
Wright, C. C. Reading Interests in Texas
from the 1830's to the Civil War.
Southwestern Hist. Rev., 54, 1951.
Gilsoul, R. Les influences ANGLO-
SAXONnes sur les lettres françaises

de Belgique de 1850 à 1880. Bruxelles, 1953.
Brughetti, R. Una nueva generación
literaria ARGENTINA, 1940-50. CA,
63, 1952, 261-81. [Social, political
and economic obstacles are many,
but a growing number of good translations affords immediate rewarding
contacts with contemporary American and European experimentation in
the novel.]
Pomes, Madalena S. Exilados de AR-
MENIA en los dominios de Pedro IV
de Aragón. Estudios de Edad Media
de la Corona de Aragón, Sección de
Zaragoza, 2, 1946.
Reiffenberg, F. A. de. Coup d'oeil sur les
relations qui ont existé jadis entre la
BELGIQUE et le Portugal. Mémoires
de l'Acad. Royale des Sciences et
Belles-Lettres de Bruxelles, 14, 1841.
Braamcamp Freire, A. Maria Brandoa: a
do Crisfal. Archivo Histórico Portuguez, 6-7, 1908-09. [Reprinted as Noticias da Feitoria de Flandres prece-
didas dos Brandões Poetas do Cancioneiro, Lisboa, 1920.]
Bussche, E. van den. Flandres et Portugal: Mémoires sur les relations qui
existèrent autrefois entre les Fla-

mands de Flandre, particulièrement ceux de Bruges, et les Portugais. Bruges, 1874. [See also La Flandre: Revue des Monuments d'Histoire et d'Antiquités, 4-8, 1872-76.]

Parker, J. H. A Research Need: The Investigation of the Relations between CANADA and Portugal and Brazil. Proceeding of Internat. Colloquium on Luso-Brazilian Studies. Washington, D. C., 1950, Nashville, 1953.

Garces, T. CATALUNYA-Italia. Revista, 21, 1935.

Givanel i Mas, Joan. El teatre estranger en llengua catalana. Ibid.

Moule, A. C. Christians in CHINA before the Year 1550. London, 1930.

Pavlovsky, M. N. Chinese-Russian Relations. New York, Philos-Library, 1949.

Larsen, S. DANMARK og Portugal i det 15de aarhundrede. Aarbøger for Nordisk Oldkyndighed og Historie, 3, 1919.

Baldensperger, F. Avec les voyageurs anglais du "Grand Tour." (ENGLAND). EA, 6, 1953, 227-30.

Carrière, J. M. Anglo-French and Franco-American Studies: A Current Bibliography. FAR, 4, 1952, 79-119.

Dobrovoljc, F. Deux épisodes de l'histoire des relations culturelles anglo-slovènes. NS, 6, 1951.

Downs, B. W. Anglo-Norwegian Literary Relations, 1867-1900. MLR, Oct., 1952.

Farinelli, A. Divagazioni erudite: Inghilterra e Italia, Germania e Italia, Spagna e Germania. Torino, 1925.

Livesay, J. L. & R. B. Davis. A Cavalier Library—1643. U. of Va. Studies in Bibliog., 6, 1954, 141-60.

Offor, R. A Collection of Books in the University Library, Leeds, printed before the nineteenth century, containing (a): translations from English into French (b): books written in French on Great Britain and on British affairs. Proc. Leeds Philos. Soc., 1-6, 1925-48.

Shillington, V. M. & Wallis Chapman. The Commercial Relations of England and Portugal. London, 1907.

Stoye, J. W. English Travellers Abroad, 1604-67. London, 1952. 479 p.

Wright, H. G. Studies in Anglo-Scandinavian Literary Relations. Bangor, 1919.

Ajnalov, D. Epizod iz snošenij Kieva s

Zapadnoj Evropoj. (EUROPE). TODRL, 3, 1936, 5-12.

Baumer, F. Main Currents of Western Thought. New York, 1952.

Belyj, A. Evropa i Rossija. Zv, 3, 1924, 52-70.

Bernard, H. Les adaptations chinoises d'ouvrages européens. Monumenta Sinica, 10, 1945.

———— Traductions chinoises d'ouvrages européens au Japon durant la période de fermeture (1614-1853). Monumenta Nipponica, 3, 1940.

Bicilli, P. Zapadnoe vlijanie na Rusi i načal'naja letopis.' Odessa, 1914.

Das Gupta, H. M. Studies in the Western Influence on 19th Century Bengali Poetry, 1857-87. Calcutta, 1935.

Demkov, M. Vlijanie zapadnoevropejskoj pedagogiki na russkuju. ZMNP, 5, 1910.

Franke, H. Europa in der ostasiatischen Geschichtsschreibung des 13. und 14. Jahrhunderts. Saeculum, 2, 1951.

Frederiksen, S. Aspects of European Influence in West Greenlandic Poetry. Midwest Folklore, 2, 1952, 251-61.

Gollwitzer, H. Europabild und Europagedanke. Beiträge zur deutschen Geistesgeschichte. München, 1951.

Hudson, G. F. Europe and China. London, 1931.

Iorga, N. Influenta occidentală şi orientală în cultura noastră. Neamul românesc, 1929.

Isopescu, C. Influssi occidentali sulla cultura romena. L'Ambrosiano, 17.XI.1942.

Jonas, F. M. Foreign Influence on the Early Press of Japan. Japan Society Transactions & Publications, 32, 1934-35.

Lessing, T. Europa und Asien. Untergang der Erde am Geist. Leipzig, 1930. 360 p.

Linden, A. L. van der. De Europeaan in de maleische Literatuur. Meppel, n.d.

Martens, F. Rossija i literaturnoe obščestvo zapadno-evropejskix narodov. VE, 3, 1881, 235-61.

Miller, O. Osnovy učenija pervonačal'nyx slavjanofilov. RM, 1-3, 1880.

Ohloblyn, O. Western Europe and the Ukrainian Baroque. An Aspect of Cultural Influences at the Time of Hetman Ivan Mazepa. AUA, 1, 1951.

Ota, S. New Poetry Movements and Occidental Poetry. In: An Introduction to Comparative Literature, ed. by Nakajima & Nakano. Tokyo, 1951.

Parry, A. Latest Westernisms in the Soviet Russian Language. Aatseel, 10, 1953, 79-81.

Pisut, M. Occidental Literatures in Soviet Literary Science. (In Slovak). SIPo, 1950.

Pumpjanskij, L. Očerki po literature pervoj poloviny XVIII veka. In: Orlov, A. (ed.) XVIII vek. Leningrad, 1935, 83-132. [Italian influences on Kantemir; German and French influences on Lomonosov.]

Pypin, A. Vopros o zapadnom vlijanii v russkoj literature. VE, 10, 1896, 660-99.

Savickij, P. Evropa i Evrazija. RM, 1-2, 1921, 119-38.

Shimmura, I. Western Influences on Japanese History and Culture in Earlier Periods (1540-1860). Tokyo, 1936.

Skripil', M. Povest' o Savve Grudcyne. TODRL, 1935, 1936, 1947.

Solov'ev, V. Mnimaja bor'ba s Zapadom. RM, 8, 1890, 1-20.

Struve, G. Hovudliner in den nyare Sovjetliteraturen. Vinduet, 6, 1952, 131-38. [A brief exposé of recent developments in Soviet literature, with the stress on its anti-Westernism. The true meaning of Socialist Realism is shown to lie in the conformity to the demands of the Communist Party.]

Taeger, F. West und Ost im Hellenismus. Hessische Blätter für Volkskunde, 41.

Tsung, Hyui-Puh. Chinese Translations of Western Literature. Chinese Social & Political Science Review, 12, 1928.

Varschavskij, S. Occidental Art and Literature in the Mirror of the Criticism of Russian Realists. (In Czech). Prague, 1951.

Veselovskij, A. Zapadnoe vlijanie v russkoj literature. Sravnitel'no-istoričeskij očerk. VE, 1881-82.

Bertoni, G. Canzonette musicali FRANCEsi e spagnuole alla corte d'Este. Modena, 1905.

Deanovic, M. Anciens contacts entre la France et Raguse. Bibliothèque Institut fr., Zagreb, 3, 1950.

Gaudin, Lois F. Bibliography of Franco-Spanish Literary Relations. New York, 1930. 71 p.

Guillemain, H. Notions de littératures étrangères envisagées dans leurs rapports avec la littérature française. Paris, 1951. 266 p.

Guyard, M. F. Les relations littéraires franco-britanniques au XIXe siècle. Année propédeutique, 7-8, 1952.

Hillard, G. Französisch-deutsches Mittlertum. Merkur, 62, 1953, 397-99. [Essentially a review of Ferdinand Lion's books Lebensquellen französischer Metaphysik and Der französische Roman im 19. Jahrhundert.]

Minis, C. Französisch-deutsche Literaturberührungen im Mittelalter. Romanist. Jb, 4, 1951, 55-123. [Well-informed critical review of research.]

Salza, Abdelkader. Alcune relazioni tra poeti francesi e italiani dei secoli XVII e XVIII. BI, 8, 1908, 56-65.

Tessier, J. Le Chevalier de Jant: Relations de la France avec le Portugal au temps de Mazarin. Paris, 1877.

Villard, Léonie. La France et les Etats-Unis: Echanges et rencontres, 1524-1800. Lyon, 1952. 407 p. (Cf RLC, 1954).

Wedkiewicz, S. Notes bibliographiques pour servir à l'histoire des relations franco-polonaises. Bull. de l'Acad. polonaise des Sciences et des Lettres. Paris, 1952-53.

Wilmotte, M. Relazione letteraria franco-spagnola. Riv. delle Nazioni Latine, I.II.1917.

Zeller, G. La France et l'Allemagne depuis dix siècles. Paris, 1932. 211 p.

Anon. Les rapports culturels GERMANo-suédois. Allemagne d'aujourd'hui, July, 1953.

Charles, R. A. French Intermediaries in the Transmission of German Literature and Culture to England, 1750-1815. Diss. Penn. State., 1952. 233 p. [In almost every instance, the French reception and translation of German literature antedated the English. Up to 1800, all English translations of German texts were based on French translations. After 1800 the French émigrés in Germany were mediators between Germany and England.]

Hoffmann, W. Deutsch-schweizerischer Kulturaustausch. Basler Nachrichten, 1.IV.1948.

Hüffer, H. J. Aus 1200 Jahren deutsch-spanischer Beziehungen. Romanist. Jb, 3, 1950, 85-123.

Kesten, H. Die gevierteilte deutsche Literatur. (Occupation Zones). Welt & Wort, 8, 1953, 1-5.

Koenigsgarten, H. F. Deutschland und Frankreich von England aus gesehen. Antares, (Baden), 1953, 12-16. [On the greater affinity of England to France than to Germany.]

Kovalevskij, M. Bor'ba nemeckogo vlijanija s francuzskim v konce XVIII i v pervoj polovine XIX stoletija. VE, 10, 1915, 123-63.

Neubert, F. Ein Jahrtausend deutsch-französischer geistiger Beziehungen. Vom Hochmittelalter bis zum Zeitalter der Aufklärung und des Rokoko. In: Studien zur Vergl. Literaturgeschichte. Berlin, 1952, 147-201. (Cf CL, 1953).

Palmer, Nettie. Some Relations between German and Australian Literatures. Proc. Australian Goethe Soc., 1951.

Varia, Die deutsch-spanische Begegnung. Sonderheft der Mitteilungen des Instituts f. Auslandsbeziehungen, 4, 1954. 35 p.

Viëtor, K. Die deutsche Literatur und die Krise der europäischen Kultur. Festschrift Strich. Bern, 1952.

Zschelletzky, H. Wechselbeziehungen der deutschen und russischen Literatur. Heute & Morgen (Schwerin), 1949.

Iorga, N. Relations culturelles GRÉCO-roumaines (d'après les livres de la Bibliothèque de Ploiești). Bull. de la Section Historique, Académie roumaine, 1920.

Toussaint, G. Formes grecques, rhythmes indiens. France-Asie, 7, 1951.

Gabriel, A. La HONGRIE et la péninsule ibérique au moyen-âge. Budapest, 1944.

Filliozat, J. Les échanges de l'INDE et de l'Empire Romain aux premiers siècles de l'ère chrétienne. Revue Historique, 201, 1949.

Loudet, S. M. Les rapports de l'Inde avec l'Occident, d'Alexandre à l'Empire Romain. Paris, 1948.

Mode, H. Indische Frühkulturen und ihre Beziehungen zum Westen. Basel, 1944.

Winternitz, M. India and the West. Visva-Bharati Quarterly, N.S., 2, 1937.

Dunleavy, G. W. Cultural Relations between Northumbria and IRELAND, 635-793. Diss. Northwestern U., 1953.

Anon. Relazioni storiche fra l'ITALIA e il Portogallo. Memorie e documenti R. Accademia d'Italia, Roma, 1940.

Bersano Begey, M. Studi recenti (1939-49) sui rapporti culturali tra l'Italia e la Polonia. RS, 1, 1952, 186-92.

Bertini, G. M. Venezia e la Spagna nel passato. Congresso Intern. per il Progresso delle Scienze di Venezia. Roma, 1938.

―――― Della prima "grammatica" italo-spagnola. In: Estudios dedicados a Menéndez Pidal, 4, Madrid, 1953, 27-35.

Cambiagi, F. (ed.). Serto di documenti attenenti alle Reali Case di Savoja e di Braganza per le Auspicatissime Nozze di Sua A.R. la Principessa Pia di Savoja con Sua Maesta Don Luigi I. Re di Portogallo. Firenze, 1862.

Coppola, N. Fratellanza italo-romena agli albori della nostra unità nazionale. NAnt, 1940.

Costanzo, S. Discurso histórico-político sobre la poesía italiana y española. In his: Opúsculos políticos y literários. Madrid, 1847.

Croce, B. Cultura italiana e cultura spagnola. In: Uomini e cose della vecchia Italia. Bari, 1927.

Emery, L. Vecchi manuali italo-tedeschi. Lingua Nostra, 9-10, 1948-49.

Erizzo, N. Sulle ambasciate e sugli ambasciatori Veneti in Portogallo. Atti dell' Ateneo Veneto, N.S., 1, 1864, 485-87.

Fernández Murga, F. La Academia napolitano-española de los Ociosos. Instituto español, Roma, 1951. 24 p.

Garofalo, F. P. Relazioni storiche fra l'Italia e il Portogallo. RI, 6, 1903.

Garrone, M. A. Per le relazioni tra Italia e Spagna. FD, 36, 1914.

Iorga, N. Quelques documents sur les rapports italo-roumains. Revue Historique du sud-est européen, 1929.

Isopescu, C. L'Italia e la Romania. Rivolta Ideale, 1925.

―――― I rapporti intellettuali italo-romeni. Ibid, 1925.

―――― Italia e Romania nel loro sviluppo storico. Rassegna Italo-Romena, 1940.

Marchesi, V. Le relazioni tra la Repubblica Veneta e il Portogallo dall'anno 1522 al 1797. Archivo Veneto, 33-

Martinelli, V. Contributi alle relazioni culturali italo-romene. Avvenire, 29. VIII.1943.

Mila y Fontanals, M. La literatura italiana y la catalana. Cataluña, 6 (Barcelona), 7.IX.1912.

Negri, P. Per le relazioni italo-spagnuole nel secolo XVII. Archivio stor. ital., 71, 1913.

Neri, F. Gli studi di questi ultimi 35 anni intorno ai rapporti culturali italo-francesi durante il Settecento. Cooperazione Intellettuale, 4-5, 1936, 27-32.

Ortiz, R. Italia e Rumania. Festschrift J. Rossi. Firenze, 1937.

———— Relaţii culturale între Italia si Spania. Anuarul Univ. din Bucureşti, 1930, 9-12.

———— Sull'importanza della dominazione fanariota in Romania come determinatrice dei contatti linguistici e letterarie italo-romeni attraverso la lingua e la letteratura neo-ellenica. Atti del V. Congresso Internazionale di Studi Bizantini, Roma, 1, 1939, 254-83.

Pavolini, A. Italia e Spagna. Saggi sui rapporti storici, filosofici ed artistici tra le due civiltà. Firenze, 1941.

Peragallo, P. Cenni intorno alla colonia italiana in Portogallo nei secoli XIV, XV e XVI. Miscellanea di Storia italiana, 3, Torino, 1904.

Rebora, P. Momenti di cultura italiana e inglese. Mazara, 1952.

Salomone, A. W. (et al). Italian Culture and the Western Tradition. New York, 1952.

Vossler, K. Italienisch-Französisch-Spanisch, ihre literarischen und sprachlichen Physiognomien. Zeitwende, 2 (München), 1926.

Zaccaria, E. Bibliografia italo-spagnuola, ossia edizioni e versioni di opere spagnuole e portoghesi 'fattesi in Italia. Carpi, 1908.

Haas, H. JAPAN und die westliche Literatur. Wahrheit, 3, 1902 & Bayrisches Jb. f. Protestant. Kultur, 1, 1908.

Barthe, R. L'idée LATINE. Institut d'Etudes Occitanes, Toulouse, 1951.

Bertoni, G. La latinità della lingua romena. Cultura neolatina, 1942.

Isopescu, C. Antiche attestazioni italiane della latinità dei Romeni. Corriere della Sera (Milano) 28.VIII.1928 & In: Saggi Romeno - Italo - Ispanici. Roma, 1943, 9-22.

———— Romanità e cultura romena. Resto del Carlino, 5.VI.1928.

———— Il movimento latinista in Romania. Rassegna Italo-Romena, 1940.

———— Umanisti italiani scoprono la latinità romena. Corriere Diplomatico Consolare, 1940.

———— L'antichità dei Romeni e il fondo latino del loro cristianesimo. La Festa, 9.VI.1940.

Öhmann, E. Romanische Randwörter der mittelhochdeutschen Zeit im Kontinental-germanischen. Zs. f. Mundartforschung, 20, 1952, 93-101.

Paiva Boléo, M. de. Os estudos de linguística românica na Europa e na América desde 1939 a 1948. Supl. bibliográfico da Revista Portuguesa de Filologia, 1. (Coimbra) 1951.

Ruffini, M. La scuola latinista romena. Piccola Bibl. Romena, Roma, 1940.

Savj-Lopez, P. Per l'alleanza della cultura latina. NAnt, 258, 1915.

Schiaffini, A. Latinità e italianità nell'-Europa di sud-est. Annuario della R. Accademia d'Italia, 14, 1942.

Vossler, K. Die Dichtungsformen der Romanen. Stuttgart, 1951. 333 p.

Simões de Paula, E. MARROCOS e suas relações con a Iberia na antiguidade. Boletim, 57, U. de São Paulo, 1946. 295 p.

OCCIDENT or WEST: See Europe, above.

Do-Dinh, P. ORIENT et Occident. France-Asie, 8, 1952.

Ehrenberg, V. Ost und West: Studien zur geschichtlichen Problematik der Antike. Prag, 1935.

Guins, G. C. East and West in Soviet Ideology. Russian Review, 1949.

Iorga, N. Choses d'Orient et de Roumanie. Bucarest, Paris, 1924.

Northrup, F. The Meeting of East and West. New York, 1946.

Rouselle, E. Begegnung von Morgen- und Abendland. Saeculum, 2, 1951.

Trovato, G. Un millennio di rapporti tra mundo mussulmano e Sicilia. Rassegna Mediterranea, 4.

Varia. Der Orient und wir. Berlin, 1935.

Vayssac, S. Sagesse orientale et science occidentale. Paris, 1949.

Young, T. C. (ed.) Near Eastern Culture and Society: A Symposium on the Meeting of East and West. Princeton U.P., 1951.

Zirmunskij, V. K voprosu o literaturnyx otnošenijax Vostoka i Zapada. VLU, 4, 1947, 100-19.

POLAND: for inter-Slavic relations, See: Slavic chapters, 690-92, 815-17, 903-04.

Pociecha, W. Cultural Relations between Poland and Italy. (In Polish). Studia dziejow Kultury, Warsaw, 1949.

Preisner, W. Stosunki literackie polsko-włoskie w latach 1800-1939 w świetle bibliografii. Toruń, 1949. 291 p.

Schmid, H. F. Les rapports polono-allemands et polono-tchèques à travers l'histoire, vus de Pologne. Coup d'oeil à l'Est, 2. (Graz) 1949.

Brazão, E. Apontamentos para a história das relações diplomáticas de PORTU-GAL com a China, 1516-1753. Lisboa, 1949.

Castello Branco, J. B. Apontamentos sobre as relações de Portugal com a Syria no seculo 12.º Memorias Acad. Real das Sciências de Lisboa ,1, 1854.

Castro de Osorio, J. O além-mar na literatura portuguesa (época dos descobrimentos). Lisboa, 1948.

Cidade, H. A literatura portuguesa e a expansão ultramarina: As idéias, os sentimentos, as formas de arte. Vol. 1: (Séculos XV e XVI) Lisboa, 1943.

Ciesielska-Barkowska, S. Les voyages de Pologne en Espagne et en Portugal au XV et XVI siècle. Arch. Neophilol. 1934.

*Faria, A. de Portugal e Italia: Ensaio de Diccionario Bibliographico. Leorne, 1898.

———— Portugal e Italia: Litteratos portuguezes na Italia, ou Collecção de subsidios para se escrever a Historia litteraria de Portugal que dispunha e ordenava Frei Fortunato Monge Cistercense. Leorne, 1905.

Figueiredo, F. de. Modernas relaciones literarias entre Portugal y España. Contribución bibliográfica. Estudio, 12, (Barcelona) 1915 & Estudos de Literatura, 1, Lisboa, 1917. 250 p.

Fonseca Pinto, A. A. da. Um inedito de Frei Fortunato. O Instituto, 24-25, 1877-78. [The item is Litteratos portuguezes na Italia, ou Collecção de subsidios para se escrever a historia litteraria de Portugal, que dispunha e ordenava Frei Fortunato Monge Cistercense.]

Iorga, N. Tara latina cea mai departata în Europa: Portugalia. Bucureşti, 1928.

Lombardi, A. Relazioni politiche fra i re del Portogallo e Firenze nella prima metà del quattrocento. Roma, 1902.

Marques Guedes, A. A aliança inglêsa:

Notas de história diplomática. 2nd ed. Lisboa, 1943.

Mendes da Luz, F. P. Alguns aspectos das relações culturais luso-espanholas. Conferencia. Madrid, 1949.

Moisés, M. A influência do ultramar na novela de cavalaria quinhentista. II. Colloquium Internacional de Estudos Luso-Brasileiros. São Paulo, 1954.

Morf, H. Die kastilianische und portugiesische Literatur. Berlin, 1909.

Paxeco, F. The Intellectual Relations between Portugal and Great Britain. Lisboa, 1937.

Pellizzari, A. Portogallo e Italia nel secolo XVI: Studi e ricerche storiche e letterarie. Napoli, 1914.

Prestage, E. The Diplomatic Relations of Portugal with France, England, and Holland from 1640 to 1668. Watford, 1925.

Rebello, J. P. O aspecto espiritual da aliança inglesa (Artigos publicados no Jornal "Novidades" durante os años de 1943 e 1944). Lisboa, 1945.

Rebello da Silva, L. A. Relações politicas e diplomáticas de Portugal com as diversas potencias do mundo. 4 vols. Lisboa, 1910.

Ricard, R. Le Portugal et la culture étrangère. Lettres Romanes, 1951.

Soveral, Visconde de. Apontamentos sobre as antigas relações politicas e commerciaes de Portugal com a Republica de Veneza. Lisboa, 1893.

Strasen, E. A. & A. Gândara. Cito séculos de historia Luso-Alemã. Berlin, 1944.

Tovar, Conde de. Portugal e Veneza na Idade-Média (até 1495). Coimbra, 1933.

Trindade Coelho, H. & G. Mattelli. (eds.) Documentos para o estudo das relações culturaes entre Portugal e Italia. 4 vols. Firenze, 1934-35.

Wolf, F. J. Studien zur Geschichte der spanischen und portugiesischen Nationalliteratur. Berlin, 1859.

Zaccaria, E. Bibliografia italo-spagnuola ossia edizioni e versioni di opere spagnuole e portoghesi fattesi in Italia. Pt. I: Edizioni. Carpi, 1907.

Iorga, N. La place des ROUMAINS dans le développement de la vie spirituelle des nations romanes. Académie Roumaine: Bull. de la Section Historique, 1920, 47-64.

———— Les influences étrangères sur la Nation Roumaine. Paris, 1921.

RUSSIA: For inter-Slavic relations, See: Slavic chapters, 690-92, 815-17, 903-04.

Berdjaev, N. Rossija i Zapadnaja Evropa. RM, 5-6, 1917, 76-81.

Berkov, P. Neispol'zovannye materialy dlja istorii russkoj literatury XVIII veka. In: Orlov, A. (ed.) XVIII vek. Leningrad, 1935, 327-76.

Dvoichenko-Markov, E. The American Philosophical Society and Early Russian-American Relations. PAPS, 94, 1950.

Kamarovskij, L. O zaključenii meždu Rossiej i Franciej literaturnoj konvencii. RM, 12, 1887, 89-97.

Kirchner, W. Russia and Europe in the Age of the Reformation. Archiv. f. Reformationsgesch., 43, 1952, 172-86.

Kovalevskij, M. Stranica iz istorii našego obščenija s zapadnoj filosofiej. VE, 6, 1915, 157-68.

Pypin, A. Drevnij period russkoj literatury i obrazovannosti. Sravnitel'no-istoričeskie očerki. VE, 1875-76.

——— Rossija i Evropa. VE, 1, 1889, 296-336.

Riasanovsky, N. V. Russia and the West in the Teaching of the Slavophiles: A Study of a Romantic Ideology. Cambridge (Mass.), 1952.

Solov'ev, V. Rossija i Evropa. VE, 2-4, 1888.

Stocki, R. S. Slavs and Teutons, the Oldest Germanic-Slavic Relations. Milwaukee, 1950.

Struve, P. Rossija. RM, 3, 1922, 101-15.

Zaozerskij, A. (ed.) Rossija i Zapad. Petrograd, 1922. 212 p.

Zenkovsky, V. Russian Thinkers and Europe. Ann Arbor (Mich.), 1952.

Smith, A. H. & Hatto, A. T. A List of English, **SCANDINAVIAN** and German Theses in the University of London. London, 1939.

Bejarano, E. Reciprocidad de influencias entre dos grandes literaturas (**SPAIN**). Revista de Menorca, 40, 1944.

Bell, R. Some Early Literary Contacts between Modern Spain and the East. Transactions Glasgow U., 13, 1947-51.

*Croce, B. Primi contatti tra Spagna e Italia. Atti Accad. Pontoniana di Napoli, 23, 1893.

*Dessoff, A. Über spanische, italienische und französische Dramen in den Spielverzeichnissen deutscher Wander-

truppen. ZVL, 4, 1891.

Farinelli, A. Ensayos y discursos de critica literaria hispano-europea con cartaprologo de R. Menéndez Pidal. Roma, 1925.

Fitzmaurice-Kelly, J. The Relations between Spanish and English Literature. Liverpool U.P., 1910.

Geers, G. J. Relaciones literarias entre España y Holanda. Estudio, 31 (Barcelona), 1920.

Gili Gaya, S. El primer diccionario español-francés (Juan Palet). Clavileño, Nov., 1951.

Henriquez Ureña, M. El intercambio de influencias literarias entre España y América durante los últimos cincuenta años (1875-1925). In: Cuba contemporánea, 41, (Habana) 1926.

Hueffer, H. I. Relaciones culturales entre España y Alemania en lo pasado y en la actualidad. Religión y Cultura, 8, (Madrid) 1929.

Levi, E. La spagna e la cultura italiana. Marzocco, 25.XI.1923.

*Mathews, E. G. Studies in Spanish-English Cultural and Literary Relations. New York, 1938.

Menéndez y Pelayo, M. História de los heterodoxos españoles. Madrid, 1880-82.

Morf, H. Die kastilianische und portugiesische Literatur. Berlin, 1909.

Terlingen, Juan H. Stroom en tegenstroom in spaanse en italiaanse letteren. Nijmegen, 1952.

Uscatescu, G. Relaciones culturales hispano-rumanas. Madrid, 1950.

Wolf, F. J. Studien zur Geschichte der spanischen und portugiesischen Nationalliteratur. Berlin, 1859. Spanish transl. by Miguel de Unamuno, notes by Menéndez y Pelayo, 2 vols., Madrid, 1895-96.

Prestage, E. & K. Mellander. The Diplomatic and Commercial Relations of **SWEDEN** and Portugal from 1641 to 1670. Watford, 1930.

*Strindberg, A. Relations de la Suède avec l'Espagne et le Portugal jusqu'à la fin du dix-septième siècle. Bol. Real Acad. de História, 18 (Madrid), 1890.

Woolley, L. **SYRIA** as the Gateway between East and West. Geographical Journal, 107, 1946.

Fahir Iz. **TURKEY** and Western Literatures. Internat. PEN, July, 1951.

WESTERN WORLD: See Europe, above.

Individual Authors

Croce, B. La corte spagnuola di AL-FONSO d'Aragona a Napoli. Atti Accad. Pontoniana di Napoli, 24, 1894.

Carpenter, R. C. Kay BOYLE. CE, 15, 1953. [The achievement of this American writer of novels and short stories who has used the European scene much in her work.]

Cone, C. B. Edmund BURKE's Library. PBSA, 44, 1950.

Shine, H. CARLYLE's Early Reading, to 1834, with an Introductory Essay on his Intellectual Development. Lexington (Ky.), 1953. 353 p.

Lejeune, Rita. Influences méridionales chez CHRÉTIEN DE TROYES. Bull. Bibliogr. de la Soc. Internat. Arthurienne, 3, 1951.

Cian, V. L'Italia e la Spaga nel secolo XVIII: G. B. CONTI e alcune relazioni letterarie fra l'Italia e la Spagna nella seconda metà del Settecento. Studi e ricerche. Torino, 1896.

Santoli, V. CROCE e le letterature boreali. RLM, 1953.

Munteano, B. Latinitatea, franta si sufletul autohton în conceptia lui O. DENSUSIANU. Analele Acad. Române: Mem. Sectiunii literare, 14, 1945, 59 p.

Drouilly, J. F. M. DOSTOIEVSKY et l'Europe en 1873. Diss. Paris, 1949.

Giusti, W. Dostoievskij e il mondo russo dell'800. Napoli, 1952. 153 p. [The book deals primarily with D's ideas and relates him to contemporary Russian thought. In the chapter "Europa e Antieuropa" D. is shown as an exponent of "Russian Europeanism."]

Grossman, L. Dostoevskij i Evropa. RM, 11, 1915, 54-93 & In: Ot Puškina do Bloka. Moscow, 1926, 171-246.

Reizov, B. O zapadnom vlijanii v tvorčestve Dostoevskogo. Izvestija Severo-Kavkazskogo Gosudarstvennogo Universiteta, 1927.

Mosely, P. E. DRAHOMANOV and the European Conscience. AUA, 2, 1952, 1-5.

Chaloner. W. H. The EGERTONS in Italy and the Netherlands, 1729-34. BRL, 32, 1950.

Cameron, K. W. EMERSON's Early Reading List. BNYPL, 55, 1951.

Melle, P. GHANDI ou la sagesse déchaînée. In: M. K. Ghandi: Expé-rience de vérité ou autobiographie. Paris, 1950.

Rintelen, F. J. von. GOETHE als abendländischer Mensch. Mainz, 1947.

Setschkareff, V. N. V. GOGOL: Leben und Schaffen. Berlin, 1953. 192 p. [Containing references to the influence of Sterne, Scott, Hoffmann, Tieck and other writers on him.]

Nelick, F. C. Oliver GOLDSMITH, Traveller. Diss. U. of Wisconsin, 1953.

Ester, Karl d'. GÖRRES und das Abendland. Neues Abendland, 3, 1948.

HARTMANN, K. A. Reiseeindrücke und Beobachtungen eines deutschen Neuphilologen in der Schweiz und in Frankreich. Leipzig, 1897. 202 p.

Belozerskaja, N. Slavjanofily, zapadniki i Gercen. (HERZEN). VE, 11, 1898, 183-201.

Gabrieli, F. Sicilia e Spagna nella vita e nella poesia di IBN HAMDIS. Miscellanea, G. Galbiati. Milano, 1951.

Pascu, S. Nicola IORGA, genio della latinità. Rassegna Italo-Romena, 1941.

Sowerby, E. M. The Catalogue of the Library of Thomas JEFFERSON. 3 vols. Washington, 1953.

Highet, G. JUVENAL's Bookcase. AJPh, 72, 1951, 369-94.

Pypin, A. Načalo devjatnadcatogo veka. Tesnaja svjaz' načatkov XIX-go veka s XVIII-m; perexodnaja époxa. Zapadnye istočniki. KARAMZIN. Zukovskij. VE, 8-9, 1895.

Korsakov, D. Iz žizni K. D. KAVELINA vo Francii i Germanii v 1862-1864 gg. (po ego perepiske za éto vremja). RM, 1899-1900.

Struve, G. Russkij evropeec. Materialy dlja biografii i xarakteristiki kn.P.B. KOZLOVSKOGO. San Francisco, 1950. 164 p.

Kudrjavcev, P. Pis'ma Petra Nikolaeviča KUDRJAVCEVA iz-za granicy (1845-47). RM, 1-9, 1898.

Fay, E. Lorenzo in Search of the Sun: D. H. LAWRENCE in Italy, Mexico and the American Southwest. New York, 1953.

Trubeckoj, S. Razočarovannyj slavjanofil (LEONTYEV). VE, 10, 1892, 772-810.

Canto, Estela. Benito LYNCH o la inocencia. Sur, 215-16, 1952, 109-13. [Although Lynch has written almost exclusively about the pampa, his approach has been eminently European.]

Fedorov, A. **MAJAKOVSKIJ** i literatura Zapada (Svjazi Majakovskogo s novejšeij zapadnoj poéziej). In: Vladimir Majakovskij. Sbornik, 1, Moscow, 1940, 94-125.

Uspenskij, I. N. Majakovskij o buržuaznoj "kul'ture" Zapada i Ameriki. Moscow, 1950.

Scott, A. L. **MARK TWAIN** Looks at Europe. SAQ, 52, 1953, 399-413.

Kuhn, Brigitta. Les orientations anglosaxonnes de Xavier **MARMIER**. Diss. Paris, 1953.

Sealts, M. M. **MELVILLE's** Reading: A Supplementary List of Books Owned and Borrowed. Harvard Library Bull., 6, 1952, 239-47.

*Ortiz, R. Radici e propaggini francesi, rumene e spagnuole della "Libertà" di Pietro **METASTASIO**. Mélanges Baldensperger, Paris, 1930, 151-62 and In: Varia romanica. Firenze, 1932.

Mokievskij, P. N. K. **MIXAJLOVSKIJ** i zapadnaja nauka. RB, 3, 1904, 45-50.

Brunet, G. Bibliothèque de **MONTESQUIEU**. In his: Fantaisies bibliographiques. Paris, 1864, 138-44.

Desgraves, L. Catalogue de la Bibliothèque de Montesquieu. Genève, 1954. 320 p.

Surtz, E. L. Thomas **MORE** and the Great Books. PQ, 32, 1953, 43-57.

Hilton, R. Doña Emilia **PARDO BAZÁN** and the Europeanization of Spain. Symposium, 6, 1953, 298-307.

Gradassi, M. Casa d'Aragona in Napoli e vita italiana nei tempi del **PONTANO**. Spoleto, 1926.

Gladkova, E. Prozaičeskie nabroski Puškina iz žizni "sveta." **PUŠKIN**. Vremennik, 6, 1941, 305-22.

Tomaševskij, B. Puškin i narodnost'. In: Puškin, rodonačal'nik russkoj literatury. Moscow, 1941, 67-100.

Vanslov, V. Zapadnoevropejskaja literatura v ocenke Puškina. In: A. S. Puškin. Sbornik statej. Moscow, 1937. 248 p.

Weidlé, W. Puškin i Evropa. SZ, 63, 1937, 220-31.

—— Puschkin und das Abendland. Merkur (Baden-Baden), 3, 1949.

Žirmunskij, V. Puškin i zapadnye literatury. Puškin. Vremennik, 3, (Moscow) 1937, 66-103.

—— Pushkin and Western Literature. In: Pushkin, Moscow 1939, 155-72.

—— Puškin und die Literatur des

Westens. Sinn & Form (Potsdam), 1949.

Bemol, M. **RILKE** et les influences. RLC, 27, 1953, 169-81.

Struve, P. S. P. **ŠEVYREV** i zapadnye vnušenija i istočniki teorii-aforizma o "gnilom," ili "gnijuščem" Zapade. Izyskanija, sopostavlenija i materialy. ZRNI, 17, 1940, 201-63.

Whitaker, V. K. **SHAKESPEARE's** Use of Learning: An Inquiry Into the Growth of His Mind and Art. Huntington Library, 1953. 366 p.

Picchio, R. L'occidentalismo conservatore di Penčo **SLAVEJKOV**. RS, 1, 1952, 124-43.

Pawlikowski, M. The King-Spirit as a Monument of Latin Civilization. (In Polish). **SŁOWACKI** Centenary Volume. London, 1951.

Sitwell, O. (ed.) **SMOLLETT's** Travels in France and Italy. London, 1949.

Praz, M. **STANLEY**, Sherburne and Ayres as Translators and Imitators of Italian, Spanish and French Poets. MLR, 20, 1925.

Gradovskij, A. Po povodu odnogo predislovija. N. **STRAXOV**: Bor'ba s Zapadom v našej literature. VE, 5, 1882, 271-88.

Florovskij, G. Pis'mo k P. B. **STRUVE** ob Evrazijstve. RM, 1-2, 1922, 267-74.

Havens, G. R. & N. L. Torrey. The Private Library of **VOLTAIRE** at Leningrad. PMLA, 43, 1928, 990-1009.

—— Voltaire's Books: a Selected List. MP, 27, 1929-30, 1-22.

—— Voltaire's Library. Fortnightly Rev., 132, 1929, 397-405.

Wilkie, R. F. Christian Felix **WEISSE** and his Relations to French and English Literature. Diss. Calif., 1953. 642 p. [W's early comedies are French in form and subject, but his later and better comedies stem from English sources and are syntheses of French and English elements. In his "Singspiele" he also turned to French comic opera for inspiration. In his tragedies he shows a trend from English historical themes cast in the form of French classical tragedy to a French subject treated with English freedom.]

Reeves, G. Thomas **WOLFE** et l'Europe. Diss. Paris, 1953.

Evans, B. I. **WORDSWORTH** and the European Problem of the Twentieth

Century.   Wordsworth   Centenary
Studies, ed. by G. T. Dunklin. Princeton, 1951.

Kallaš, V. Poétičeskij djad'ka čertej 1
ved'm nemeckix i anglijskix. (ZHU-
KOVSKY). RM, 4, 1902, 138-57.

D. THE MODERN WORLD

IV. SPANISH CONTRBUTIONS.

Influences upon Individual Countries

Kiddle, L. B. The Spanish Language as
a Medium of Cultural Diffusion in
the Age of Discovery. American
Speech, 27, 1953, 241-56.

Miaja de la Muda, A. De la existencia de
una escuela internacional española de
los siglos XVI y XVII. Madrid, 1949.

Vossler, K. Die Bedeutung der spanischen
Kultur für Europa. In his: Südliche
Romania. Leipzig, 1950, 243-80.

———— Spanien und Europa. München,
1952. 206 p.

Ballesteros-Gaibrois, M. La vida cultural
en la AMÉRICA española en los siglos
XVI y XVII. In: Díaz-Plaja (ed.) Historia general de las literaturas hispánicas. III. Renacimiento y barroco.
Barcelona, 1953.

Boggs, R. S. Caribbean Ballads of the
Spanish Conquest. In: Wilgus, A.
(ed.) The Caribbean: Contemporary
Trends. Gainesville (Fla.), 1953, 91-
99.

Bühler, C. F. Iberian Incunabula in
America. Library Quart., 23, 1953,
281-83.

Cowles, Ella N. A Vocabulary of American Spanish Based on Glossaries Appended to Literary Works. Diss. U. of
Michigan, 1952.

Delk, Lois J. & J. N. Greer. Spanish Language and Literature in the Publications of American Universities. A
Bibliography. Texas Hisp. Studies 4,
(Austin), 1952. 211 p.

Espinosa, A. M. Spanish Tradition Among
the Pueblo Indians.   Festschrift
Archer M. Huntington, Wellesley
(Mass.), 1952, 131-41.

Kiddle, L. B. Spanish Loan Words in
American Indian Languages. Hisp.,
35, 1952, 179-84.

Leonard, I. A. Books of the Brave: Being
an Account of Books and Men in the
Spanish Conquest and Settlement of
the Sixteenth Century New World.
Harvard U.P., 1949. Spanish Transl.:
Los Libros del Conquistador. Mexico,
1953. [Contains a valuable appendix

of documents not contained in the
original edition.]

Morreale, Margherita. La Biblioteca del
Congreso de los Estados Unidos y sus
actividades hispánicas.   Arbor, 23,
1952, 106-13.

Ornstein, J. La labor hispanista de la
Biblioteca del Congreso norte-ameri-
cano. Clavileño, 4, 1953, 39-43.

Palacín, G. B. La lengua española de
América. Le lingue del Mondo, 17,
1952, 4-5.

Reparaz-Ruiz, G. de. Les études his-
paniques aux Etats-Unis jusqu'en
1939. BH, 48, 1946.

Stimson, F. S. Spanish Themes in Early
American   Literature   in   Novels,
Drama, and Verse, 1770-1830. Diss.
U. of Michigan, 1953.

Hoppe, H. R. Spanish Actors at the Court
in Brussels 1614-18, (including Francisco López, autor). (BELGIUM).
Bull. of the Comediantes, 5, 1953, 1-3.

Kolker, Sister Mary D. Spanish Legends in
ENGLISH and American Literature,
1800-1860. Diss. Catholic U. Washington, 1952.

McCann, Eleanor M. The Influence of
Sixteenth and Seventeenth Century
Spanish Mystics and Ascetics on some
Metaphysical Writers.   Diss. Stan-
ford U., 1953.

Metford, J. C. J. British Contributions
to Spanish and Spanish-American
Studies. London, 1950. 86 p. (Cf. CL,
1953).

Russell, P. E. English Seventeenth Century Interpretations of Spanish Literature. Atlante (London), 1, 1953,
65-77.

Salazar Chapela, E. Clásicos españoles en
Inglaterra. CA, 11, 1952, 256-61.

Foulché-Delbosc, R.   Bibliographie des
voyages en Espagne et en Portugal.
(FRANCE). Paris, 1896. 349 p.

Isopescu, C. "L'Espagne littéraire." Os-
servatore Romano, 23.XII.1949.

Kurz, H. The Spanish. In his: European
Characters in French Drama in the
Eighteenth Century. New York, 1916,
45-85.

Morel-Fatio, A. Catalogue des manuscrits

espagnols et des manuscrits portugais
(dans la Bibliothèque Nationale).
Paris, 1892.
Reparaz-Ruiz, G. & H. E. Davis. Hispanic
and Hispanic-American Studies in
France. Hispanic-American Historical
Rev., 26, 1946.
Bertrand, J. J. A. Los comienzos del Hispanismo alemán. (GERMANY). Clavileño, March, 1952.
Loomis, C. G. Some Spanish Proverbs in
Seventeenth-Century German. RPh,
6, 1953, 281-83.
Geers, G. J. De studie van spaanse in-
vloeden op de nederlandse littera-
tuur. (HOLLAND). NP, 37, 1953,
193-202.
Almagiá, R. Un fiorentino in Spagna al
principio del sec. XVI. (ITALY).
Festschrift Gino Luzzatto. Milano,
1950.
Chasles, P. Etudes sur l'Espagne et sur
les influences de la littérature espagnole en France et en Italie. Paris,
1847.
Farinelli, A. La Spagna e i romantici
d'Italia. NAnt, 387, 1936.
Ferrara, O. El siglo XVI a la luz de los
embajadores venecianos. Madrid,
1952. 498 p.
Gutiérrez, C. Españoles en Trento.
Madrid, 1951.
Pepe, G. Il mezzogiorno d'Italia sotto
gli Spagnuoli. Firenze, 1952. 237 p.
Wade, G. E. A Seventeenth-Century Ital-
ian Looks at the Spanish. Hisp., 1952,
217-18.
Gil Benumeya, R. Hispanismo en el LI-
BANO. Clavileño, Jan., 1952.
Cintra, L. F. L. (ed.) Crónica geral de
Espanha de 1344. Edicão crítica do
texto PORTUGUES. Lisboa, 1951.
Figueiredo, F. de. España en la moderna
literatura portuguesa. In: Estudos de
Literatura, 2. ser. Lisboa, 1918.
Hoenerbach, H. Spanien in der Staats-
kanzlei der Mamluken. (TURKEY).
Romanist. Jb, 3, 1950, 254-80.

Amadis, Romances, Comedias

Isopescu, C. O Amadis de Gaula. Osserva-
tore Romano, 6.VIII.1950.
Lázaro, Elena & J. López de Toro. Ama-
dis de Grecia por Tierras de Cuenca.
Bibliofilia, 6, 1952, 25-28.
Parker, J. H. & A. G. Reichenberger. A
Current Bibliography of Foreign Pub-
lications Dealing with the Comedia.
Bull. of The Comediantes, 4, 1952.

Cervantes and Don Quijote

Ares Montes, J. Cervantes en la litera-
tura portuguesa del siglo XVII.
Anales Cervantinos, 2, (Madrid)
1952, 193-230.
Barber, Leonore. Florians Don Quijote-
Übersetzung. Diss. Heidelberg, 1951.
Bertrand, J. J. A. Cervantes en el país
de Fausto. Madrid, 1950.
Camara Cascudo, C. da. Don Quijote no
folclore do Brasil. Rev. de Dialecto-
logia y Tradiciones Populares, 8,
(Madrid), 1952.
Carilla, E. Cervantes y América. Buenos
Aires, 1951. 70 p.
Corrales Egea, J. Notas a una aventura
quijotesca del Cardenal de Retz.
Anales Cervantinos, 2 (Madrid), 1952,
368-71.
Darmangeat, P. Cervantès et nous. Eu-
rope, 76, 1952, 97-102.
Díaz Plaja, G. Don Quijote en el país de
Martín Fierro. Madrid, 1952. 186 p.
Eguía Ruiz, C. La hispanidad en tierras
uruguayas: Un gran cervantista, Don
Arturo Estanislao Xalambrí. Bol.
Biblioteca Menéndez Pelayo, 27, 1951,
365-78.
Ferrer, Olga P. Las Almas muertas de
Gogol y Don Quijote. Cuadernos de
Literatura, July, 1950, 201-14.
Figueiredo, F. de. O tema do Quijote na
literatura portuguesa do século XVIII.
In: Estudos de Literatura, 3 ser.,
Lisboa, 1921.
———— O tema de Quijote na literatura
portuguesa do século XIX. Ibid., 4 ser.,
Lisboa, 1924.
Geers, G. J. Cervantes en wij. (Holland).
Critisch Bulletin, 18, 1951, 373-81.
Gehle, H. Hardy und Cervantes. Diss.
Berlin, 1951.
Hinz, J. (L. Carroll's) Alice Meets the
Don. SAQ, 52, 1953, 253-66.
Iorga, N. Shakespeare şi Cervantes. Drum
Drept, 1916.
Kaplan, D. The Lover's Test Theme in
Cervantes and Mme de Lafayette. FR,
26, 1953, 285-90.
López Estrada, F. Don Quijote en Lima.
Anales Cervantinos, 1 (Madrid), 1951,
332-36.
Lubac, A. Robinson Crusoe, Don Quijote,
El Idiota. Ibid., 2, 1952, 372-73.
Mirabent, F. Sobre un aspecto del cer-
vantismo alemán. Rev. de Ideas Es-
téticas, 10, 1952, 115-39.
Parker, J. H. Influencia del Quijote en el

extranjero. Publ. trimestral, U. de San Carlos 7, (Guatemala), 1947, 57-73.

Rhoades, Sister Mary Teresa. Was Mark Twain Influenced by the Prolog to Don Quixote? Mark Twain Quart., 9, 1952, 4-6.

Santayana, G. Tom Sawyer and Don Quixote. Ibid., 1-3.

Savj-Lopez, P. Don Chisciotte e l'Italia. Secolo, June, 1916.

Schürr, F. Der Don Quijote als Ausdruck der abendländischen Seele. Freiburg i.B., 1952.

Sciacca, M. F. El caballero vivo de esta Europa moribúnda. Clavileño, Nov., 1951.

Speziale, A. Il Cervantes e le imitazioni nella novellistica italiana. Messina, 1914.

Sullivan, M. W. La influencia de Cervantes y de su obra en Chile. Anales Cervantinos 2, (Madrid), 1952, 287-310.

Don Juan

Doolittle, J. The Humanity of Molière's Don Juan. PMLA, 68, 1953, 509-34.

*Figueirido, F. de. Donjuanismo e antidonjuanismo em Portugal. In: Critica do Exilio. Lisboa, 1930, 181-260.

Hall, V. Joyce's Use of Da Ponte and Mozart's Don Giovanni. PMLA, 66, 1951, 78-84.

Prunaj, G. B. Le tre leggende eterne: Il Cid, Don Giovanni, Faust. Palermo, n.d.

Sauvage, Micheline. Le cas de Don Juan. Paris, 1953. 106 p.

Smirnov, A. Obraz Don Žuana u Mol'era. UZLU-FN, 8, 71-84.

Sretenskij, N. Šekspirizm Bajrona v Donžuane. Učenye Zapiski, Rostov Pedagogical Institute, 1, 1938, 159-84. (With short summaries in French and English.)

Tejada, F. E. de. Il superhombre y Don Juan. Esudios Americanos, April, 1952.

Worthington, Mabel P. Don Juan: Theme and Development in the Nineteenth Century. Diss. Columbia U, 1953.

Picaro and Lazarillo

Caneva, R. Picaresca: Anticaballería y realismo. U. de Antioquia, 28, 1953, 373-89.

Carballo Picazo, A. El señor d'Ouville y el Lazarillo de Tormes. Rev. Biblio-

gráfica y Documental, 5, 1951, 223-28.

Frutos Gómez de las Cortinas, J. El anti-héroe y su actitud vital. Cuad. de Lit., 7, 1950, 97-143.

Günther, H. Gestalt und Wandlungen des deutschen Schelmenromans. Welt & Wort, 10, (Tübingen), 1955, 1-5.

Guillen, C. The Anatomies of Roguery: A Comparative Study of the Origins and Nature of Picaresque Literature. Diss. Harvard, 1953.

Lovett, G. H. Lazarillo de Tormes in Russia. MLJ, 36, 1952, 166-74.

May, T. E. Pícaro. A Suggestion. RR, 43, 1952, 26-33.

Pabisch, Marie. Picaresque Dramas of the 17th and 18th Centuries. Göttingen, 1909. 112 p.

Pereda Valdés, I. La novela picaresca y el pícaro en España y América. Montevideo, 1950. 142 p. [A series of loosely connected essays which, at their best, are delightfully written and highly suggestive. Factually they add nothing.]

Roland, Brother A. La psicología de la novela picaresca. Hisp., 36, 1953, 423-26.

Schneider, H. La primera traducción alemana del Lazarillo de Tormes. (1614). Clavileño, July, 1953, 56-58.

Other Spanish Authors

Atkins, S. Goethe, CALDERÓN, and Faust: Der Tragödie Zweiter Teil. Gr, 28, 1953, 83-98.

Rehm, W. Schiller und das Barockdrama. In: Götterstille und Göttertrauer. Bern, 1951.

Ritter, F. de. El gran teatro del mundo. Rev. Nacional de Cultura, 14 (Caracas), Nov., 1952, 133-53. [Plato, Calderón, Hofmannsthal, Pirandello.]

Hanke, L. Bartolomé de las CASAS and the Spanish Empire in America: Four Centuries of Misunderstanding. PAPS, 97, 1953, 26-30.

Ugalde, L. Las Casas and the Black Legend. Boston Public Lib. Quart., 5, 1953, 97-106.

*Milner, Z. GÓNGORA et Mallarmé. Esprit Nouveau, 1, 1920, 285-96. [The two poets of the condensed image.]

Spell, J. R. Indulgencia para todos (by M. E. GOROSTIZA) en Austria y Alemania. RIA, 17, 1953, 293-300.

Fellheimer, Jeanette. The Episode of "The Villain of the Danube" in Fen-ton's Golden Epistles. (GUEVARA). MLQ, 14, 1953, 331-34.

Vézinet, F. IRIARTE et Florian (la fable littéraire). In his: Molière, Florian et la littérature espagnole. Paris, 1909.

Copleston, F. C. David Hume and St. JOHN OF THE CROSS. The Month, N.S., 8, 1952, 69-81.

LEÓN EBREO: See under Platonism, 260 & 725.

*Cotronei, B. Una commedia di LOPE DE VEGA e i Promessi Sposi. Rassegna bibliogr. della lett. ital., 7, 1899.

Jobit, P. De Lope de Vega à Jean Anouilh. Clavileño, July, 1952, 1-4.

Bentley, E. El poeta en Dublin (García LORCA). Asomante, 9, 1953, 44-58.

Batllori, M. Le LULLIsme de la renaissance et du baroque: Padoue et Rome. Actes du XIe Congrès Internat. de Philosophie, 13 (Bruxelles), 1953, 7-12.

Ward, R. S. An Interpretation of a Psalm of Life with Reference to MANRIQUE's Coplas. Festschrift S. E. Leavitt. Washington, 1953, 191-98.

Miró, Clemencia. Gabriel MIRÓ y América. Revista Nacional de Cultura (Caracas), 14, 1953, 83-88. [Contacts and correspondence with, and reception by, Spanish American writers.]

Coyle, W. MOLINOS: "The Subject of the Day" in "The Ring and the Book" (Browning). PMLA, June, 1952.

Rogers, F. M. Os quatro dromedários do Infante Dom PEDRO: Uma fonte de Guillaume Apollinaire, Gómez de Santisteban. II. Colloquium Internacional de Estudos Luso-Brasileiros, São Paulo, 1954.

Hendrix, W. S. QUEVEDO, Guevara, Lesage, and the Tatler. MP, 19, 1921-22, 177-86.

Domenicali, D. A Bibliography of the Works by and about Ramón José SENDER in the English Language. Bull. of Bibliog., 20, 1951.

Tucker, J. E. Castillo SOLORZANO's Garduña de Sevilla in English Translation. PBSA, 46, 1952, 154-58.

Ferrater Mora, J. SUÁREZ y la filosofía moderna. Notas y Estudios de Filosofía, 2, (Tucumán), 1951, 269-94 and In: JHI, 14, 1953, 528-47.

García Blanco, M. Versiones italianas de las obras de UNAMUNO. Quaderni Iberoamericani (Torino), 13.

Seal, L. Unamuno y Pirandello. Ital., 29, 1952, 193-99.

*Willers, H. Le diable boîteux (Lesage). El diablo cojuelo (VÉLEZ GUEVARA). Diss. Rostock. Erlangen, 1935. Also In: RF, 49, 1935, 215-316.

Juneo, A. Antonio VIEIRA en México. La carta atenagórica de Sor Juana Inés de la Cruz. Arquivo histórico de Portugal, 1, 1932-34, 288-302.

Ricard, R. Antonio Vieira y Sor Juana Inés de la Cruz. Miscelanea Americanista, 2, (Madrid) 1951, 301-27.

Spanish Influences upon Individual Authors

Real, C. A. del. Noticias sobre España en Elio ARISTIDES de Esmirna. Madrid, 1950. 24 p.

*Croce, B. Traiano BOCCALINI, il nemico degli spagnuoli. In his: Poeti e scrittori del pieno e del tardo Rinascimento, 2, (Bari) 1953, 255-97 & In: Estudios dedicados e Menéndez Pidal, Madrid, 1952, 217-27.

Hart, T. R. Friedrich BOUTERWEK, A Pioneer Historian of Spanish Literature. CL, 5, 1953, 351-61.

Kaegi, W. España y la Controreforma en la obra de BURCKHARDT. Colección O crece o muere. Madrid, 1952. 40 p. & In: Annali Scuola Norm. Sup. di Pisa, 21, 1951, 158-73.

Guerrieri Crocetti, C. La lirica di CAMOES. Genova, 1939.

Giusso, L. CAMPANELLA e la Spagna. Idea, 2.III.1952.

Ferraro, S. Bibliografia di Benedetto CROCE hispanista. 1. (1885-1900). Quaderni Iberoamericani, 14, 1953.

Gmelin, H. España en la Divina Comedia (DANTE). Clavileño, July, 1953.

Cordasco, F. Spanish Influence on Restoration Drama: George DIGBY's Elvira (1663?). RLC, 27, 1953, 93-98.

FARINELLI, A. Le monde hispanique dans ma dernière oeuvre. In: La mission de l'Espagne, Paris, 1941, 296-313.

FIGUEIREDO, F. de. Viagem atraves da Espanha literária. Estudos de Literatura, 5a Ser., São Paulo, 1951.

Ernst, F. GRIMMELSHAUSENs Simplizissimus und seine spanischen Verwandten. Merkur, 7, 1953, 753-64. [Compares, beyond the question of "influence," Simplizissimus with Spanish picaresque novels from Lazarillo to El Gran Tacaño and Marcos de Obregón. Stresses the closeness to the Spanish tradition, minimizes the significance of the "Parzifal" tradition.]

Guicciardini, P. L'andata in Ispagna in un diario inedito di Francesco **GUICCIARDINI** ambasciatore fiorentino di Ferdinando il Cattolico. Atti della Soc. Colombaria, 1930-31.

────── Ancora sul Guicciardini in Ispagna. Marzocco, 37, 1932.

────── Diario del viaggio in Ispagna di Francesco Guicciardini. Firenze, 1932.

Vazquez-Arjono, C. Spanish and Spanish-American Influences on Bret **HARTE**. RH, 76, 1929.

Aubrun, C. V. (ed.) Le Chansonnier espagnol d' **HERBERAY DES ESSARTS**. Bordeaux, 1951. 300 p.

Laplane, G. Victor **HUGO** y España. Clavileño, March, 1953.

Adams, T. R. Washington **IRVING**: Another Letter from Spain. AL, 25, 1953, 354-58.

Devos, J. P. Un tableau de l'Espagne à la fin du XVIe siècle (**JEHAN L'HERMITE**). Lettres romanes, Nov., 1953.

Ortiz, R. **LEOPARDI** e la Spagna. Appunti. Bucarest, 1923.

Brunetière, F. La question de Gil Blas. (**LESAGE**). In: Histoire et littérature, 2, (Paris) 1891, 235-69.

Isopescu, C. Le Sage e il teatro spagnuolo. Idea, 27, 1949.

Robolsky, H. Sur l'originalité de Gil Blas. Stettin, 1857. 25 p.

Vic, J. La composition et les sources du Diable boîteux de Lesage. RHL, 27, 1920, 481-517.

Healy, Sister M. Aquinas. Spanish Influences on **LONGFELLOW**. Hisp., 35, 1952, 301-04.

Grönvold, M. La vida feliz de Egron **LUNDGREN** en España. Clavileño, Sept., 1953.

Russell, P. E. A Stuart Hispanist: James **MABBE**. BHS, 30, 1953, 75-84.

Williams, S. T. Some Spanish Influences on American Fiction: **MARK TWAIN** to Willa Cather. Hisp., 36, 1953, 133-36.

Figueiredo, F. de. Oliveira **MARTINS** e a Hespanha. In: Historia dum Vencido da Vida. Lisboa, 1930, 141-82.

Parturier, M. Rendez-vous espagnols de Prosper **MÉRIMÉE**. RP, 60, 1953, 63-74. [Letters of 1853 concerning the writer's trip to Spain in that year, dealing partly with contemporary events in Spain but mostly with Mérimée's personal relations, particulary with women.]

Arias, A. **MONTALVO** en España. América 37, (Quito), 1951-52, 37-49. [The Ecuadoran's contacts with, and indebtedness to, Spain.]

Rosenbaum, S. C. Henry de **MONTHERLANT** and Spain. BHS, 29, 1952, 138-47.

Knight, K. G. **MOSCHEROSCH'** Novel Soldatenleben. GLL, 7, 1953, 48-55. [Relates one of Moscherosch' "Gesichte" to the Spanish picaresque tradition and claims for the story the distinction of being the first original German prose fiction.]

Mead, R. G. Manuel González **PRADA**: Peruvian Judge of Spain. Spanish-American Attitudes toward Nineteenth Century Spain. PMLA, Sept., 1953, 696-715.

Zardoya, Concha. **SANTAYANA** y España. Insula, 7, 1952.

Lida de Malkiel, Maria. Para las fuentes españolas de algunos sonetos burlescos de **SCARRON**. RLC, 27, 1953, 185-91.

Williams, S. T. Spanish Influences on the Fiction of William Gilmore **SIMMS**. HR, 21, 1953, 221-28.

Remenyi, J. J. Jeno **TERSANSZKY**, Writer of Picaresque Stories. SAQ, 52, 1953, 391-98. [Tersanszky is not a great writer, but the genuine humor, the ironic spirit of his stories and novels and their picaresque features deserve the attention of the discriminating reader.]

Alekseev, M. **TURGENEV** i ispanskie pisateli. LK, 11, 1938, 136-44.

Sánchez y Escribano, F. Actitud neoclásica de **VOLTAIRE** ante el Barroco español. MLJ, 37, 1953, 76-77.

V. PORTUGUESE CONTRIBUTIONS

Influences upon Individual Countries

Anon. O português dos jornais portugueses no estranjeiro. Revista de Portugal, 3, 1943.

Bell, A. F. G. Portuguese Bibliography. Oxford, 1922.

Cidade, H. Influência da Expansão Ultramarina na Literatura. In: Baião, et al., História da Expansão Portuguesa no Mundo, 3, Lisboa, 1937-40.

———— Os Portugueses no Renascimento: Sua contribuição para a mundividência quinhentista. Revista da Faculdade de Letras de Lisboa, 17, 1951.

Consiglieri Pedrozo, Z. Influencia dos descobrimentos dos portugueses na historia da civilisação: Conferencia. Lisboa, 1898.

———— Catalogo bibliographico das publicações relativas aos descobrimentos portugueses. Lisboa, 1912.

Cortesao, J. L'expansion des Portugais dans l'histoire de la civilisation. Lisboa, 1930.

Farinelli, A. Viajes por España y Portugal desde la edad media hasta el siglo XX: Divagaciones bibliograficas. Madrid, 1920 & In: Nuevas y antiguas divagaciones bibliograficas. 3 vols., Roma, 1942.

Foulché-Delbosc, R. Bibliographie des voyages en Espagne et en Portugal. Paris, 1896. 349 p.

Freyre, G. O mundo que o português criou. Rio de Janeiro, 1940.

Mercadal, J. G. Viajes de extranjeros por España y Portugal: Desde los tiempos remotos hasta fines del siglo XVI. Madrid, 1952.

Parker, J. H. Some Aspects of the Portuguese Contribution. Canadian Mod. Lang. Review, 5, 1948.

Axelson, E. South-East AFRICA, 1488-1530. London, 1940.

Anon. Os Portuguêses em New Bedford. (AMERICA). O 5.º Centenario des Açores na Nova Inglaterra. New Bedford, 1932.

Azevedo, A. de. Portugal na América do Norte. In: A América do Norte na literatura portuguêsa. Bol. Sociedade de Geografia de Lisboa, 69, 1951.

Carvalho, E. de. Os Portugueses na Nova Inglaterra. Rio de Janeiro, 1931.

Gayton, Anna H. The "Festa da Serreta" (Azores) at Gustine (California). Western Folklore, 7, 1948.

———— Luso-Californian Culture and its Research Needs. Proceedings Internat. Colloquium on Luso-Brazilian Studies, 1950. Nashville, 1953.

Holmes, U. T. Portuguese Americans. In: Our Racial and National Minorities (ed. F. J. Brown and J. S. Roucek). New York, 1937.

Lang, H. R. The Portuguese Element in New England. JAF, 1892.

Pap, L. Portuguese-American Speech: An

Outline of Speech Conditions among Portuguese Immigrants in New England and Elsewhere in the United States. New York, 1949.

Soares, C. California and the Portuguese. How the Portuguese Helped to Build up California. Monograph Written for Golden Gate International Exposition San Francisco 1939. Lisbon, 1939.

Taft, D. R. Two Portuguese Communities in New England. New York, 1923.

Welsh, Doris V. A Catalog of The William B. Greenlee Collection of Portuguese History and Literature and the Portuguese Materials in the Newberry Library. Chicago, 1953.

Dalgado, Monsenhor S. R. Influência do vocabulário português em línguas ASIÁticas (abrangendo cêrca de cinqüenta idiomas). Coimbra, 1913. [Engl. trsl. by Xavier Soares: Influence of Portuguese Vocables in Asiatic Languages. Baroda, India, 1936.]

———— Glossário luso-asiático. 2 vols. Coimbra, 1919-21.

Gândara, A. Isabel, Filha de el-rei D. João I: Prolongamento histórico de Joanna d'Arc. (BELGIUM). Lisboa, 1954. [About Isabel, Duchess of Burgundy.]

Godin, O. L. Princes et princesses de la famille royale de Portugal ayant par leurs alliances régné sur la Flandre: Rapports entre la Flandre et le Portugal de 1094 à 1682. 10e Congrès Internat. des Orientalistes, Lisboa, 1892.

Looten, C. Isabelle de Portugal, duchesse de Bourgogne et comtesse de Flandre (1397-1471). RLC, 18, 1938.

Lopes, J. M. Les Portugais à Anvers au XVIe siècle. Anvers, 1895.

Martel Patricio, Maria Magdalena de. Princesses du Portugal, Souveraines de Flandres, 1430-1930. Printed Lecture dated Portugal, Dec. 1930 about the 15th century Isabel, being a hommage to the 20th century Queen Elisabeth of Belgium, granddaughter of King Miguel of Portugal.

Sousa Viterbo. D. Isabel de Portugal, Duqueza de Borgonha: Notas documentaes para a sua biographia e para a historia das relações entre Portugal e a côrte de Borgonha. Archivo Historice Portuguez, 3, 1905.

Freyre, G. Um BRASILeiro em Terras Portuguêsas. Rio de Janeiro, 1953.

Jarry de Mancy, A. & F. Denis. Tableau

historique, chronologique de la littérature portugaise et brésilienne, depuis son origine jusqu'à nos jours. In: Jarry de Mancy, A.: Atlas historique et chronologique. . . Paris, 1831.

Livermore, H. V. (ed.) Portugal and Brazil: An Introduction. Oxford, 1953.

Malheiro Dias, C. et al. História da Colonização Portuguesa do Brasil. 3 vols. Porto, 1921-24.

Paiva Boléo, M. de. Filologia e história: A emigração açoriano para o Brasil. Biblos, 20, 1944 & Coimbra, 1945.

Costa, F. O árcade Curvo de Semêdo na poesía anglo-americana: Influências literárias peninsulares em alguns poetas ingleses do começo do seculo XIX. (ENGLAND). Bol. Academia das Sciências de Lisboa, 12, 1917-18.

Figaniere, F. F. de la. Catalogo dos manuscriptos portuguêzes existentes no Museu Britannico. Lisboa, 1853.

Gonçalves Rodrígues, A. A lingua portuguesa em Inglaterra nos séculos XVII e XVIII. Biblos, 27, 1951.

Livermore, H. V. The "Privilege of an Englishman in the Kingdoms and Dominions of Portugal." Atlante, 2, 1954. [About a small book published in London, 1736, with text in both English and Portuguese.]

MacAulay, Rose. They Went to Portugal. London, 1946. Translated into Portuguese by Maria F. Gonçalves & Alvaro Doria, Porto, 1950. [About Englishmen who have gone to Portugal throughout the ages: the Crusaders, William Beckford, Byron, Southey, the port-shippers (established in the North of Portugal since the 17th century, etc.)]

Thomas, H. Short-title Catalogue of Portuguese Books and of Spanish-American Books Printed before 1601 Now in the British Museum. RH, 65 & London, 1926.

*——— English Translations of Portuguese Books before 1640. Library, 7, 1926 & In: Rivista da Universidade de Coimbra, 11, 1933.

——— Short-title Catalogue of Portuguese Books Printed before 1601 Now in the British Museum. London, 1940.

Tovar, Conde de. Catálogo dos manuscritos portugueses ou relativos a Portugal existentes no Museu Britânico.

Lisboa, 1932. [Supplements Figaniere, above.]

Coutinho, B. X. A Revolução de 1640 na literatura FRANCEsa. In: Ensaios: Varia camoniana e outros estudos, Porto, 1941.

Matos, L. de. Les Portugais à l'Université de Paris entre 1500 et 1550. Coimbra, 1950. 245 p.

——— Les Portugais en France au XVIe siècle: Etudes et documents. Coimbra, 1952.

Morel-Fatio, A. Catalogue des manuscrits espagnols et des manuscrits portugais [in the Bibliothèque Nationale]. Paris, 1892.

Watkins, W. A. Portuguese Literature in France. Symposium, 4, 1950.

Cordeiro, L. Portuguezes fóra de Portugal: Uma Sobrinha do Infante Imperatriz da Allemanha e Rainha da Hungria. (GERMANY). Lisboa, 1894. [About Leonor, wife of Friedrich III.]

Horch, H. J. Postwar Development of Luso-Brazilian Studies at German Universities. Proceedings Internat. Colloquium in Luso-Brazilian Studies, 1950. Nashville, 1953.

Sousa Viterbo. D. Leonor de Portugal, Imperatriz da Allemanha: Notas documentais para o estudo biographico d'esta princesa e para a historia das relações da corte de Portugal com a casa d'Austria. Archivo Historico Portuguez, 7, 1909, 432-40.

Burnell, A. C. A Tentative List of Books and Manuscripts Relating to the History of the Portuguese in INDIA Proper. Mangalore, 1880.

Campos, J. J. History of the Portuguese in Bengal. Calcutta, 1919.

Faria, A. de. Portugal e ITALIA: Elenco de manuscriptos portuguezes ou referentes a Portugal existentes nas Bibliothecas de Italia. Leorne, 1899.

Norton, L. Os Portugueses no Japão. (1543-1640). (JAPAN). Lisboa, 1952.

Figueiredo, F. de (ed.) Viajantes espanhoes em Portugal: Textos de seculo XVIII. (SPAIN). São Paulo, 1947.

Lang, H. R. Cancioneiro Gallego-Castelhano. New York, 1902.

Martinez-Ferrando, J. E. Pere de Portugal "Rei dels Catalans" vist a través dels registres de la seva Cancellerai. Barcelona, 1936.

Individual Portuguese Authors

Gonçalves Rodrígues, A. Mariana ALCO-FORADO: História e crítica de uma fraude literária. 2nd ed. Coimbra, 1943.

García, C. Camilo e Sóror Mariana por detrás das grades. Porto, 1945. [Contains the French text of the Lettres Portugaises.]

Smith, R. C. A Pioneer Teacher: Father Peter BABAD and His Portuguese Grammar. Hisp., 28, 1945. [Father Peter Babad, of the Society of St. Sulpice of Baltimore, taught the first course in Portuguese at an American University and wrote the first Portuguese grammar published in the U.S. Born and died in France (1763-1846).]

Aquarone, J. B. Chateaubriand admirateur de CAMOENS. In: Mélanges Le Gentil. Paris, 1949.

Baumgarten, S. Camões et la sensibilité hongroise. Bull. des Etudes Portugaises et de l'Inst. fr. au Portugal, 13, 1949.

Colaço, T. R. Os Lusíadas e a Espanha. In: D. Quichote, Rei de Portugal. Lisboa, 1953.

Costa, F. Camões, exemplar e modêlo de modernos sonetistas ingleses: Elizabeth Browning e Catarina de Ataide. Bol. Academia das Sciências de Lisboa, 11, 1916-17.

*Coutinho, B. X. Camoëns en France au XVIIe siècle. In: Ensaios: Varia camoniana e outros estudos. Porto, 1941.

—— Um precursor dos estudos camonianos em França: Timóteo Lécussan Verdier. Ibid.

Paxeco, Elza. Camões e Elizabeth Barrett. In: Estudos em três línguas. Lisboa, 1945.

Peixoto, A. Camões e o Brasil. In: Ensaios. Coimbra, 1932.

Rónai, P. La fortune intellectuelle de Camões en Hongrie. Revista da Faculdade de Letras de Lisboa, 7, 1941, & In: Ocidente, 26, 1945.

Rüegg, A. Luis de Camões und Portugals Glanzzeit im Spiegel seines Nationalepos. Basel, 1925.

*Storck, W. Camoens in Deutschland: Bibliographische Beiträge zur Gedächtnisfeier des Lusiadensängers. Kolozsvár, 1879. 2nd ed., 1880.

Warnier, R. La chaire Camoëns à Nice, Centre Universitaire Mediterranéen, 1937-41. Coimbra, 1942.

Agan, J. E. CORREA DA SERRA. Penn. Mag. of History & Biography, 49, 1925. [About the Abade José Francisco Corrêa da Serra (1750-1823), Portuguese Minister in Washington from 1816 to 1820. In 1815, he lectured on botany at the U. of Pennsylvania. He had earlier initiated the publication of the famous Collecção de livros ineditos de historia portugueza.]

Battelli, G. Due celebri monaci portoghesi in Firenze nella prima metà del quattrocento: L'Abate GOMES FERREIRA da Silva e Velasco di Portogallo. Archivio Storico Ital., 95, 1938.

—— Due lettere inedite dell'Abate Gomes a Cosimo de' Medici. Biblos, 16, 1940.

Martinez Ferrando, J. E. Tragedia del Insigne Condestable Don PEDRO DE PORTUGAL. Madrid, 1942.

Battelli, G. Una dedica inedita di Ambrogio Traversari all'Infante Dom Pedro di Portogallo, Duca di Coimbra (1392-1449). Rinascita, 2, 1939.

—— O Infante Dom Pedro, Duque de Coimbra, em Florença. Portucale, 13, 1940. [This article should be used with caution.]

Calmette, J. Dom Pedro, roi des Catalans, et la cour de Bourgogne. Annales de Bourgogne, 18, 1946. [About the poet Pedro, Constable of Portugal (1429-66).]

Brito, Rocha. O Português Francisco SANCHES. Bull. des Etudes Portugaises, June, 1940.

*Coralnik, A. Zur Geschichte der Skepsis: Francesco Sanchez. Arch. f. Geschichte d. Philosophie, 27, 1913-14.

*Iriarte, J. Kartesischer oder Sanchezischer Zweifel? Diss. Bonn. Bottrop i.W., 1935.

Moreira de Sâ, A. Os Precursores de Descartes. Lisboa, 1944. [He points out that Francisco Sanches anticipated Descartes.]

Beau, A. E. GIL VICENTE na Alemanha. Coimbra, 1939.

Livermore, Ann. Gil Vicente and Shakespeare. Proceedings Internat. Colloquium on Luso-Brazilian Studies, 1950. Nashville, 1953.

Portuguese Influences upon Individual Authors

*Solman, A. H. The Sources of CALDE-RÓN's El Principe Constante. Oxford, 1950.

Escagües y Javierre, I. Miguel de CER-VANTES y la geografía de Portugal. Rev. Bibliográfica y Documental, 2, 1948. [P. 131-32 contain a bibliography on Cervantes and Portugal.]

*Saunal, D. CHATEAUBRIAND et le Portugal. RLC, 23, 1949.

Le Gentil, G. Ferdinand DENIS, iniciador dos estudos portuguesese brasileiros. Biblos, 4, 1928.

Vasconcellos, J. de. (ed.) Voyage de JEHAN VAN-EYCK (Viaje de Juan Van-Eyck), 1428-30. Revista de Guimarães, 14, 1897. [Contains the French and Spanish texts of the narrative and the editor's commentary. Van Eyck went to Portugal to paint Isabel's portrait for the Duke of Burgundy.]

Baker, C. The Source-book for Hudson's Green Mansions. PMLA, 61, 1946. [Suggests Lady MORGAN's novel The Missionary (3 vols., London, 1811), about a Portuguese missionary in India.]

MURR, C. G. von. Portugesische (sic!) Litteratur. Journal zur Kunstgeschichte & zur allg. Litteratur, 4-17, 1777-89. [Murr had a large correspondence, in Latin, with persons in Portugal. He gives a running account of new books, chiefly literary, and of many other topics, a large number of them political. These articles show that Portugal is of interest to the rest of Europe because of the Academy movement, the literary Arcadias, the earthquake, the Marquis of Pombal, and the expulsion of the Jesuits.]

QUILLINAN, Dorothy Wordsworth. Journal of a Few Months' Residence in Portugal, and Glimpses of the South of Spain. 2 vols. London, 1847.

Schwartz, W. August Wilhelm SCHLE-GELS Verhältnis zur spanischen und portugiesischen Literatur. Halle a.S., 1914.

SOUTHWELL, R. The History of the Revolutions of Portugal from the Foundation of that Kingdom to the Year 1667, with Letters of Sir Robert Southwell During his Embassy there. London, 1740.

VII. FRENCH CONTRIBUTIONS.

Influences upon Individual Countries

Kareev, N. Francuzskaja revoljucija v istoričeskom romane. Petrograd, 1923.

Martineau, A. Histoire des colonies françaises et de l'expansion de la France dans le monde. Paris, 1929.

Rivarol, A. De l'universalité de la langue française. Berlin, 1784 & Paris, 1785.

Roumiguière, Henriette. Le français dans les relations diplomatiques. Berkeley, 1926. 340 p.

Cazalot, J. Langages français du Maghreb et dans les pays islamiques. (ASIA-AFRICA). Revue de la Mediterranée, 8, 1951.

Baissac, M. C. Etude sur le patois créole mauricien. Nancy, 1880. 233 p.

Barquissau, R. L'Asie française et ses écrivains, avec une bibliographie indochinoise. Paris, 1947.

Faucon, P. Le Théâtre Norodom, foyer de culture française. (In Viêt-Nam). France-Asie, 9, 1953.

Nguyen-thanh-Guiny. Le Viêt-Nam au contact de la culture française. Ibid.

Brodin, P. L'Université française de New-York. (AMERICA) France-Amérique, 1953.

Brown, J. L. Influence de la littérature française sur la littérature américaine. Ibid.

Daviault, P. L'élément canadien-français de l'anglais d'Amérique. Proc. & Trans. Royal Soc. of Canada, III.46. 1952, 5-18.

Gordon, B. R. Early Translations of French Romantics in Mexico. Symposium, 7, 1953, 62-70. [The full force of French romanticism reached Mexico in the late forties and early fifties.]

Joyaux, G. J. The French Press in Michigan. Mich. Hist, 36-37, 1952-53.

Maya, R. Francia en la literatura colombiana. Bolívar (Bogotá), 20, 1953, 841-55. [Good summary review of French literary influences in Colombia.]

McWilliams, R. G. (trsl. & ed.) Fleur de Lys and Calumet: Being the Pénicaut Narrative of French Adventure in Louisiana. Louisiana State U.P., 1953, 316 p. (Cf. FR, 1953).

Milly, A. de. Le théâtre français aux Etats-Unis. Age Nouveau, 72.

Perzan, M. L'oeuvre des Franco-Américains (Louis Dantin, Rosaire Dion-Levesque). Ibid., 67.

Peyre, H. La littérature française contemporaine vue d'Amérique. Dialogues, Oct., 1952.

Struble, G. G. The French in Pennsylvania Prior to 1800. FR, 26, 1953, 50-58.

Thevet, A. Les Français en Amérique pendant la deuxième moitié du XVIe siècle. 1. Le Brésil et les Brésiliens. Paris, 1953. 348 p.

Tinker, E. L. Bibliography of the French Newspapers and Periodicals in Louisiana. Proc. Am. Antiquarian Soc., 42, 1932, 247-370.

Lambrechts, W. Une chambre de rhétorique française au XVIIIe siècle à Anvers. (BELGIUM). Lettres Romanes (Louvain), 1953.

Byrne, M. S. C. (ed.). Claudius Holyband: The French Littleton (1609). (ENGLAND) Cambridge U.P., 1953. 252 p.

Derocquigny, J. A Contribution to the Study of the French Element in English. Lille, 1904. 176 p.

Hassan, I. H. French Symbolism and Modern British Poetry: With Yeats, Eliot, and Edith Sitwell as Indices. Diss. U. of Pa., 1953.

Hobson, H. The French Theatre To-Day: An English View. London, 1953.

Hughes, Helen S. Notes on Eighteenth-Century Fictional Translations. MP, 17, 1919-20, 225-31.

Robinson, J. K. A Neglected Phase of the Aesthetic Movement: English Parnassianism. PMLA, 68, 1953, 733-54.

Rommel, G. W. The Concept of France in England in the Restoration Period. Diss. Northwestern U., 1953.

Temple, Ruth. The Critic's Alchemy: A Study of the Introduction of French Symbolism into England. New York, 1953.

Clappier, L. Paris vaut bien un voyage. (GERMANY). Allemagne d'aujourd'hui, July, 1953.

Colberg, K. et al. Französische Dramen auf deutschen Bühnen (1951). Das literarische Deutschland, II.22 (Heidelberg), 1951.

Fromm, H. Bibliographie deutscher Übersetzungen aus dem Französischen 1700-1948. 6 vols. Baden-Baden, 1950-53. [The last volume includes a list of German translations of French language writings by authors of German nationality (e.g. Frederick the Great, Leibniz), anthologies of French literature in German, and an extensive index of translators.] (Cf. Archiv, 189, 1953.)

Garat, J. Théâtre dans les ruines. NL, 1.X.1953. [Report on theatrical life in Berlin and productions of French plays there (L'Avare, Anouilh's Médée); also discusses French efforts to stage Büchner and Kleist.]

*Olivier, J. J. Les comédiens français dans les cours d'Allemagne au XVIIIe siècle. 4 vols. Paris, 1901-05.

Rehm, W. Römisch-französischer Barockheroismus und seine Umgestaltung in Deutschland. In: Götterstille und Göttertrauer, München, 1951, 11-61.

Adelman, J. Bibliographie de quelques oeuvres françaises traduites en HÉBREU. Le Flambeau (N.Y.), 10, 1951, 28-30.

Smaele, P. de. Hoe verstaan we met de studie van den invloed van de franse letterkunde op de Nederlandse? (HOLLAND). NP, July, 1952.

Libiszowska, Z. L'histoire des influences littéraires françaises en POLOGNE au XVIIe siècle. (In Polish). Prace Polonistyczne, 9 (Wroclaw), 1951.

Pankowski, Marian. Uwagi o poezji. Kultura, April, 1953, 57-65. [Relationship between contemporary Polish and French poetry is discussed.]

Bever, P. J. L. van. Présence de la France au 18e siècle: L'introduction de l'illuminisme au PORTUGAL. Alumni, June, 1952.

Matos, L. de. Les Portugais à l'Université de Paris entre 1500 et 1550. Coimbra, 1950. 245 p.

Warnier, R. La Gazette française du Portugal, 1884-85. Bull. des Etudes Portugaises et de l'Inst. fr. du Portugal, 16, 1952.

Iorga, N. Influenta francesă în ROMANIA. Neamul românesc, 28, 1921.

—— Idées et formes littéraires françaises dans le sud-est de l'Europe. Paris, 1924.

*Ortiz, R. L'influsso dei romantici francesi sulla poesia romena. Cultura, 1910.

Radulesco, L. H. Portée morale et sociale du théâtre français chez les

Roumains au XIXe siècle. Revue des Etudes Roumaines, 1, 1953.

Mooser, R. A. Contribution à l'histoire de la musique RUSSE. L'opéra-comique français en Russie au XVIIIe siècle. Genève, 1932. 56 p.

Picard, G. Le romantisme français et l'Espagne. (SPAIN) Hisp., 5, 1922.

Söllner, R. Die französischen Lehnwörter im Spanischen. Diss. München, 1949.

Maixner, R. Les débuts de l'Académie YOUGOSLAVE et la France. Annales de l'Institut fr. à Zagreb, 1, 1952.

Diderot and the Encyclopédie

Chinard, G. L'Encyclopédie et le rayonnement de l'esprit encyclopédique en AMÉRIQUE. Cahiers de l'Assoc. internat. des Etudes fr., (Paris), May, 1952.

Lough, J. Le rayonnement de l'Encyclopédie en Grande Bretagne. (ENGLAND). Ibid.

———— The Encyclopédie in Eighteenth Century England. YFS, Oct. 1952.

Lunen, W. Appeal for an English Edition of Diderot's Jack the Fatalist. Contemporary Issues (London), July, 1953.

Jacoby, D. Diderot in Leipzig (GERMANY). Euphorion, 6, 1899, 645-49.

Schalk, F. Le rayonnement de l'Encyclopédie en Allemagne. Cahiers de l'Assoc. internat. des Etudes fr., 1952.

———— Die Wirkung der Diderot'schen Enzyklopädie in Deutschland. GRM, 34, 1953, 50-57. [Very poor reception in Germany because of the mixed, sometimes rather negative reception of the encyclopédie in France itself and because the spiritual climate of the German enlightened culture was too different from that of France.]

Dresden, S. L'Encyclopédie aux Pays-Bas (HOLLAND). Cahiers de l'Assoc. internat. des Etudes fr., 1952.

Busnelli, M. D. Diderot et l'ITALIE; reflets de vie et de culture italiennes dans la pensée de Diderot, avec . . . un essai bibliographique sur la fortune du grand encyclopédiste en Italie. Paris, 1925. 305 p.

Guggenheim, Susanna. Drammi e teorie drammatiche del Diderot, e loro fortuna in Italia. EI, 3, 1921.

Venturi, F. L'Encyclopédie et son rayonnement en Italie. Cahiers de l'Assoc.

internat. des Etudes fr. July, 1953.

Fabre, J. L'Encyclopédie en Pologne (POLAND). Ibid.

Codignola, E. Diderot e le origini dell' utilitarismo pedagogico in Francia: il piano di una Università RUSSA. Riv. pedagogica, 1917, 380-407.

Fellows, O. E. & N. L. Torrey. Notes on Diderot's Fortunes in Russia. In: Diderot Studies. Syracuse U.P., 1949.

Lang, D. M. L'Encyclopédie en Russie. Cahiers de l'Assoc. internat. des Etudes fr., 1952.

Tourneux, M. Les manuscrits de Diderot conservés en Russie. Archives des missions scientifiques et litt., 12, 1885, 439-74.

Sarrailh, J. Notes sur l'Encyclopédie en Espagne (SPAIN). Cahiers de l'Assoc. internat. des Etudes fr., 2, 1952.

Guyot, C. Le rayonnement de l'Encyclopédie en Suisse (SWITZERLAND). Ibid.

Gamillscheg, E. Diderots Neveu de Rameau und die GOETHEsche Uebersetzung der Satire. Akad. der Wiss. & Lit. Mainz, 1953. (Cf. RLC, 1954). [A thorough study, based on Dieckmann's finds, of the various texts of the Neveu. Comes to conclusion that the text Goethe used was an older version of the final Ms., possibly an early copy, made perhaps by Grimm or his secretary, Meister.]

Tiersot, J. GLUCK and the Encyclopedists. Musical Quart., 16, 1930, 336-57.

Crocker, L. G. Diderot's Influence on ROUSSEAU's First Discours. PMLA, 52, 1937, 398-404.

Gastinel, G. Rousseau et la philosophie encyclopédiste. In: Leçons faites sur Rousseau. Paris, 1912, 67-88.

Havens, G. R. Diderot and the Composition of Rousseau's First Discourse. RR, 30, 1939, 369-81.

Hubert, R. Rousseau et l'Encyclopédie. Paris, 1928. 137 p.

*Green, F. C. Autour de quatre lettres inédites de Diderot à John WILKES. RLC, 25, 1951.

Other French Authors

Morrissette, B. T. S. Eliot and Guillaume APOLLINAIRE. CL, 5, 1953, 262-68.

Hermans, R. Un témoin inattendu de l'influence de BACULARD d'ARNAUD en Allemagne: le Père Girard (1754-1850). NP, Jan., 1951.

*Inklaar, D. François Thomas de Baculard d'Arnaud, ses imitateurs en Hollande et dans d'autres pays. 's-Gravenhage, 1925. 426 p.

Ahnebrink, L. Dreiser's Sister Carrie and BALZAC. Symposium, Nov., 1953.

Baldensperger, F. Balzac à l'étranger. In: Balzac, Le Livre du Centenaire. Paris, 1953.

Benson, C. Yates and Balzac's Louis Lambert. MP, 49, 1952, 242-47.

Charlier, G. Ce que les lettres étrangères doivent à Balzac. In: Balzac, Le Livre du Centenaire. Paris, 1953.

Efimova, Z. Bal'zak i russkie žurnaly XIX veka. XL, 9, 1935, 53-57.

Korwin-Piotrowska, Sophie de. Balzac en Pologne. Essai de bibliographie. Paris, 1933.

Neubert, F. Balzac und Deutschland. In: Studien z. Vergl. Literaturgeschichte. Berlin, 1952.

Strzalkowa, M. Les traductions polonaises de Balzac. C. R. Académie des Sciences Polonaises, 52, 1951.

Taylor, A. C. La fortune de Balzac en Angleterre. In: Le Livre du Centenaire. Paris, 1953.

Simonsen, V. L. Josuah Sylvester's English Translation of du BARTAS' La première Semaine. Orbis Litterarum, 8, 1952, 259-85.

Ure, P. Two Passages in Sylvester's du Bartas and their Bearing on Shakespeare's Richard II. N&Q, 198, 1953, 374-77.

Antognini, T. D'Annunzio e BAUDELAIRE. Lett. mod., July, 1953.

Leakey, F. W. Baudelaire and Mortimer. FS, April, 1953.

*Malkiewicz, M. Asnyk et Baudelaire. Bull. de l'Acad. Polonaise des Sciences et Lettres (Paris), 1951.

Sugar, M. de. Baudelaire et R. M. Rilke. Etude d'influence et d'affinité spirituelle. Diss. Paris, 1953.

Weindling, S. Stefan George als Übersetzer Baudelaires. Diss. Penn. State U., 1953. 192 p. [George's acquaintance with the Fleurs du Mal, incompleteness of "Die Blumen des Bösen," faithfulness of translation, discussion of George's philosophy of life in his translation etc.]

Lichtenstein, E. Gottscheds Ausgabe von

BAYLES Dictionnaire. Heidelberg, 1915. 151 p.

Joyaux, G. J. The Reception of Pierre-Jean de BÉRANGER in America: 1818-48. FR, 26, 1953, 268-77.

Budrecki, L. Dziwaczny przemyt. Życie literackie, 3, 1953. [A sharp criticism of BERNANO's writings in connection with Polish translations of L'Imposture and Joie.]

Aden, J. M. Dryden and BOILEAU: the Question of Critical Influence. SP, 50, 1953, 491-509.

Rosenberg, A. Some Hitherto Unnoticed Evidence of Boileau's Influence in England. N&Q, 197, 1952.

Isenberg, K. Der Einfluss der Philosophie Charles BONNETS auf F. H. Jacobi. Borna-Leipzig, 1906. 65 p.

Gotaas, Mary C. BOSSUET and Vieira: A Study in National, Epochal and Individual Style. Washington, 1953. 136 p. (Cf. FS, 1954).

*Sauter, E. Herder und BUFFON. Rixheim, 1910. 94 p.

Peck, L. F. The Monk and Le Diable Amoureux. MLN, 68, 1953, 406-08. [A close analysis to show that M. G. Lewis in The Monk was not indebted to CAZOTTE's book.]

Blayney, Margaret S. Sir John Fortescue and Alain CHARTIER's Traité de l'Espérance. MLR, 48, 1953, 385-90.

Andreu, F. CHATEAUBRIAND, ambasciatore a Roma, e il Padre Gioacchino Ventura. Roma, 1948.

Chapman, A. Atala and Niágara: Further Comment. MLN, 68, 1953, 150-54. [Corrections of Menéndez y Pelayo about Heredia's borrowing from Chateaubriand, which turns out to be less extensive and significant than has been supposed.]

Legendre, M. Chateaubriand et l'Espagne. Occident, Rev. Internat. d'Hispanisme, 1940.

Nemesio, V. Chateaubriand e Garrett na Ilha Graciosa (one of the Azores Islands). Illustração, 16.X.1926.

Žirmunskij, V. Vokrug Kavkazskogo plennika Puškina. Lit. Mysl', 2, 1923, 110-23.

Hatto, A. T. On CHRÉTIEN and Wolfram. MLR, 44, 1949, 380-85.

Richey, Margaret. The Independence of Wolfram von Eschenbach in Relation to Chréstien de Troyes. MLR, 47, 1952.

Temple, Maud. CHRISTINE DE PISAN and the Victorian Revival: An Essay on Some of the Mediaeval Elements in French Classical Criticism. Diss. Harvard, 1913.

Dewaule, L. CONDILLAC et la psychologie anglaise contemporaine. Paris, 1892. 331 p.

Haraszti, Z. John Adams on CONDORCET; his Comments on The Outline of the Progress of the Human Mind Now First Published. More Books, 5, 1930, 473-99.

Benjamin CONSTANT: See Swiss Contributions, 617 & 890.

Hewett-Thayer, H. W. Rilke and François COPPÉE. GR, 27, 1952, 294-97.

Almeida, A. A. de. O Cartesianismo em Portugal nos séculos XVII e XVIII. (DESCARTES) Proceedings Internat. Colloquium on Luso-Brazilian Studies, 1950. Nashville, 1953.

*Andrade, A. A. de. Descartes em Portugal nos séculos XVII e XVIII. Brotéria, Nov., 1950.

Radulesco, L. H. Mihaïl Kogâlniceanu, traducteur de DUMANOIR. RLC, July, 1953.

Nielsen, A. J. Bibliography of Alexandre DUMAS père in Denmark, Norway and Sweden; Works translated and printed, 1830-52. Copenhagen, 1952.

Reich, B. Djuma, Bal'zak, Gor'kij. LK, 6, 1934, 155-71.

Kirk, R. (ed.) The Moral Philosophie of the Stoicks, Written in French by Guillaume DU VAIR, Englished by Thomas James. New Brunswick (N. J.), 1951.

ENCYCLOPÉDIE: See Diderot, above.

Just, L. FÉNELONs Wirkung in Deutschland. In: J. Kraus & J. Calvet (eds.), Fénelon, Persönlichkeit und Werk. Baden-Baden, 1953, 35-62. [Popularity of the translations and adaptations (Neukirch) of Télémaque as well as of the religious (Geistliche Schriften), aesthetic and political works of Fénelon.]

Malkiewicz-Strzalkowa, M. Fénelon en Pologne. Bull. de l'Acad. Polonaise des Sciences et des Lettres. Paris, 1953.

*Clavería, C. FLAUBERT y La Regenta (Clarín). In: Cinco estudios de literatura española moderna. Salamanca, 1945, 9-28.

———— Unamuno y la enfermedad de

Flaubert. In: Temas de Unamuno. Madrid, 1953.

Conn, E. H. The Impact of Madame Bovary on the English Novel (1857-1915). Diss. Columbia U., 1952.

*Helms, F. von. German Criticism of G. Flaubert. Columbia U.P., 1939.

Smith, I. H. Tourguénew, Flaubert et leurs amis.! Diss. Paris, 1950.

Sobolevskij, N. Irodiada Flobera v perevodax Turgeneva i Ejxengol'ca. LK, 11, 1934, 187-93.

Spencer, P. Flaubert en Angleterre. Les Amis de Flaubert, 2, 1951.

Riasanovsky, N. V. FOURIERism in Russia: An Estimate of the Petraševcy. ASEER, 12, 1953, 289-302.

Folkierski, W. Ut pictura poesis ou l'étrange fortune du De Arte Graphica de Du FRESNOY en Angleterre. RLC, 27, 1953, 385-402.

Renauld, Jeanne F. Gabriele d'Annunzio tributaire d'Eugène FROMENTIN. RLC, 27, 1953, 204-11.

Anon. Essai d'une bibliographie des traductions polonaises des ouvrages d'André GIDE. Bull. de l'Acad. polonaise des Sciences et des Lettres, Paris, April, 1952.

Lang, Renée (ed.) Gide et Rilke. Correspondance (1909-26). Paris, 1953. (Cf NL, 12.II.1953).

———— Rilke, Gide et Valéry. Boulogne-sur-Seine, 1953.

Zelenski-Boy, T. André Gide et Witold Wojtkiewicz. Bull. de l'Acad. polonaise des Sciences et des Lettres, Paris, April, 1952.

Amador Sánchez, L. Reminiscencias españolas de Victor HUGO. Atenea (Chile), 30, 1953, 270-83. [Significance of Hugo for Spain of past and present.]

Askenazy, S. Victor Hugo et la Pologne. Bull. de l'Acad. polonaise des Sciences et des Lettres. Paris, April, 1952.

Barrère, J. B. Victor Hugo et la Grande-Bretagne. RLC, 28, 1954, 137-67.

Billeskov Jansen, F. J. Victor Hugo dans les écoles danoises. In: L'Age d'Or. Copenhagen, 1953.

Krebs, A. Victor Hugo et l'Amérique. Rapports France-Etats-Unis, July, 1952.

Kubacki, W. Widmo Fantiny. Przeglad kulturalny, 25, 1953. [Massalski's Jan Podstolic and V. Hugo's Les Misérables.]

Rudnicka, J. La première traduction polonaise des Misérables. Zeszyty Wroclawskie, 6, 1952.

Tan, D. Q. Victor Hugo et l'âme Viétnamienne. France-Asie, 8, 1952.

Wedkiewicz, S. Victor Hugo et la Pologne. Bull. de l'Acad. polonaise des Sciences et des Lettres, Paris, May, 1953.

Turner, M. The Influence of LA BRUYÈRE on the Tatler and the Spectator. MLR, Jan., 1953.

Reizov, B. Val'ter Skott i Princessa Klevskaja (Mme. de LA FAYETTE). LS, 2, 1935, 211-15.

Lugli, V. Emilio de Marchi traduttore di LA FONTAINE. In: Dante e Balzac. Napoli, 1952.

Floripe, R. O. Rubén Darío y Jules LEMAITRE: una fuente secundaria de Azul. RIA, 17, 1952, 285-92. [Lemaître as a source, particularly, of "El rey burgués".]

Allen, D. C. A Note on Donne's Elegy VIII. (Jean de LERY). MLN, 68, 1953, 238-39.

Abel, D. LE SAGE's Limping Devil and Mrs. Bullfrog (Hawthorne). N&Q, 198, 1953.

Mouton, L. Un prétendu supplément du Gil Blas de Lesage: L'histoire de Don Rodriguez Vexillario. RHL, 44, 1937, 77-83.

Wetzel, G. The Source of Poe's The Man That Was Used Up. N&Q, 198, 1953.

Souffrin, Eileen. Pierre LOUYS et Swinburne. RLC, 27, 1953, 211-12.

Aulard, A. John Adams, MABLY et la Révolution d'Amérique. Révolution fr., 70, 1917, 555-62.

Gutia, J. Ungaretti e MALLARMÉ. RLM, Oct., 1952.

Hartman, G. H. An Interpretation of Four Modern Poets. (Mallarmé, Valéry, Rilke, Eliot). Diss. Yale, 1953. 299 p.

Ilsley, M. H. Four Unpublished Letters of Stéphane Mallarmé to Stuart Merrill. YFS, 9, 1952, 155-61.

Reyes, A. Mallarmé en castellano. Atenea (Concepcion), 12.

Voigt, F. A. Gerhart Hauptmanns Drama Die Tochter der Kathedrale. GRM, 3, 1953, 1-12. [Shows which works influenced Hauptmann's drama. Voigt accepts Heuser-theory that Lai of MARIE DE FRANCE' "Frene" influenced Hauptmann's "Tochter" as far

as subject-matter (Stoff) is concerned, but he finds other influences too. A clear relationship to Shakespeare's plays can also be seen (Tempest).]

Tilley, A. MARIVAUDage. MLR, 25, 1930, 60-77.

Dent, R. W. Pierre MATTHIEU: Another Source for Webster (on Henry IV). HLQ, 17, 1953, 75-82.

Ross, C. R. Le conteur américain O. Henry et l'art de MAUPASSANT. Diss. Strasbourg, 1925. [Maupassant explained a posteriori by the O'Henry twist.]

Sorber, Gudrun. Maupassant in Deutschland. Diss. Göttingen, 1949.

*San-Giorgiu, J. Sébastien MERCIERS dramaturgische Ideen im Sturm und Drang. Basel, 1921.

Humbertclaude, P. Ueda Akinari et Prosper MÉRIMÉE. Bull. Maison Franco-Japonaise, 7, 1936.

Parturier, M. Rendez-vous espagnole de Prosper Mérimée. RP, Dec., 1953, 63-74.

Deanović, M. MOLIÈRE à Raguse au XVIII siècle. RLC, 28, 1954, 1-15.

Goggin, L. P. Fielding and the Select Comedies of Mr. de Molière. PQ, 31, 1952, 344-50.

Humbert, Beate. Die Lustspiele Wicherleys und Stradwells in ihrer Beziehung zu den Komödien Molières. Diss. Hamburg, 1950.

Iorga, N. Molière et les Roumains. Bull. de la Section historique Académie Roumaine, 1923.

Leipoldt, Karin. Molière und Holberg. Diss. Leipzig, 1946.

Merian-Genast, E. Die Technik der komischen Charakteristik bei Molière und Goldoni. RF, 64, 1952, 114-39. [A close study in comparative characterology of the comedy.]

Davril, R. Un disciple de MONTAIGNE en Angleterre: le chevalier William Cornwallis. Annales, Faculté des Lettres, Toulouse, Dec., 1952.

Henderson, E. H. Montaigne and Modern Philosophy. Personalist, 34, 1953, 278-89.

Hodgen, Margaret. Montaigne and Shakespeare Again. HLQ, 16, 1952, 23-42.

Krüger, K. Montaignes Essais und ihre Einwirkungen auf das dramatische

Schaffen John Websters. Diss. Hamburg, 1949.

Marichal, J. Montaigne en España. NRFH, Jan., 1953, 259-78.

Schirmer-Imhoff, R. Montaigne und die Frühzeit des englischen Essays. GRM, 3, 1953.

Thorpe, L. Pieter van Veen's Copy of Montaigne. RLM, July, 1952, 168-79.

Villey, P. L'influence de Montaigne sur les idées pédagogiques de Locke et de Rousseau. Paris, 1911. 270 p.

────── Montaigne et François Bacon. Paris, 1913. 109 p.

Bonno, G. MONTESQUIEU's Esprit des lois and its Significance for the Modern World. FAR, 2, 1949, 1-11.

Crane, R. S. Montesquieu and British Thought. Journal of Political Economy, 49, 1941, 592-600.

Crisafulli, A. S. A Neglected English Imitation of Montesquieu's Lettres Persanes: Letters from an Armenian. MLQ, 14, 1953, 209-16.

Janet, P. Comparaison des théories morales et sociales de Montesquieu et de Jean-Jacques Rousseau. Rev. polit. & litt., 9, 1871, 556-61.

Masson, A. Naissance et fortune de l'Esprit des lois. La Revue, litt., histoire, arts et sciences des deux mondes, 1, 1948, 701-10.

Tchernoff, J. Montesquieu et J. J. Rousseau. Rev. du droit publique, 19-20, 1903.

Axelrad, A. J. Sur une source possible de la Sophonisbe de John Marston (N. de MONTREUX). RLC, 27, 1953, 182-85.

Bennie, P. Søren Kierkegaard, the PASCAL of the North. Meanjin, 4 (Melbourne), 1945, 97-99.

Guitton, J. Pascal et Leibniz. Etude sur deux types de penseurs. Paris, 1951.

Peyre, H. Friends and Foes of Pascal in France Today. YFS, 12, 1953, 8-18. (Also references to Germany, e.g. Nietzsche.)

Chinard, G. (ed.) The Correspondence of Jefferson and Du Pont de Nemours, with an introduction on Jefferson and the PHYSIOCRATS. Baltimore, 1931. 293 p.

Mikhailovski, N. K. PROUDHON i Belinski. In: Otechestvennye zapiski, 1875.

Stössinger, F. Diskussion mit Zeitschriften: Von PROUST zu Broch. NSR, 21, 1953, 440-46. [Discusses the almost complete neglect of Proust in Germany.]

Barański, H. Mikołaj Rey i Franciszek RABELAIS. Widnokrag, 24, 1953. [A comparison of world views.]

Gyergyai, A. Rabelais en Hongrie. Europe, 31, 1953.

Haffen, L. Johann Fischart, humaniste alsacien, "Rabelais de l'Allemagne." Ibid. 155-66. [A discussion of F's adaptation of Gargantua, 40 years after the original was published, and of his presentation of the Pantagruéline Pronostications, called the "grandmother of all prophetic almanacs." F. through his Alsatian background appears as the ideal intermediary between France and Germany.]

Porcher, J. Rabelais à travers les siècles. In: Hommage à Rabelais. NL, 9.IV. 1953.

Roe, F. C. A Double Centenary: Sir Thomas Urquhart and his Translation of Rabelais. Aberdeen U. Review, 35, 1953, 120-29.

Münchow, Maria. Alfieri und RACINE. Diss. Berlin, 1946.

Trigiani, A. Il teatro raciniano e i melodrammi di Pietro Metastasio. Torino, 1951.

Duhamel, P. A. Milton's Alleged Ramism (RAMUS). PMLA, 67, 1952, 1035-53.

Ong, W. S. J. Hobbes and Talon's Ramist Rhetoric in English. Transactions Cambridge Bibliogr. Soc., 3, 1951.

────── Peter Ramus and the Naming of Methodism: Medieval Science through Ramist Homiletic. JHI, April, 1953.

────── Ramus et le monde anglo-saxon d'aujourd'hui. RLC, 28, 1954, 57-66.

Coulling, S. M. B. RENAN's Influence on Arnold's Literary and Social Criticism. Florida State U. Studies, 5, 1952, 95-112.

Rivoallan, A. Un admirateur anglais de Renan: Matthew Arnold. Nouvelle Revue de Bretagne, Sept., 1952.

Barrère, J. J. Romain ROLLAND et Malvida. FS, April, 1950.

Grappin, P. Romain Rolland et Hermann Hesse. EG, Jan., 1952.

McClain, W. H. & Zohn H. Zweig and Rolland: The Literary and Personal Relationship. GR, 28, 1953, 262-81.

ROMAN DE RENART: See Reynard, 139, 711.

ROMAN DE LA ROSE: See also: Jean de Meung, 523.

Magoun, F. P. Chaucer's Sir Gawain and the Roman de la Rose. MLN, 67, 1952, 183-85.

Rolland, R. La Marseillaise en Allemagne. (ROUGET DE LISLE). In: Goethe et Beethoven. Paris, 1930, 243-51.

J.-J. ROUSSEAU: See Swiss Contributions, 611-15 & 888-90.

Bonnerot, J. Quelques correspondants anglais et américans de **SAINTE-BEUVE:** 1. Mme. Harriet Beecher-Stowe. EA, Nov., 1952.

Joyaux, G. J. George **SAND,** Eugène Sue and The Harbinger. FR, 27, 1953, 122-31. [Favorable opinions of the literary qualities and socialist tendencies of Sand and translations of Consuelo and The Countess of Rudolstadt in the Fourierist journal refuted generally held beliefs in America which were usually based on moralistic strictures.]

MME. DE STAEL: See Swiss Contributions, 615-16 & 890.

Bergholz, H. Was Washington Irving **STENDHAL's** First American Critic? RLC, 27, 1953, 328-39.

Dechamps, J. Sur Stendhal et un de ses amis belges. Bull. Classe des Lettres de l'Acad. Royale de Belgique, 38, 1952.

Stein, M. Stendhal et B. E. Fogelberg. Les relations scandinaves de Henri Beyle. Ord och Bild, June, 1952 & Le Divan, Oct., 1952.

Struve, P. Puškin o Stendale i Bal'zake. Rossija, 22, 1928.

Bonno, G. (ed.) Lettres inédites de **SUARD** à Wilkes. Berkeley, 1932.

Benítez Claros, R. Antonio Flores y Eugenio **SUE.** Revista de Literatura, 2, 1952.

Feilbogen, S. Smith und **TURGOT**; ein Beitrag zur Geschichte und Theorie der Nationalökonomie. Wien, 1892. 170 p.

Lhombreaud, R. A. **VERLAINE** et ses amis d'Angleterre. RHLF, July, 1953, 363-70.

Zack, Doris-Jeanne. Verlaine in England, 1872-96. Diss. Columbia U., 1952.

Lugli, V. Carducci et de **VIGNY.** Lett. Moderne, July, 1951

Dukor, I. Fransua Vijon v tvorčestve

Antokolskogo. (**VILLON**). LK, 11, 1934, 109-20.

Adamski, J. (ed.) L'enfant prodigue de **VOLTAIRE,** traduit en polonais par S. Trembecki en 1780. (In Polish). Wrocław, 1951.

Beaunier, A. Voltaire en Prusse. RDM, 25, 1915, 216-27.

*Bianquis, Geneviève. Goethe et Voltaire. In: Etudes sur Goethe. Dijon, Paris, 1951, 91-98.

Dimares, C. T. La fortune de Voltaire en Grèce. Festschrift O. & M. Merlier. Athens, 1953.

Drouhet, C. G. Alexandrescu si Voltaire. In: Omagiu lui I. Bianu. Bucureşti, 1927. (Cf. RLC, 1928.)

Jordan, L. Die Münchener Voltairehandschriften. Archiv, 129, 1912, 388-429.

Sainte-Beuve, C. A. Correspondance de Voltaire avec la duchesse de Saxe-Gotha. In: Causeries du lundi, 15, Paris, 1862.

Trudel, M. L'influence de Voltaire au Canada. 2 vols. Montréal, 1945.

Arrighi, P. **ZOLA** et De Sanctis. RLC, 27, 1953, 438-46.

Barreur, S. Zola en Hongrie. Europe, Nov., 1952.

Beregi, T. Prestige de Zola en Hongrie. In: Présence de Zola. Paris, 1953.

Brown, C. S. Zola 50 Years After. UTQ, 21, 1952, 325-29.

Cazaux, M. Zola en Suède. RLC, 27, 1953, 428-37.

Colburn, W. E. Zola in England, 1883-1903. Diss. U. of Illinois, 1953.

Collet, G. P. Un disciple irlandais de Zola. Journal de Genève, 19-20.X. 1952.

González de Mendoza, J. J. L'influence de Zola sur le roman mexicain. In: Présence de Zola. Paris, 1953.

Macchia, G. Zola et la critique italienne. Ibid.

Matitch, D. Fragment d'une étude yougoslave sur Zola. Ibid.

Mitov, D. Zola en Bulgarie. Europe, Nov., 1952.

Nikolaev, V. Emil' Zola i sovremennost'. IAN OLJa, 12, 1953, 28-39. [Zola's influence (mainly ideological) today.]

Nowakowski, J. The Quarrel over Zola in Poland. (In Polish). Wrocław, 1951.

Salvan, A. J. Lafcadio Hearn's Views on the Realism of Zola. PMLA, 67, 1952, 1163-67. [Opinions gleaned

from New Orleans newspapers and
correspondence revealing somewhat
confused attitudes. Hearn was lauda-
tory about Zola's artistic evocation of
a sordid world, but generally con-
demned the lack of idealism in different works.]

French Influences upon Individual Authors

Baym, M. I. The Garret on the Avenue
du Bois: An Essay on Henry ADAMS
and France. YFS, 10, 1953, 43-53.

Denis, S. Le voyage en France d'AL-
PHONSE V de Portugal. BH, 36,
1934.

Nardi, J. D'ANNUNZIO ed alcuni scrittori francesi. Cesena, 1951.

Malkiel, María R. L. de. La leyenda de
BÉCQUER "Creed en Dios" y su pre-
sunta fuente francesa. CL, 3, 1953,
235-46.

Tiersot, J. BEETHOVEN, musicien de la
Révolution Française. RP, 17, 1910,
733-60.

Dresch, J. (ed.) Louis BÖRNE: Etudes
sur l'Histoire et les Hommes de la
Révolution Française (avec introduction et commentaire). Lyon, Paris,
1952. 153 p. [Although Börne's German text has little bearing on Franco-
German literary relations, the Introduction must be considered a very
important contribution to the subject. Börne's activities in Paris are
fully analysed.]

Dolansky, J. The Echo of the Commune
in Paris in the Works of the Czech
Poet Svatopluk CECH. (In Czech).
SloP., March, 1951.

Lubac, A. La France et le français dans
le Persiles. Anales CERVANTinos
(Madrid), 1951, 111-30.

Pellegrini, C. CROCE e la letteratura
francese. RLM, April, 1953.

Ortiz, R. Ricordi di letture provenzali e
francesi nella "Comedia" di DANTE.
Atti della R. Accad. di Archeologia.
Napoli, 1914.

Soler, W. G. John DICKINSON's Ode on
the French Revolution. AL, 25, 1953,
287-92.

Dorovatovskaja-Ljubimova, V. Francuz-
skij buržua. (Material k obrazam
DOSTOEVSKOgo). LK, 9, 1936, 202-
17.

Aden, J. M. The Question of Influence
in DRYDEN's Use of the Major

French Critics. Diss. U. of N.C., 1951.

Oprescu, G. ELIADE-RADULESCU și
Franța. Dacoromania, (Cluj) 1923.
(Cf. RCL, 1927).

*Hedgecock, F. A. David GARRICK et
ses amis français. Paris, 1911. 283 p.
& London, 1911, 442 p.

Faber du Faur, K. von. Stefan GEORGE
et le symbolisme français. CL, 5,
1953, 151-66. [Keen analysis of what
attracted George to, and of what re-
pelled him from, the French symbolists. In fact, George was more of a
Parnassian than he was a symbolist.]

Gibelin, J. Une source possible des Af-
finités Electives de GOETHE. RLC,
27, 1953, 191-93.

Neubert, F. Goethe und Frankreich bis
zu Schillers Tode. In: Studien zur
vergl. Litgesch., Berlin, 1952, 55-93.

Ortiz, R. GOLDONI și Franța. Convor-
biri Literare, (București), 1924, 653-
85 & Mem. Acad. Romana, 1924, 231-
318.

Sieburg, H. O. Les remarques de GRILL-
PARZER sur la littérature française.
Allemagne d'Aujourd'hui, 4, 1953.

F. M. GRIMM: See also 49.

Danzel, T. W. Letters of Grimm to Gottsched. In his: Gottsched und seine
Zeit. Leipzig, 1855, 343-54.

Jones, Anne C. Frederick-Melchior Grimm
as a Critic of Eighteenth Century
French Drama. Bryn Mawr (Pa.),
1926. 69 p.

Gicovate, B. The Poetry of Julio HER-
RERA Y REISSIG and French Symbolism. PMLA, 68, 1953, 935-42.

Bianquis, Geneviève. HOFMANNSTHAL
et la France. RLC, 27, 1953, 301-18.
[From the trip to Southern France
1892 to the meeting with Maeter-
linck in Paris, 1900. Greatest influence of Balzac; also Molière, Hugo,
Musset.]

——— HÖLDERLIN et la Révolution
Française. EG, 7, 1952, 105-116.

Chapman, R. The Earl of Surrey in
France (H. HOWARD). TLS, 7.III.
1952.

Garten, H. G. La France dans l'oeuvre
de George KAISER. Allemagne d'Aujourd'hui, July, 1953.

Chuquet, A. KLOPSTOCK et la Révolution Française. In: Etudes d'Histoire,
2e Sér., Fontemoing, n.d.

Mouton, J. LÉONARD DE VINCI et la

France. Nouv. Revue Canadienne, 2, 1953, 112-16.

*Aronson, A. LESSING et les classiques français. Montpellier, 1935. 279 p.

Murdock, Eleanor E. Oscar LEVERTIN: Swedish Critic of French Realism. CL, 5, 1953, 137-50. [A clear, concise catalogue of Levertin's views, expressed mostly in journalistic criticism in the 1890s, of Zola, the Goncourts, Huysmans, Stendhal, etc. There is little attempt to synthesize or draw conclusions.]

Lough, J. (ed.) LOCKE's Travels in France, 1675-79. Cambridge U.P., 1953. 309 p. (Cf. Rev. des Sciences humaines, 1953.)

O'Bear, Elizabeth D. The Significance of France in the Writings of Heinrich MANN. Diss. Ohio State, 1953. [Distinguishes three periods: the first shows purely literary interests (Schlaraffenland patterned after Bel-Ami, interest in Flaubert; translation of A. France's Histoire Comique); in the second period he turned to the Italian Renaissance and viewed French literature from the angle of the "superman" (interest in Les Liaisons Dangereuses, also in Stendhal); in the third he turned toward French democratic ideals (Zola, Hugo, Rousseau, Voltaire; Die Armen patterned after Germinal).]

*Nolhac, P. de. Un poète rhénan ami de la Pléiade, Paul MELISSUS. Paris, 1923. 96 p.

Borowy, W. La troisième partie des Aïeux de MICKIEWICZ et le théâtre français. Bull. de l'Acad. polonaise, Paris, May, 1953.

Davenport, B. C. (ed.) Governor MORRIS: A Diary of the French Revolution, 1789-93. 2 vols. Boston, 1939.

Dening, M. Some Remarks on MÖSER's Treatment of French and English Language and Literature in Über die deutsche Sprache und Literatur. Festschrift A. Lodewyckx, Melbourne, 1951, 22-28.

Kress, D. M. The Weight of French Parnassian Influence in the Modernistic Poetry of Manuel Gutierre NÁJERA. RLC, 12, 1932, 555-71. [Stresses stylistic vs. ideological influence.]

Williams, W. D. NIETZSCHE and the French. Oxford, 1952. 206 p. (Cf. CL, 1953; FS, NP, MLN, 1954). [Convincing analysis of the influence of French literature from the 17h to the 19th centuries on the thought and personality of Nietzsche. Attributes to France the change from speculative philosophy to interest in moral and psychological problems. Treats effect of Montaigne, La Rochefoucauld, Pascal, Rousseau, Stendhal, Mérimée, and Bourget.]

Monsterleet, J. Note sur PA CHIN et les maîtres qui l'ont formé. RLC, 28, 1954, 89-92.

Hilton, R. Spanish Preconceptions about France, as Revealed in the Works of Emilia PARDO BAZÁN. BHS, 30, 1953, 193-204.

Preisendanz, Hermine. Die Romane der Gräfin Emilia Pardo Bazán und der französische Naturalismus. Diss. Heidelberg, 1941.

Holmes, U. T. Samuel PEPYS in Paris and Other Essays. Chapel Hill, 1954. 65 p.

Kenner, H. Ezra POUND and the Light of France. YFS, 10, 1953, 54-64.

Neubert, F. PUSCHKIN und die französische Kultur. Studien z. vergl. Litgesch. Berlin, 1952.

Cuenou, V. Les années d'apprentissage de C. F. RAMUZ à Paris. Diss. Paris, 1953.

Lemos, M. RIBEIRO SANCHES, a sua vida e a sua obra. Porto, 1911. [About the 18th-century writer and friend of the Enlightenment. His Cartas sobre a educação da mocidade were published in Cologne in 1760.]

Olden, P. H. RILKE on Paris. Two Letters from Duino. BA, 27, 1953, 33-35. [Text with commentary of letters of Oct. 23, 1911 and Feb. 9, 1912 with glowing description of Paris.]

Grosclaude, P. J.-J. ROUSSEAU à Lyon. Lyon, 1933.

Vermale, F. Jean-Jacques Rousseau en Savoie. Chambéry, 1922.

Aquarone, J. B. Francisco SANCHES em Montpellier. Bracara Augusta, Revista Cultural da Câmara Municipal de Braga. 21.IV.1952.

Sendrail, M. Francisco Sanches em Toulouse. Ibid.

Lenz-Medoc, P. Max SCHELER und die französische Philosophie. Philosoph. Jb, 61, 1951.

Reboul, P. Fr. SCHLEGEL à Paris. Projet

d'y constituer une académie allemande, 1802. Rev. Sciences Humaines, 65, 1952, 27-32.

Ure, P. SHAKESPEARE's Play and the French Sources of Holinshed's and Stow's Account of Richard II. N&Q, 198, 1953, 436-39.

Osborn, A. W. Sir Philip SIDNEY en France. Paris, 1932. 171 p.

SIEBURG, F. Je passais au bord de la Seine. Paris, 1953. 254 p. [Translation of the author's Unsere schönsten Jahre. Ein Leben mit Paris. Tübingen, 1950.] (Cf. MF. 1.VII.1953.)

Sanders, C. R. Lytton STRACHEY and French Literature. SAQ, April, 1954, 238-59.

Gravier, M. STRINDBERG, traducteur de lui-même. Mélanges Michaëlsson. Gottenbourg, 1952.

Lefèvre, A. Thèmes médiévaux normands dans la poésie de UHLAND. RLC, 27, 1953, 322-28. [Wace's Roman de Rou and other sources.]

Groult, P. Le diable picard de Gil VICENTE. Bull. des Etudes Portugaises et de l'Inst. fr. au Portugal, 16, 1952.

Teyssier, P. Essai d'explication du passage en picard de l'Auto das Fadas de Gil Vicente. Ibid., 14, 1950, 223-45.

Günther, H. Paris als Erlebnis: Frank WEDEKIND und Paris. Antares, June, 1953, 3-8. [Brief account of W's six visits to Paris, between 1891 and 1914. It was less the artistic & literary life of Paris than life itself that fascinated him here. In Paris W. found his own medium and style; he wrote his "Bänkelsängerlieder," his Lulutrilogy and "Marquis von Keith" here, among shorter works. Few contacts with French writers.]

Schön, E. Französische Einflüsse in Oskar WILDEs Werken. Diss. Hamburg, 1948.

Vanicek, Hilde. Der Einfluss der französischen Lyrik auf Anton WILDGANS, Stefan Zweig und Felix Dörmann. Diss. Wien, 1952.

VIII. ENGLISH CONTRIBUTIONS

Influences Upon Individual Countries

Ballam, H. & R. Lewis. The Visitors' Book: England and the English as Others Have Seen Them, 1500-1950. London, 1950.

Werner, W. L. English for the World. SRL, 4.X.1952.

Dickason, D. H. The Daring Young Men: The Story of the AMERICAn Pre-Raphaelites. Indiana U.P., 1953.

Dorsey, S. P. Early English Churches in America, 1607-1807. Oxford U.P., 1952.

Patridge, E. & J. W. Clark. British and American English Since 1900. New York, 1951.

Pyles, T. Words and Ways of American English. New York, 1952.

——— British Titles of Nobility and Honor in American English. American Speech, 28, 1953, 69-79.

Reed, C. E. English Archaisms in Pennsylvania German. Publ. of Am. Dialect Soc., 19, 1953.

Schorer, C. E. English Loan Words in Puerto Rico. American Speech, 28, 1953, 22-25.

Sansom, C. AUSTRALIAn Speech. Quart. Journal of Speech, 39, 1953, 470-76.

Greet, W. C. A Report on English in EUROPE. Ibid., 465-69.

Kirkconnell, W. Common English Loan Words in East European Languages. Winnipeg, 1952. 22 p. (Cf. BA, 1953).

Beckwith, F. The Bibliothèque Britannique, 1733-47. (FRANCE). Library, Ser. IV, 12, 1931-32, 75-82.

Guyard, M. F. L'image de la Grand-Bretagne dans le roman français, 1914-40. Diss. Paris, 1953.

Lanson, G. Formation et développement de l'esprit philosophique au XVIIIe siècle: l'influence anglaise. RCC, 17, 1909, 721-36.

McCutcheon, R. P. The Journal des Scavans and the Philosophical Transactions of the Royal Society. SP, 21, 1924, 626-28.

*Sichel, J. Die englische Literatur im Journal étranger. Ein Beitrag zur Geschichte der literarischen Beziehungen zwischen England und Frankreich im 18. Jahrhundert. Darmstadt, 1907. 75 p.

Oppel, H. Der Einfluss der englischen Literatur auf die deutsche. (GERMANY). In: Deutsche Philologie im Aufriss III (ed. by W. Stammler). Berlin, 1954, 47-143.

Price, L. M. English Literature in Germany. UCPP, 37, 1953. 548 p. (Cf. GQ, MLQ, ESs, 1954).

Robson-Scott, D. W. German Travellers in

England, 1400-1800. Oxford, 1953, 238 p.

Feldman, A. B. English Playwrights in the Netherland Wars. (HOLLAND). N&Q, 197, 1952, 530-33.

—— Playwrights and Pike-Trailers in the Low Countries. Ibid., 198, 1953, 184-87.

Roberts, W. English Books in Holland, 1744. TLS, 29.I.1938.

Myrick, A. B. Some Notes on ITALIAN Borrowings from England in the Eighteenth Century. Diss. Harvard, 1904.

Bryan, J. I. English Books and JAPANESE Readers. Japan Society Transactions & Publications, 35, 1937-38.

Saito, T. English Literature in Japan. In: Western Influences in Modern Japan, (ed. Nitobe). Chicago, 1931.

Smith, E. English Literature in NORWAY around 1900. Norseman, 6, 1948.

Thesen, R. England in Norwegian Eyes. Ibid., 10, 1952.

*Machado, L. S. Os Ingleses em PORTUGAL. Biblos, 12-15, 1936-39. [A historical study on the period of the Crusades and Reconquest.]

Alekseev, M. O svjazjax russkogo teatra s anglijskim v konce XVII-načale XVIII vv. (RUSSIA). UZLU, 87 (Saratov), 1943, 123-40.

Harper, K. E. & B. Booth. Russian Translations of Nineteenth-Century English Fiction. NCF, 8, 1953, 188-97. [Some raw bibliographical material, illustrating the fortunes of English writers, especially the lesser known ones, in Russia in the second half of the 19th century.]

Livermore, H. V. An Early English Play described by a SPANISH Visitor (1522). Atlante, 1, 1953, 28-31.

Mata Carriazo, J. de. Inglaterra y los ingleses vistos por un cronista castellano. Rev. de Estudios Políticos, 44, 1952, 65-90.

*Schindler, J. Das Bild des Englaenders in der Kunst- und Volksliteratur der deutschen Schweiz von 1798-1848. (SWITZERLAND). Zürich, 1950.

Horowitz, M. YIDDISH Translations of English Literature. Jewish Book Annual, 11, 1952, 136-53.

Filipović, R. Les débuts des études anglaises en Croatie. (YUGOSLAVIA). Zbornik radova, Zagreb, 1591.

Shakespeare

Parkhurst, C. E. A Comparative Analysis of Selected Opera Libretto Adaptations of the Romeo and Juliet Legend. Diss. Northwestern U. 1953.

Madariaga, S. de. On Translating Hamlet. Shakespeare Survey (ed. A. Nicoll). Cambridge U.P., 1953, 106-11.

Cohen, H. Shakespeare in Charleston on the Eve of the Revolution. (AMERICA). SQ, 4, 1953, 327-30.

Davidson, L. J. Shakespeare in the Rockies. Ibid., 39-49.

Schoff, F. G. Aspects of Shakespearean Criticism, 1914-50: A Commentary Centered on British and American Criticism of Hamlet. Diss. U. of Minnesota, 1953.

Eisner, Doris. Sieben Jahre Shakespeare in Oesterreich (1945-51). (AUSTRIA). JbShG, 87-88, 1952, 180-87.

Chang Chen-Hsien. Shakespeare in CHINA. In: Shakespeare Survey (ed. A. Nicoll). Cambridge U.P., 1953, 112-16.

Rund, M. B. An Essay Toward a History of Shakespeare in DENMARK. Minneapolis, 1920.

*Bösser, R. Shakespeare's Romeo and Juliet in französischer Bearbeitung. (FRANCE). Frankfurt, 1907. 132 p.

Keys, A. C. Les adaptations musicales de Shakespeare en France jusqu'en 1870. Diss. Paris, 1933. 237 p.

—— Shakespeare in France. An Early Stage Adaptation. AUMLA: Australasian Universities' Mod. Lang. Assoc. (Melbourne), Aug., 1953, 15-20.

Lambin, G. Sur les traces d'un Shakespeare inconnu: Shakespeare à Paris. LM, Nov., 1953.

Taupin, R. Le mythe de Hamlet à l'époque romantique. FR, 27, 1953, 15-21.

Vigo Fazio, L. Come Parigi apprezzò Shakespeare. In: Francia coi poeti. Catania, 1952, 41-52.

Gregor, J. Was ist uns Hamlet? (GERMANY). JbShG, 87-88, 1952, 9-25.

Richter, C. A. Beiträge zum Bekanntwerden Shakespeares in Deutschland. 2 vols. Breslau, 1909-10.

Sehrt, E. T. Die Shakespeareforschung 1937-1952 in Deutschland und der Schweiz. Anglia, 71, 1952, 50-81.

Stroedel, W. Bühnenbericht über Shakespeare auf der deutschen Bühne, 1950-52. JbShG, 87-88, 1952, 174-80.

Decroos, J. Deutschlands Einfluss auf die

Shakespeare-Pflege im Niederländischen Sprachgebiet. (HOLLAND). Ibid., 116-57.

Draper, J. W. Shakespeare and INDIA. In: Etudes de littérature moderne. Annales de Toulouse, Nov., 1953, 1-12.

Minoru, T. Shakespeare in JAPAN. Japan Society Transactions and Publications, 36, 1938-39 & Tokyo, 1940.

*Shanai, R. G. Shakespeare vu par les ORIENTaux. Paris, 1932.

Iorga, N. Shakespeare in româneste. (RUMANIA). Ramuri, 1922.

Gibian, G. Shakespeare in Soviet RUSSIA. Russian Rev., 11, 1952, 24-34.

Radlova, Anna. Kak ja rabotaju nad perevodom Šekspira. LS, 3, 1934, 138-45.

Sehrt, E. T. Shakespeareforschung 1937-52 in Deutschland und der Schweiz. (SWITZERLAND). Anglia, 71, 1952, 50-81.

Wilson, A. H. The Influence of Hamlet upon CHEKHOV's The Sea Gull. Sesquehanna U. Studies, 4, 1952, 309-16.

Orsini, N. CROCE e la critica shakespeariana. RLM, 4, 1953, 145-54.

Vanderhoof, Mary (ed.) Hamlet: A Tragedy adapted from Shakespeare (1770) by Jean François DUCIS. PAPS, 97, 1953. 55 p. (Cf. SQ, 1953).

Ryan, Marjorie. The Shakespearean Symbolism in The Sound and the Fury. FAULKNER Studies, 2, 1953, 40-43.

Donner, A. H. Svenska Översättningar av Shakespear's Macbeth. I: Schillers inflytande på GEIJERS Översättning. Humaniora, 20 (Abo), 1950. 148 p.

Norwood, E. Stefan GEORGE's Translation of Shakespeare's Sonnets. MDU, 44, 1952, 217-24.

Flatter, R. The Veil of Beauty: Some Aspects of Verse and Prose in Shakespeare and GOETHE. JEGP, 50, 1951.

Kaufmann, W. Goethe versus Shakespeare: Some Changes in Dramatic Sensibility. PR, 19, 1952, 621-34.

Uhler, J. F. Goethe and Shakespeare. In: Goethe After Two Centuries (ed. C. Hammer). Baton Rouge (La.), 1952, 97-102.

Fogel, Ada. J. GOLDBERG's Yiddish Translation of Hamlet. Yidishe Shprakh, 12, 1952, 1-11.

Banachévitch, N. A propos d'un vers des Contemplations sur un vers d'Hernani. (HUGO). RLC, 28, 1954, 206-11.

Samuel, R. H. Shakespeares Heinrich IV und Heinrich von KLEIST. Festschrift

A. Lodewyckx, Melbourne, 1951, 12-15.

*Haak, P. Die ersten französischen Shakespeare - Uebersetzungen von LA PLACE und Le Tourneur. Diss. Berlin. Steinau, 1922. 94 p.

Taupin, R. The Myth of Hamlet in France in MALLARMÉ's Generation. MLQ, 14, 1953, 432-47.

Polak, A. L. The Tempest and The Magic Flute. (MOZART). English, 9, 1952, 2-7.

Baum, B. Tempest and Hairy Ape: The Literary Incarnation of Mythos. (O'NEILL) MLQ, 14, 1953, 258-73.

Wolff, Tatiana A. Shakespeare's Influence on PUSHKIN's Dramatic Work. In: Shakespeare Survey, 5 (ed. A. Nicoll), Cambridge U.P., 1952, 93-105.

Wittlinger, K. Hans ROTHE und die Shakespeare-Forschung. JbShG, 87-88, 1952, 158-73.

Parks, E. W. SIMMS' Edition of the Shakespeare Apocrypha. In: Studies in Shakespeare, Miami, 1952, 30-39.

Iorga, N. O traducere din Shakespeare: Macbeth de C. Al. STEFANESCU. Neamul românesc literar, 1912, 68-71.

Andersson, M. STRINDBERG's Master Olof and Shakespeare. In: Essays and Studies of English Language and Literature, 11 (Copenhagen), 1952.

Kerman, J. VERDI's Otello, or Shakespeare Explained. Hudson Rev., 6, 1953, 266-77.

Arndt, R. Zur Entstehung von VOLTAIRE's Zaïre. Marburg, 1906. 55 p.

*Havens, G. R. Voltaire and English Critics of Shakespeare. American Legion of Honor Mag., 15, 1944, 177-86.

Stovall, F. WHITMAN's Knowledge of Shakespeare. SP, 49, 1952, 643-69.

———— Whitman, Shakespeare, and the Baconians. PQ, 31, 1952, 27-38.

———— Whitman, Shakespeare, and Democracy. JEGP, 51, 1952, 457-72.

Legouis, E. La Terre de ZOLA et le Roi Léar. RLC, 27, 1953, 417-27.

Other English Authors

Brown, F. A. ADDISON's Imagination and the Gesellschaft der Mahlern. MLQ, 15, 1954, 57-66.

*Gelobter, Hanna. Le Spectateur von Pierre Marivaux und die englischen moralischen Wochenschriften. Limburg, 1936. 94 p.

Kazanskij, B. V. Zapadnye obrazcy Sovremennika. Puškin. Vremennik, 6, 1941, 375-81.

Mainwaring, Marion. ARNOLD und Tolstoi. NCF, 6, 1952, 269-74.

King, N. J. Jane AUSTEN in France. Ibid., 8, 1953, 1-26. [Evaluation of French translations from 1815 to the end of the century. Deals mainly with Mme. de Montolieu's distorted version of Sense and Sensibility, giving numerous extracts from the English and French. Ends with summary of critical opinions in France. Though Jane Austen was generally misunderstood in 19th century France, recent critical works have studied her admirably.]

Adam, C. E. Influence de BACON aux XVIIe, XVIIIe et XIXe siècles. In his: Philosophie de François Bacon. Paris, 1890. 437 p.

Miller, V. Kant i Békon v ix otnošenii k isxodnym problemam metodologii i filosofii. NISGU, 5, 1929, 3-30.

Pollak, Marion. BOSWELL's Johnson and Eckermann's Goethe. Proc. Australian Goethe Soc. (Melbourne), 1950.

Dugas, J. H. The Literary Reputation of the BRONTES, 1846-1951. Diss. U. of Illinois, 1952.

Childs, H. E. Emily Dickinson and Sir Thomas BROWNE. AL, 22, 1951.

Leroy, O. A French Bibliography of Sir Thomas Browne. London, 1931. 97 p.

Schmitt, H. A. & J. C. Weston. Ten Letters to Edmund BURKE from the French Translator of the Reflections on the Revolution in France. Jour. Mod. Hist., 24, 1952, 406-23.

Barzun, J. BYRON and the Byronic. AM, 192, 1953, 47-52.

Brodskij, N. Bajron v russkoj literature. LK, 4, 1938, 114-42.

Feiss, E. Melville as a Reader and Student of Byron. AL, 24, 1952, 186-94.

Granjard, H. Le Byronisme de Mácha. RLC, 28, 1954, 24-39.

Heutschel, C. The Byronic Teuton. Aspects of German Pessimism, 1800-1833. London, 1939.

Korninger, S. Lord Byron und Nikolaus Lenau. In: English Miscellany, 3 (ed. M. Praz). Roma, 1952.

Mortier, R. La réaction d'un critique classique devant Byron. (Vandenbourg). RLV, July, 1951.

Rosaldo, R. Un traductor mexicano de Byron. RIA, 17, 1952, 243-52. [On Roa Bárcena's translation of Mazeppa.]

Svirin, N. K voprosu o bajronizme Puškina. LS, 2, 1935, 184-210.

*Turdeanu, E. Oscar of Alva de Byron. Izvoare apusene si reflexe românesti. In: Studii literare. Sibiu, 1944.

Žirmunskij, V. Bajron i sovremennost'. UZLU-FN, 8, 1941, 284-91.

Reece, J. B. New Light on Poe's The Masque of the Red Death. MLN, 68, 1953, 114-15. [Sees Thomas CAMPBELL's Life of Petrarch as a possible source for Poe's story.]

*Clavería, C. Unamuno y CARLYLE. In: Temas de Unamuno. Madrid, 1953.

Kirby, T. A. Theodore Roosevelt on CHAUCER and a Chaucerian. MLN, 68, 1953, 34-37.

Purdy, R. R. Chaucer Scholarship in England and America: A Review of Recent Trends. Anglia, 70, 1952, 345-81.

Webb, J. A Russian Chaucer (Chekhov). Meanjin, 10 (Melbourne), 1951, 287-90.

Gulick, S. L. A CHESTERFIELD Bibliography to 1800. Chicago, 1935. 114 p.

Stone, E. Melville's Pip and COLERIDGE's Servant Girl. AL, 25, 1953, 358-60.

Himelick, R. Thoreau and Samuel DANIEL. AL, 24, 1952, 177-85.

Bastide, C. The Strange Adventures of the Translator of Robinson Crusoe, the Chevalier de Thémiseul. (DEFOE). In: Anglo-French Entente. London, 1914.

Dottin, P. Robinson Crusoë en France. In: La vie et les aventures étranges et surprenantes de Daniel Defoe. Paris, 1924.

Gates, W. B. A Note on Cooper and Robinson Crusoe. MLN, 67, 1952, 421-22.

Peterson, W. M. Gide and Defoe. N&Q, 197, 1952, 202-03.

Rodway, A. E. Moll Flanders and Manon Lescaut. Essays in Criticism, 3 (Chicago), 1953, 303-20. [Although Prévost does draw heavily on Moll Flanders for Manon, he does it in such a way as to recreate the story in his own manner.]

Bolge, F. W. Recent Criticism of DICKENS. NCF, 8, 1953, 171-87. [An examination of the Marxist, Freudian, and symbolic approaches to the interpretation of Dickens, and an account of the influence of Edmund Wilson on Dickens' criticism since 1934.)

Grubb, G. G. The American Edition of All the Year Round. PBSA, 47, 1953, 301-04.

Gallup, D. T. S. ELIOT, a Bibliography, Including Contributions to Periodicals and Foreign Translations. London, 1953.

Greene, E. J. H. T. S. Eliot et la France. Paris, 1952. 248 p. (Cf. RR & MLN, 1954).

Gwynn, F. L. Faulkner's Prufrock and Other Observations. JEGP, 52, 1953, 63-70. [Mildly interesting, detailed comparison of Faulkner's novel Mosquitoes with T. S. Eliot's Prufrock and other earlier poems to show the considerable use Faulkner made of Eliot material in his abortive early satirical novel.]

Morrissette, B. A. T. S. Eliot and Guillaume Apollinaire. CL, 5, 1953, 262-68.

Roe, F. C. T. S. Eliot and France. Aberdeen U. Review, 1952.

Simons, J. W. Eliot and his Critics. Commonweal, 57, 1953, 515-16.

Waldschmidt, C. Die Dramatisierungen von FIELDING's Tom Jones. Wetzlar, 1906. 104 p.

Helming, V. P. Edward GIBBON and Georges Deyverdun, Collaborators in the Mémoires littéraires de la Grande Bretagne. PMLA, 47, 1932, 1028-49.

Norton, J. E. A Bibliography of the Works of Edward Gibbon. London, 1940. 256 p.

Barwick, G. F. Notes from the First French Translation of The Vicar of Wakefield. (GOLDSMITH). Library, NS, 5, 1904. 134-45.

*Carrière, J. M. Notes on Arnaud Berquin's Adaptations from English Poetry. RR, 26, 1933, 335-40.

Harth, P. Goldsmith and the Marquis d'Argens. N&Q, 198, 1953, 529-30.

Seeber, E. D. & H. H. Remak. Les oeuvres de Charles-Michel Campion. Indiana U.P., 1945. (Cf. Introduction).

Manly, J. M. On the Question of the Portuguese Translation of GOWER's Confessio Amantis. MP, May, 1930.

Northup, C. S. A Bibliography of Thomas GRAY. New Haven, 1917. 296 p.

Starr, H. W. A Central-American Translation of Gray's Elegy. N&Q, 197, 1952, 203-04.

Davy, G. Thomas HOBBES et J.-J. Rousseau. Oxford, 1953. 29 p. [Counterbalancing the generally held belief of the antithesis of these two writers, this concise and pithy lecture reviews the points of coincidence and the influence of Hobbes on Rousseau.]

Thielemann, L. Diderot and Hobbes. In: Diderot Studies, 2, Syracuse, 1953, 221-78.

Mossner, E. C. The Continental Reception of HUME's Treatise, 1739-41. Mind, NS, 56, 1947, 31-43.

Cohen, B. Hawthorne's Mrs. Bullfrog and The Rambler. PQ, 32, 1953, 382-87. [Comparison of Hawthorne's tale and JOHNSON's essays dealing with marriage to suggest that Hawthorne may have drawn on Johnson for his attempt at a satirical tale.]

Metzdorf, R. F. The First American Rasselas and Its Imprint. PBSA, 47, 1953, 374-76.

——— Samuel Johnson in Brunswick. MLN, 68, 1953, 397-400.

Tello, J. Un experimento en español. Bolívar, 17 (Bogotá), 1953, 345-62. [An attempt to show that JOYCE's Finnegans Wake could be translated into Spanish.]

Cordasco, F. Thomas Paine and the History of JUNIUS: A Forgotten Cause Célèbre. JEGP, 52, 1953, 226-28.

Spector, R. D. The American Publication of Heron's Edition of the Letters of Junius. N&Q, 197, 1952, 275-76.

Eaves, T. C. D. An Early American Admirer of KEATS. (Simms). PMLA, 67, 1952, 895-98.

Hill, D. L. KIPLING in Vermont. NCF, 7, 1952, 153-70.

McAdow, B. Kipling in Colorado. Western Humanities Rev., 6, 1952, 205-06.

Super, R. H. LANDOR'S American Publications. MLQ, 14, 1953, 360-74.

Hallowell, R. E. C. J. Dorat, Opponent of the Drame bourgeois and Critic of the English Theatre. (LILLO). FR, 25, 1952, 355-63.

Bastide, P. Sieyès et les philosophes. (LOCKE). Rev. de synthèse, 17, 1939, 137-57.

Brown, F. A. On Education: John Locke, Christian Wolff, and the Moral Weeklies. UCPP, 36, 1952, 149-71.

Hahn, J. Voltaires Stellung zur Frage der

menschlichen Freiheit in ihrem Verhältnis zu Locke und Collins. Borna-Leipzig, 1905. 53 p.

Keim, A. Helvétius: sa vie et son oeuvre, d'après ses ouvrages, des écrits divers et des documents inédits. Paris, 1907. 719 p.

Marsh, J. O. The Spanish Version of Sir John MANDEVILLE's Travels: A Critical Edition. Diss. U. of Wisconsin, 1950.

Bailey, Dorothy D. American Literary Criticism of George MEREDITH. 1860-1917. Diss. U. of Wisconsin, 1952.

Fogle, F. MILTON Lost and Regained. HLQ, 15, 1952.

Kramer, C. Les poèmes épiques d'André Chénier. NP, 5, 1919, 210-18.

Stevens, D. H. Reference Guide to Milton from 1800 to the Present Day. Chicago, 1930. 302 p.

Zimmerman, L. F. Some Aspects of Milton's American Reputation to 1900. Diss. U. of Wisconsin, 1951.

Hennig, J. Goethe and Lalla Rookh. (MOORE). MLR, 48, 1953, 445-50.

Rubertis, A. de. Per la traduzione degli Amori degli Angeli di Tommaso Moore. Boll. Storico Pisano, 19, 1950, 169-76.

Schoeck, R. J. Another Renaissance Biography of Sir Thomas MORE. (by Antonio Maria Graziani). ES, 34, 1953, 115-17.

Brunet, P. L'introduction des théories de NEWTON en France au XVIIIe siècle avant 1738. Paris, 1931. 355 p.

Remak, H. H. Fontaine über seine Ballade Die Jüdin (PERCY). MLN, 53, 1938, 282-87.

Branca, V. Alfieri e la ricerca dello stile (POPE). Firenze, 1949.

*Duchâteau, O. Pope et Voltaire. An Essay on Man (1734); Discours en vers sur l'homme (1734-37). Greifswald, 1875. 56 p.

Hoffmann, A. Voltaires Stellung zu Pope. Königsberg, 1913. 95 p.

Howard, L. The American Revolt against Pope. SP, 49, 1952, 38-65.

*La Harpe, Jacqueline de. Le Journal des Savantes et la renommée de Pope en France au XVIIIe siècle. UCPP, 1933.

Holmes, W. C. Pamela Transformed (RICHARDSON). Musical Quart., 38, 1952, 581-94. [Goldoni's play and libretto based on Pamela, and the opera

of Piccini using the libretto. This opera, La buona Figliola, was performed in London, in 1767, in a wretched English "translation."]

Lohse, Mina. Die Liaisons dangereuses von Laclos in ihrem Verhältnis zu den Romanen RICHARDSONS and Crébillons. Diss. Hamburg, 1950.

Van Tieghem, P. Le Roman Sentimental en Europe de Richardson à Rousseau (1740-61). RLC, 20, 1940.

West, T. W. D. G. ROSSETTI and Ezra Pound. RES, 4, 1953, 63-67.

Townsend, F. G. The American Estimate of RUSKIN, 1847-60. PQ, 32, 1953, 69-82.

*Lukács, G. Puškin i Val'ter Skott (SCOTT). LK, 4, 1937, 106-11.

Pommier, J. Diderot avant Vincennes. (SHAFTSBURY). Paris, 1939. 119 p.

Schlegel, Dorothy. Shaftesbury and the French Deists. Diss. U. of N.C., 1954.

Tuveson, E. The Importance of Shaftesbury. ELH, 20, 1953, 267-99.

Scherrer, G. F. James SHIRLEYs Nachruhm. Zürich, 1951. 102 p.

Jacquot, J. Sir Hans SLOANE and French Men of Science. Notes & Records of Royal Society & Politics, 10, (London) 1952.

Risch, D. SMOLLETT und Deutschland. Deutschlandbild und Aufnahme in Deutschland. Diss. Göttingen, 1950. 175 p.

Hazard, P. Une source anglaise de l'abbé Prévost. (STEELE). MP, 27, 1929-30, 339-44.

Tronskaja, M. Iz istorii sternianstva. Teodor Gippel. (STERNE). UZLU-FN, 9, 1944, 210-35.

Varese, C. Linguaggio Sterniano e linguaggio Foscoliano. Firenze, 1947. [Interesting comparative study on imitative restrictions.]

Cox, J. M. Treasure Island and Tom Sawyer. (STEVENSON). Folio, 18, 1953, 7-21.

Triller, Eugenia. Pierwsze polskie wydanie "Podrózy kapitana Gulliwera." (SWIFT). Ze Skarbca Kultury, 1, 1953, 117-19.

Bergman, H. Whitman and TENNYSON. SP, July, 1954, 492-504.

Tryon, W. S. Nationalism and International Copyright: Tennyson and Longfellow in America. AL, 24, 1952, 301-02.

Tobias, R. C. American Criticism of **THACKERAY**. NCF, 8, 1953, 53-65. [The vagaries of Thackeray's reputation as a novelist from the publication of Vanity Fair through his second lecture tour of 1855.]

*Hirsch, A. James **THOMSON**: see traducteurs et ses critiques en France. RELV, 42, 1925.

Crocker, L. G. John **TOLAND** et le matérialisme de Diderot. RHL, 53, 1953, 289-95.

Ilchester, G. S. Madame du Deffand to **WALPOLE**. TLS, 19.VI.1948.

Irvine, L. L. Walpole and Mme. du Deffand. In his: Ten Letter-Writers. London, 1932, 49-65.

Koven, Anna de. Horace Walpole and Madame du Deffand: an Eighteenth Century Friendship. New York, 1929. 199 p.

Wardropper, B. W. Cadalso's Noches lúgubres and Literary Tradition. (**YOUNG**). SP, 49, 1952, 619-30.

English Influences upon Individual Authors and Works

Gál, I. **BABITS** és az Angol Irodalom. Debrecen, 1942. 140 p.

Dédéyan, C. **BALZAC** et l'Angleterre. In: Balzac, Le livre du centenaire. Paris, 1953.

Lebègue, R. Les modèles et les sources des Anglais de Balzac. Ibid.

Whitmore, P. J. S. English Thought and Learning in the Works of Pierre **BAYLE**. FS, April, 1954, 141-48.

Bowers, R. H. **BORRICHIUS** Recommends Some English Poets (1683). N&Q, 198, 1953.

Majut, R. Georg **BÜCHNER** and Some English Thinkers. MLR, 48, 1953, 310-22.

Brown, H. **BUFFON** and the Royal Society of London. Festschrift G. Sarton, New York, 1946, 141-65.

Braga, T. Os Doze da Inglaterra. Porto, 1902. [About a chivalric episode in the Lusíades (**CAMOENS**).]

Magalhãis Basto, A. de. Cavalarias dos Doze de Inglaterra. In: Poeira dos Arquivos. Porto, 1935.

Jacquot, J. Sébastien **CASTELLION** et l'Angleterre. BHR, 15, 1953.

Colie, Rosalie L. Jacob **CATS** and the English Puritan Marriage Tradition. NP, 37, 1953, 42-50.

Legros, R. P. André **CHÉNIER** en Angleterre. MLR, 19, 1924, 424-34.

Lombardo, A. La letteratura inglese nella criica di **CROCE**. RLM, April, 1953.

Brochard, L. Henry D.AVRAY, le Mercure de France et l'Angleterre. Diss. Paris, 1953.

Wade, I. O. **DESTOUCHES** in England. MP, 29, 1931-32, 27-47.

Pienaar, W. J. B. English Influences in Dutch Literature and Justus Van **EFFEN** as Intermediary. Cambridge U.P., 1929. 260 p.

Gaudin, Lois F. Les lettres anglaises dans l'**ENCYCLOPÉDIE**. New York, 1942. 256 p.

Venturi, F. Le origini dell'Enciclopedia. Firenze, 1946. 164 p.

Llorens, V. El original inglés de una poesía de **ESPRONCEDA**. NRFH, 5, 1952, 418-22.

Reboul, P. Le voyage de **FIÉVÉE** en Angleterre. Revue des Sciences Humaines, July, 1953.

Packer, W. A. Karl Stuart: A Neglected Phase in the Development of Theodor **FONTANE**'s Attitude toward England. Papers Michigan Acad. of Sci., Arts, & Letters, 38, 1952, 467-74.

Hennig, J. **GOETHE**'s Translation from the Annals of Philosophy, 1816. JEGP, 50, 1951.

Mor, A. Julien **GREEN** e la cultura anglosassone. Lett. moderne, Nov., 1951.

Stein, W. B. A Possible Source of **HAWTHORNE**'s English Romance. MLN, 67, 1952, 52-55.

Marchand, J. (ed.) François Armand Frédéric, duc de **LA ROCHEFOUCAULD**: A Frenchman in England (1784). Cambridge U.P., 1933. 256 p.

Mülhöfer, Lisl. Abbé J. B. **LE BLANC**, sein Leben und sein Werk; ein Beitrag zur Geschichte der Anglomanie im Frankreich des 18. Jahrhunderts. Würzburg, 1936. 87 p.

Ruff, S. Edith. Jean-Louis de **LOLME** und sein Werk über die Verfassung Englands. Berlin, 1934. 108 p.

Bonno, G. La constitution britannique devant l'opinion française de **MONTESQUIEU** à Bonaparte. Paris, 1931. 317 p.

Cestre, C. Les sources anglaises de l'Esprit des lois. Rev. Philomathique de Bordeaux, 12, 1909, 145-58.

Kingsley, M. The British Constitution; l'Esprit des lois. In his: French Liberal Thought in the Eighteenth Century. Boston, 1929, 147-69.

Trease, Billy D. José Joaquín de MORA: A Spaniard Abroad. Diss. U. of Michigan, 1953.

Hazard, P. L'amitié franco-anglaise ne date pas du XXe siècle. Déjà l'abbé PRÉVOST . . . NL, 18.III.1939.

—————— Prévost et l'Angleterre, état des travaux. In: Etudes critiques sur Manon Lescaut. Chicago U.P., 1929, 85-99.

Staab, J. Das Journal étranger unter dem Abbé Prévost und seine Bedeutung für die literarischen Beziehungen zwischen England und Frankreich im Zeitalter der Aufklärung. Erlangen, 1912. 72 p.

Irvine, D. D. The Abbé RAYNAL and British Humanitarianism. Journal Mod. History, 3, 1931, 564-77.

Crosby, Emily A. Une romancière oubliée: Madame RICCOBONI, sa vie, ses ouvrages, sa place dans la littérature anglaise et française du XVIIIe siècle. Paris, 1924. 190 p.

Havens, G. R. The Sources of ROUSSEAU's Edouard Bomston. MP, 17, 1919, 13-27.

Mornet, D. (ed.) La Nouvelle Héloïse. Paris, 1925. (Cf. Introduction).

Schinz, A. Rousseau et les Anglais. In his: La pensée de Jean-Jacques Rousseau; essai d'interprétation nouvelle. Northampton, (Mass.) & Paris, 1929.

Texte, J. Rousseau et la littérature anglaise. In his: Jean-Jacques Rousseau et les origines du cosmopolitisme littéraire au XVIIIe siècle. Paris, 1895.

Röstvig, Maren-Sofie. Casimire SARBIEWSKI and the English Ode. SP, July, 1954, 443-60.

Muyden, B. van (ed.) A Foreign View of England in the Reigns of George I and George II; the Letters of Monsieur César de SAUSSURE to his Family. London, 1902. 384 p.

Bassett, E. L. SILIUS ITALICUS in England. CP, 48, 1953, 155-68.

Ascoli, G. VOLTAIRE: Le voyage en Angleterre et Les Lettres philosophiques. RCC, 25, 1924, 275-87.

Cohn, A. Voltaire a-t-il écrit en anglais deux essais ou bien trois? Mélanges G. Lanson. Paris, 1922, 250-53.

Strachey, L. Voltaire and England. In his: Books and Characters. New York, 1922. 115-41.